Taking It to the Streets

Taking It to the Streets

Public Theologies of Activism and Resistance

Edited by Jennifer Baldwin

LEXINGTON BOOKS
Lanham • Boulder • New York • London

Published by Lexington Books
An imprint of The Rowman & Littlefield Publishing Group, Inc.
4501 Forbes Boulevard, Suite 200, Lanham, Maryland 20706
www.rowman.com

6 Tinworth Street, London SE11 5AL

Copyright © 2019 by The Rowman & Littlefield Publishing Group, Inc.

All rights reserved. No part of this book may be reproduced in any form or by any electronic or mechanical means, including information storage and retrieval systems, without written permission from the publisher, except by a reviewer who may quote passages in a review.

British Library Cataloguing in Publication Information Available

Library of Congress Cataloging-in-Publication Data Available

ISBN 978-1-4985-9010-5 (cloth)
ISBN 978-1-4985-9012-9 (pbk.)
ISBN 978-1-4985-9011-2 (electronic)

Contents

Preface: Vulnerability, Righteous Anger, and Protest: Forming Public Theologies of Activism and Resistance   vii
Jennifer Baldwin

I: Forming Action   1

1 Feel Awful? How to Identify Trump's Politics of Abuse and Subvert It   3
Susan Brooks Thistlethwaite

2 A Womanist Perspective on the Election of Donald Trump: What Pastors Are Called to Do   15
Linda E. Thomas

3 Warriors of Compassion: Coordinates on the Compass of Compassion-Based Activism   25
Frank Rogers

4 Disrupting the Public Square: Prophetic Pastoral Care and Witness in Times of Trauma   43
Michelle A. Walsh

5 Protest and Resistance as the Liturgy of the People   59
Jennifer Baldwin

II: Cultural Resourcing for Activism   73

6 "Because I'm Your Mother, That's Why": Scientific Authority and the March for Science   75
Lisa Stenmark

7   Black Theology and Hip-Hop Theology: Theologies of
    Activism and Resistance   87
    Willie Hudson

8   "Saint Hillary," On Unserious Activism   101
    Tony Hoshaw

9   Love Trumps Hate: Images of Political Love from Pussyhat
    Makers   115
    Donna Bowman

10 Achieving Reproductive Justice: Theology and Activism   129
    Thia Cooper

III: Militarism and Resistance to State Violence   **147**

11 Why Resistance Fails?   149
    Olli-Pekka Vainio

12 Homeland Theology?: Decolonizing Christianity and the Task
    of Public Theology   163
    Hille Haker

13 Political Theology in the Trump Era: Sacrificial Frameworks in
    the US "Neoliberal Disimagination Machine"   179
    Kelly Denton-Borhaug

14 A Spirituality of Activism: The Chicago Air and Water Show   197
    Robert Bossie

Index   207

About the Contributors   209

Preface

Vulnerability, Righteous Anger, and Protest:
Forming Public Theologies of Activism and Resistance

Jennifer Baldwin

MEETING VULNERABILITY

If I were asked to encapsulate my understanding of the intentions and values of Jesus of Nazareth, I would point to the teaching in Matthew 25:31–46. In these verses, Jesus identifies those who have fulfilled the vision of God and those who have impeded the health of God's community. Those who are invited to rejoice with God are the ones who provided food to the hungry, drink to the thirsty, hospitality to the stranger, clothing to those in need, health care to sick, and companionship to those imprisoned. When the people asked when they had provided these forms of care to the King, he replied "I tell you the truth, whatever you did for one of the least of these, you did for me."[1] Likewise, to those who neglected the hungry and thirsty ones, the stranger, the ones in need of material support, the ill or imprisoned, the King rebukes and casts away.

At the very heart of Jesus's narrative stands, in concrete terms, the commandment to love your neighbor as yourself. While these visions of need and either provision or neglect are essentially timeless, they do strike particular resonance in our current political climate as legislation is passed to reduce funding of services like Meals on Wheels, pipeline construction threatens the water supplies of Indigenous communities and Flint continues to go years with toxic water, asylum seekers are arrested and their children foundationally traumatized by family separation, minimum wage stagnation makes it nearly impossible to meet basic material needs even while working full time, accessibility to functional and affordable health care is stripped away, and the prison industrial complex in the United States houses a greater percentage of the national population than any other country while also requiring persons to potentially risk their lives (in the case of prisoners fighting wildfires in California) for $1 a day. If our "Christian" nation were to face the King in Jesus's tale, there is no doubt that we would fail the task of caring for the least of these!

As we reflect and subsequently act on our response-ability as people who claim to take the words, actions, and intentions of Jesus seriously, we ultimately must contend with how we offer care toward the most vulnerable people and populations in our midst. Unfortunately, the notion of vulnerability as an invocation for care and source of empathy is nearly antithetical to many of our formative national narratives including the "self-made man," "tough and independent cowboy conquering the wild west," the near frenzy of the USA as #1, or the assumption that the leader of the United States will remain the "leader of the free world" by default. When national pride is centered on wealth, military power, and/or domination of others across contexts, the vulnerable ones must be cast aside or annihilated in order to preserve the appearance being the best. Unfortunately in an effort to preserve national pride, we forfeit many of the foundational components of a healthy and prosperous society. Prosperity cannot be limited to the wealth of those who make the rules or are most visible in our media-driven society; true prosperity includes a sustainable, healthful life in which all of the basic needs of life are adequately met and many of the joys of life are accessible—this is the true measure of life, liberty, and pursuit of fulfillment/happiness. This is the vision Jesus offers in Matthew 25.

EMBRACING JUST ANGER

The ways in which we, as individuals and as a society, offer or neglect care to persons in their particular form of vulnerability reflect our core commitments, character, and innate sense of justice. Justice is primarily the desire for opportunity equality, liberation, and right relationship. When we notice the victimization of the vulnerable or unjust uses of power and influence toward our self or others, we, rightly, experience the sensations and affect of anger. Anger is a primary emotion and like all emotions has an essential survival function. Sadness facilitates the formation of empathy and drawing in social support. Disgust keeps us at a safe distance from objects that can spread disease. Fear helps us stay appropriately alert to danger. Interest draws us toward novelty to increase our resources for life. Surprise readies our attention and body for response. Joy generates connections, play, and exploration. While all emotions have a survival benefit (especially when in balance and fluid adaptability with other emotions according to the present situation), historically and popularly the emotion of anger consistently gets a bad rap. We are often told that anger is destructive, necessarily unproductive, and frequently dangerous and this is accurate when the seeds of anger are suppressed, dismissed, or exiled and grow into the explosion of violence and rage. Anger is to be exiled and avoided at all costs in a civil society. Anger, like other emotions, can be problematic when overly denied (apathy) or overly expressed (violence, rage, etc.); however, it does not have to be expressed through violence, rage, or destruction. In its purest manifestation, anger is the acknowledgment of injustice and the motivation toward corrective action. Anger is that small voice inside that says "this isn't right, this isn't ok" and provides us with the motivation and energy to make changes.

Anger as a balanced and attended to motivation for change toward greater justice in our lives, society, relationships, and the world is a good and productive thing. It fuels us to gather together in one voice and proclaim "Enough!" Anger that finds expression in corporate movements for change can be highly productive—even transformative. Anger focused on justice and nonviolent behavioral strategies is our primary resource for opposing systems that fuel injustice, oppression, and the perpetuation of intergenerational and communal trauma. It is the resource of collective power for those in society who are often excluded from institutionalized structures of social influence and agency. Birthed from suffering, protective anger for justice can be life-affirming, life-granting, and aimed toward the hope of a healthy and resilient society.

COMPASSION, MOBILIZATION, AND RESISTANCE

Anger is an affective indicator of injustice Where there is a visceral awareness of injustice, there is suffering, sorrow, and/or pain. Awareness of and compassion toward vulnerability and suffering are the twin roots of just anger and right resistance. Compassion is what keeps anger focused toward justice reclamation and away from dissolution into traumatic rage. Additionally, compassion motivates action by those with less social vulnerability "on behalf of" those who are more socially vulnerable. The mobilization of resistance movements in the immediate aftermath of the "travel ban" in January 2017 and the explosion of actions in response to family separation in the summer of 2018 are two clear instances of the combination of vulnerability, agency, compassion, just anger, and mobilization by persons with skills well suited to meet the need caused by injustice. Furthermore, they illustrate the movement from abuses of governmental power to vulnerability and injury of persons on the margins of social structures of power to the activation of compassion and agency by third parties willing to act on behalf of others.

This movement from ab/use and injury to compassion and action fuels public responses of activism and resistance.

There are periods in a nation's civil history when the tides of social unrest rise into waves upon waves of public activism and resistance of the dominant uses of power. In American history, activism and public action including and extending beyond the Women's Suffrage, the Million Man March, protests against the Vietnam War, the Civil Rights Movement, Boston Tea Party, Black Lives Matter, and Stonewall Rebellion are hallmarks of transitional or liminal moments in our development as a society. These critical periods marked by increases in public activism and political resistance are opportunities for a society to once again decide who we will be as a people. Will we move toward a more perfect union in which all persons gain freedom in fulfilling their potential or will we choose the perceived safety of the status quo and established norms of power? Whose voices will be heard? Whose will be silenced through intimidation or harm? Ultimately, these are theological questions and they stand at the center of this book.

OVERVIEW

Public Theologies of Activism and Resistance is an edited volume that explores the critical intersection of public theology, political theology, and communal practices of activism and political resistance. This volume is also intended as the sister/companion volume of *Navigating Post-Truth and Alternative Facts: Religion and Science as Political Theology*[2] which explores questions of epistemology, affect, and knowledge within our current and increasingly populist political context. If that volume takes up the concern of how to get our bearings, this text explores what we should do and resources for engaging in productive public action. It is organized into three parts. The first part focuses on responses to the societal, governmental, and cultural context that solidified with clarity during 2016 presidential election cycle in the United States and in the following administration. Additionally, it provides lenses and resources for engaging in productive public actions. Part 2 explores cultural resources of sustaining activism and resistance as well as some of the key issues at stake in public action. The third part centers on militarization and resistance to state violence. Taken in concert, these three sections work together to provide frames for understanding while also keeping us engaged in the concrete action to mobilize social change. The overarching aim of the volume is to promote critical discourse regarding the dynamics of activism and political resistance and highlight some of the key social movements of our era and how they intersect with religious or theological themes.

Part 1, "Forming Action," opens with Susan Brooks Thistlethwaite's clear and honest clarion call to resist the current presidential administrations "politics of abuse." Dr. Thistlethwaite argues that the reason so many people currently feel awful and are moved toward activism as a remedy to feelings of helplessness or hopelessness is rooted in governmental actions that mirror the abuses of power and relationship present in patterns of domestic violence. She unreservedly names the politics of abuse as a means of facilitating accountability, revealing parallel characteristics of domination and violation, and offering resources for subversion and resilience. Linda Thomas then urges us to consider ways in which religious and community leaders can respond to the systems of oppression and politics of abuse that both predated the current presidential administration and have been amplified under the tone and model set in the Oval Office. She advocates the role of the pastor as a self-aware leader offering hope and understanding . . . even for those with whom we disagree. Frank Rogers leads us through reflections and resources for compassion as a centering lens for resistance. Drawing on insights from Internal Family Systems and with clear and compelling narratives, Rogers guides us in understanding core principles that inform and cultivate healthy and productive compassion-based social activism. He advocates for action that is centered, creative, boundaried, inclusive, empowered, and grounded. Michelle Walsh draws connections between trauma, activism, and the need for a prophetic pastoral care that is equipped to meet the needs of suffering communities and persons. She leads us through the development of a pastoral care praxis that is fully open to receiving and being transformed by the testimony and witness of survivors of traumatic experiences and asks if we have the courage to truly honor the disruptive and constructive renderings of trauma. Finally, Jennifer Baldwin directs attention to the notion of civil protest and resistance as the honorable work and liturgy of the people. She argues that public social demonstrations are the people's means of communicating discontent or limits on the actions of representative leaders in between election cycles or when elections become suspect. As such the forms, prevalence, and focus of activism and protest demonstrate the shared values, limits, and hopes of the community and offer a boundaried space in which to claim our collective identity.

The second section explores various cultural resources for activism. Lisa Stenmark discusses the role and impact of authority in our social sphere. Reflecting on the March for Science, she problematizes authority that demands response solely on the basis of perceived authority; in other words, "because I said so" is not an adequate motivator for change or submission. She explicates several different forms of authority and concludes that public engagement is more effective than public fiat. Willie Hudson explores connections between Black theology, Hip-hop theology, hip-hop music and culture, and inner-city spiritual development. He states that Hip-hop and Black theologies offer a salvific theological option for persons living within systems of oppression and are resources for activism. Boldly naming the challenges and spiritual resources of resiliency of the inner-city, Hudson identifies dimensions of Hip-hop and Black theologies that offer correctives to the deficiencies of traditional Christian rhetoric. Tony Hoshaw wades into the intersections of aesthetics, politics, and gay subculture (as an action rather than an identity marker) in his chapter on Hillary as a gay icon. He offers the lens of "unserious activism" as a counter to the hyperseriousness of conflictual political discourse. "Hillary" as an aesthetic figure of subversive politics and activism represents the dynamics between the conventional and the defiant in both stark and subtle ways. From hairstyles to political policies, "Hillary" and gay politics seek to queer the space between love and resistance. As Hoshaw invites us to explore the intersections of the conventional and the deviant, Donna Bowman presents us with reflections on knitted pussyhats. Utilizing surveys and interviews, Bowman knits and weaves together various strands of intention and hope that lead to participation in the Women's March and in the crafting of the iconic pussyhats. Participatory physical action in the Women's March and symbolic action of the pussyhats, according to Bowman, often emerged from participants religious and non-religious understandings of both the successes and failures of love and care in our personal, social, and political lives. While the subject of Bowman's research is a political symbol of love and resistance, Thia Cooper offers an expansive and concrete analysis of the stakes at play in the areas of reproductive justice. With the installation of Justice Kavanaugh to the Supreme Court, the landmark and culturally contested verdict *Roe v. Wade* is under new threat. Cooper directs our attention beyond the well-worn arguments around abortion rights and towards a breadth of concerns about a woman's ability to become or to not become pregnant. Discourse about reproductive justice must include mindfulness of the sociological, economic, racial, and history of reproductive freedom and reproductive abuse in the United States.

Part 3, "Militarism and Resistance to State Violence," centers on histories of international aggression, the need for decolonization of religion and theology, critiques of military dependency, and an example of sustained public action and spirituality to resist the normalization and valorization of military weaponry. Writing from a European/Finnish context, Olli-Pekka Vainio offers an eerily familiar account of the political history of the Russian-backed Civil War in Finland in 1918 and its consequences. He traces political strategies of intimidation and control that center on the instillation of fear, disruption of critical thinking, and patterns of cognitive bias that are designed to split communities and foster suspicion and violence toward one's neighbor. Vainio offers this historical retelling as a warning in our current context of corruption and resistance. Moving from Europe to the United States, Hille Haker problematizes the notion of homeland theology. She beckons us to critically and courageously examine our long-ago and not-so-long-ago histories of violence and problematic defense of "homeland" and how these narratives are whitewashed in order to preserve the image of valorous Christian nation. Haker argues that we must "decolonize" theology in order to engage in public theologies of global ethics, healing, justice, and liberation. One requirement of decolonizing theology and moving toward a just and healthy society is a full acknowledgment and critique of the US's national obsession with military power. Kelly Denton-Borhaug examines our public pedagogies and how they contribute to the rise of post-truth and nearly unfettered growth of the military and a sacrificial war-culture. She argues that the "disimagination machine" gains sacred traction through civil religious rhetorical frames of "the ultimate sacrifice of war." In the end, this dynamic hinders citizens from critical appraisal of their own reality and working toward justice and peacebuilding. The final chapter in this section and the book offers an intimate reflection on a 28-year practice of activism and resistance to state violence. Bob Bossie, a military veteran, priest, and activist, guides us through his journey of activism as a spiritual commitment and practice thus drawing together many of the themes of the book. His reflection connects the impact of violence and trauma, our national obsession with military might, an expansive awareness of our global connections and desire for justice, compassion, and moral agency, and our desire to be connected with God and God's vision of wholeness for the world.

Public theologies and practices of activism and resistance are ultimately about participating in the crafting of God's vision for creation in our shared global world. What are our shared values, hopes, vulnerabilities, and desires? On some level, we all know that life is both fragile and remarkably resilient. Will we be a part of the forces that capitalize on the fragility of human and global life or will we seek to harness our innate capacities for compassion, courage, just anger, clarity, and curiosity to support those in need, cultivate the honor of desiring "enough" rather than "all," and foster resiliency and balanced flourishing. The values we hold dear often require protection and a willingness to claim the vision of what can be. Protest, activism, and resistance to the structures, policies, and systems of oppression, opportunism, domination, and harm are, at times, necessary actions and are worthy of theological reflection and support. Each of the authors illuminate various features of activism and resistance as a spiritual, civic, and political mandate in our time. They invite us to join the movement of action, compassion, wisdom, and agency toward health, liberation, and justice.

NOTES

1. Matthew 25:40, NIV.

2. Jennifer Baldwin, ed., *Navigating Post-Truth and Alternative Facts: Religion and Science as Political Theology* (Lanham: Lexington Books, 2018).

REFERENCES

Baldwin, Jennifer, editor. *Navigating Post-Truth and Alternative Facts: Religion and Science as Political Theology.* Lanham: Lexington Books, 2018.

I

Forming Action

Chapter One

Feel Awful? How to Identify Trump's Politics of Abuse and Subvert It

Susan Brooks Thistlethwaite

The political philosophy of Donald Trump is modeled on domestic violence. In a striking number of ways, his administration demonstrates the same abusive power that domestic abusers use. In fact, we can say that the United States doesn't have a president any more, we have an "Abuser-in-Chief."[1]

Those on the receiving end of this abusive treatment can feel powerless, despairing, fearful, and without value. In short, they can feel awful. That is how the abuser wants you to feel. It is deliberate and, in this particular climate, I want to argue this is a political strategy.

We can effectively subvert and reject a politics of abuse, but first we have to respect that the abuse is real and the pain it causes is real.

Abusers try to make you feel awful by exploiting your vulnerabilities, and taking away your sense of self-esteem and personal control. Then they try to tell you that you don't feel what you feel, that you're just "imagining things."

Well, you're not. I'm not. I feel like I'm being abused. Perhaps you do too.

Thus, when I claim we have an "Abuser-in-Chief," I am not speaking metaphorically. Donald Trump's conduct in office and his policies exactly follow the pattern of domestic abusers.

THE POLITICS OF ABUSE: IT'S ALL ABOUT POWER AND CONTROL

The National Domestic Violence hotline[2] defines domestic abuse as a "pattern of behaviors used by one partner to maintain power and control" over the other.

In this chapter, the abusive pattern of domestic violence that parallels the political philosophy of the Trump administration is characterized primarily by the following:

- The abuser insults, demeans, or shames you.
- The abuser controls the money and does not give you money for needed expenses.
- The abuser threatens you with or causes you physical harm.
- The abuser lies about the abuse and denies what is happening.
- The abuser intimidates you with guns, knives or other weapons.
- The abuser threatens the children.

The Abuser Insults, Demeans, or Shames You

In Trump world, that abusive behavior of insult, demeaning, or shaming often appears as texts. It is hard, in fact, to keep up with the firehose of insulting, demeaning, or shaming rhetoric coming from Trump, but the *New York Times* has attempted a list that they keep updating.[3] The list is informative on the pattern of abuse as "power and control" since many groups are subject to this kind of rhetoric.

One telling example is the National Football League (NFL) players who kneel to protest racism and police violence. Trump's tweets call them "weak" and/or "out of control." The idea that the powerful men who play football are "weak" is, of course, objectively false, but the signal phrase is "out of control."

American football is a racist structure. The owners and fans are primarily white, and approximately 70 percent of the players are African American. With those kinds of tweets, Trump is reaching into the racist ideology of control and its underlying fear of strong African American men, even when they are engaging in nonviolent protest. These NFL players, the racists would hold, should not be allowed to exercise their First Amendment rights. Thus, their principled protest is turned into a threat against this country.

Muslim Americans are similarly insulted, demeaned, and shamed in Trump tweets. Some researchers have posited a link between Trump tweets and hate crimes against Muslims. Researchers found a correlation between anti-Islam tweets in a given week, and the FBI hate crime data for the period immediately following.[4] This link is correlational rather than necessarily causal. In fact, some posit that Trump's hateful rhetoric simply gives license to people who already held prejudiced views simply to express them.

In the realm of domestic violence, however, these two ideas, the causal or the license, may be more closely related than one might think.

I have done domestic violence counseling as well as workshops over many years. In one facility where I volunteered as a domestic violence counselor, the man who did the court-ordered domestic violence sessions for abusive men recounted to me an exchange he had with one of the men in his group:

"I need to stop the drinking," the man had said. "That's what makes me hit her." The counselor said he had countered, "Did you ever think that you drink so that you can hit her?"

I believe abuse is a seductive exercise of power, and the Trump tweets are that kind of seduction, the drug that reduces inhibition to permit hate to flourish and this is creating an abusive pattern among his supporters.

The Abuser Controls the Money, Does Not Give You Money for Needed Expenses

Another area where the ideology of abusive power and control can be seen as practiced by this administration is in relation to health care. Abusers will try to exert control over finances, even refusing to pay for needed health care of their partners. The Trump administration has waged a vicious and sustained attack on the Affordable Care Act, up to and including imperiling insurance coverage for preexisting conditions.[5]

The massive tax cuts for the rich have not stimulated the economy; in fact, the deficit is exploding and the Trumpians in Congress are taking aim at Medicare and Medicaid, critical programs for health care for seniors and for the poor in order to "balance the budget."[6] "Balance the budget" is code for "cut entitlements." People who cannot get needed health care suffer and ultimately die from this neglect. Yet, Trump promised on the campaign trail to protect these vital programs.[7] Will he do so?

The Abuser Threatens You with or Causes You Physical Harm

The threat of physical harm and even death is at the core of abusive ideologies of power and control. Abusers use physical threat, as well as actual physical harm, with great frequency. This is why domestic violence is called violence.

Nuclear war is an existential threat to all life on the planet. It is, in a sense, the ultimate physical violence that can be inflicted. Trump has a history of effectively threatening and withdrawing threats against the world. For example, he surprised the military by requesting a "10-fold" increase in nuclear weapons as the rhetoric with North Korea heated up, and then claiming nuclear proliferation is a great threat. There are actually numerous examples of these contradictions.[8]

In foreign affairs, this is reflected in the puzzlement (with an undertone of barely muted alarm) expressed by foreign policy experts over Trump's inconsistency. Richard N. Haass, the president of the Council on Foreign Relations, has noted, "Trump has rejected a detailed pact that kept Iran out of the nuclear weapons business for a decade, while embracing a vague communiqué that allows North Korea to keep its nuclear weapons for years, and possibly forever."[9]

Playing off North Korea by flattering Mr. Kim, while then threatening Iran, is classic abuser behavior. There is never any sense of safety—the lack of a sense of safety is, itself, a climate of abuse. Abusers want to create a climate of instability and unsafety so their victims will constantly be in a state of alarm, creating the physical conditions that lead to post-traumatic stress disorder.

No wonder so many of us feel awful. We have a right to.

The Abuser Lies about the Abuse and Denies What Is Happening

There is no evidence so far that Trump keeps his word. This is consistent with domestic abuse. Abusers are congenital liars and they will especially lie about the abuse. The *Washington Post* has been tracking Trump's lying since the beginning of his presidency. He has lied more than 3,000 times, they document, not even halfway through 2018.[10] The pattern is clear. Lying is the default of both Trump and domestic abusers.

The consistent lying behavior has its own terminology, called "gaslighting," taken from a classic film. In the article "Donald Trump Is Gaslighting America," published in 2016, the author, Lauren Ducca, pinpointed the abusive political behavior of lying and denying you are lying:

> To gaslight is to psychologically manipulate a person to the point where they question their own sanity, and that's precisely what Trump is doing to this country. He gained traction in the election by swearing off the lies of politicians while constantly contradicting himself, often without bothering to conceal the conflicts within his own sound bites. He lied to us over and over again, then took all accusations of his falsehoods and spun them into evidence of bias. At the hands of Trump, facts have become interchangeable with opinions, blinding us into arguing amongst ourselves as our very reality is called into question.[11]

Trump took this to a whole new level after his so-called Summit in Helsinki, Finland, with Vladimir Putin (another practitioner of abusive politics). Trump returned home to the United States to a firestorm of controversy over his failure to confront Putin for what US intelligence has consistently said was election interference planned and targeted by Russians in 2016, most likely directly by Putin. Trump changed one word from "I don't see a reason why it would be Russia," to an out of context "I don't see a reason why it wouldn't be Russia," a weak and largely unbelievable nonretraction.[12] The change was transparently false, and then largely disappeared.

This is a dangerous pattern of deception at this point, as the foundation of democratic process as free and fair elections is undermined.

Intimidates You with Guns, Knives, or Other Weapons

Nuclear weapons are certainly weapons, but the relationship between guns and abuse requires specific attention. Guns are a central factor both in the fact that the United States is the deadliest country in the developed world for women, and the strong and growing influence of the National Rifle Association (NRA) in Trumpworld.

Through "femme fatales, lavish Moscow parties and dark money," the Russians may have spent as much as a decade in infiltrating the NRA, and influencing its efforts to help elect Trump and keep him in power. Steven Hall, chief of Russian operations for the CIA until 2015, believes, "The Russians were seeking a "mechanism by which they can, sort of, control the NRA."[13]

In my view, the NRA is the single greatest factor in why the United States is gun mad culture. The NRA significantly funds legislators whose sole job it seems to be is to defeat sensible gun legislation that the majority of Americans want, spending 60 million dollars in 2016 alone on pro-gun politicians including Trump.[14]

Women who have left abusive situations have told me that their abusive partner would take out a gun and hold it on them, even sometimes holding it to their head, while yelling at them. These women are not in the staggering statistics on the relationship between guns and domestic violence that turns deadly. The presence of a gun in a domestic violence situation makes it five times more likely that a woman will be killed. But their lives are wrecked by the presence of a gun in the home even if the gun is never fired.

The river of guns that flows through the United States, its homes, its streets, its malls, its movie theaters, its communities, and, of course, its schools is drowning our society. Gun violence poses a direct and immediate threat to every single American. Every American, no matter what your politics, lives with this threat and it is abusive.

The Abuser Threatens the Children

Abusers often threaten children as a means of control, and Trump has ripped children, even babies and toddlers, from the parents' arms and put them in cages. Hearing their cries has been a decisive moment for many in indicting this abusive administration.[15]

Massive demonstrations around the country followed revelations about this abhorrent abuse of children and families.[16]

In domestic violence contexts, women often make plans to leave when the abusive partner threatens the children. The threat to children is central to the abuse of power exercised by batterers. Their contempt for vulnerability is their signature.

We now face a Supreme Court appointment that may very well signal the reversal both of marriage equality and women's reproductive freedom, as well as perhaps other constitutionally protected rights. This makes many feel especially vulnerable in their marriages and/or their very bodies. This is a threatened loss of control over our own lives and well-being.

No wonder so many of us feel awful.

HOW TO SUBVERT A POLITICS OF ABUSE

Naming the politics of abuse as abuse is the first step in subverting it, but there are other crucial steps. They are:

- Claim your own feelings.
- Identify areas where you already exercise agency.
- Expand areas where you can exercise more agency.
- Cultivate supportive community.
- Be creative.
- Celebrate.

Claim Your Own Feelings

The first thing is to claim you feel what you feel. If you feel awful, feel awful. Don't let anybody, even with the best of intentions, tell you "well, now it's not so bad and . . ." My feelings are mine, your feelings are yours and if we feel awful, nobody can tell us differently.

I have done Bible studies with domestic violence survivors for many years, and I have found the Psalms of Lament to be essential for this work. Over 50 of the Psalms in the Hebrew Bible are these prayers that come from deep pain. Jesus quotes a Psalm of Lament from the cross, "My God, my God, why have you forsaken me?" (Psalm 22) When we are abused, we can feel God has abandoned us and there is none to help.

It is validating for our politics of subversion to lament what is happening to our country. It is not a new thing in American history that some with power will organize to exploit and control others, but there is a particular virulence to the cruelty of these times, and crying out about that is warranted.

Claiming what you feel, and what is really happening in this nation, is a step on the path to taking back control from the Abuser-in-Chief.

Identify Areas Where You Already Exercise Agency

Your own agency in your life and in your society is the most crucial shift many have made in the last decades to choose liberation over oppression.

In fact, this has been an important shift that has taken place in theology, not only in Christian theology but in many religious perspectives in the last four or five decades. This shift is broadly called the "theologies of liberation." There are important differences among these theologies, as those who engage them do so from their own contexts. A common theme, however, is the nature of the human being.

In older, and more conservative theological perspectives, the human being was often considered under the subject heading of "sin." The human condition was one of fallen sinfulness and the chief theological challenge was how divine agency worked to redeem the sinful human.

In a major change, the theologies of liberation considered the human being as a subject in her or his or their own right, and considered especially the human being who was oppressed by social and economic conditions that rendered them nonhumans. These humans were treated as objects to be acted upon by their oppressors, not subjects in their own right. In short, only some people were considered fully human in politics, economics, and, in truth, in theology.[17]

Liberation theology itself has needed liberation, however, and over time the dimensions of the interrelated oppressions of race, gender, sexual orientation, and ableism have been identified and more liberative liberation theologies have emerged. This is still taking place.

But at the heart of all of these is that central insight that oppressed people claim agency in history when they act and refuse to be acted upon.

When it comes to domestic violence, a vivid example from when I had done volunteer counseling comes to my mind about how human agency is crucial. A woman came to see me whose husband tried to assert control over every aspect of her life. He knew she loved coffee and he forbade her to have coffee and he would hit her if he suspected she had drunk coffee. She told me about the great lengths to which she would nevertheless go in obtaining coffee, brewing it, drinking it, burying the grounds in the backyard and hiding the remaining coffee in a different place in order to defy him. I affirmed her efforts to assert her own will in this way, and from this one act of doing what she wanted, she began to realize she could make an escape plan. She hid money away from the home, along with clothes and items she valued, and she eventually did get away.

Being an agent in your own life, and asserting your right to act rather than be acted upon, is fundamental to subverting domestic violence and subverting a politics of abuse.

First, recognize ways in which you are already asserting control. What do you choose to see and hear? What are your political choices and how are you exercising them? Do you refuse to allow people to bully you online or in person about your political choices?

All of these and more are ways you and I are likely already asserting agency and refusing to be messed with by the Abuser-in-Chief.

Expand Areas Where You Can Exercise More Agency

It has been very important to me to continue to limit my intake of the news, and to take in news in forms and at times when I see fit. Perhaps you already do the same, but if not, try that.

Limit your intake of the news. Make your own choices and do so consciously. For example, I never listen to or read the texts of the Abuser-in-Chief. I have perfected the art of scanning past them in reading online or newspaper sources. I severely limit television news for this reason, and because at times you may see the face or hear the voice. I choose not to see or hear that.

Becoming more politically active is also crucial. Register to vote if you have not done so, and actively work to help others register to vote. Go to candidates forums and express your opinions. Join marches for causes with which you agree. Get the app "Five Calls" and regularly call your congressional representatives and tell them your views on how they should vote. Support candidates with whom you agree. While expressing our views to friends as on Facebook can be satisfying, such expressions have been termed "slacktivism" as we do not get out into the public square and influence others.

I have found that something important happens to you when you physically join a march or a demonstration. We exercise agency with our bodies in very important ways, ways that last long past the march. We are often oppressed directly through what is done to our bodies, so physically resisting in nonviolent ways is very empowering.

Cultivate Supportive Community

Take a hard look at your current communities. Is your family supportive of your activities and attitudes of subversion? If they undermine you, limit contact and/or politely refuse to be on the receiving end of negativity.

It does no good to assert that you are an agent in your own life and then belong to a religious community that denies that in you, both practically and theologically. There is, as is well known, a high correlation between white, conservative, Christian evangelicalism and Trump support. It has been consistently high. No one should be surprised by this, though some claim to be.

The structure of this kind of Christian theology is hierarchal, patriarchal, homophobic, and racist.[18] But, in my experience, Christian "liberals" or the so-called mainline can be undermining of agency in more subtle ways. Some African American churches, students, and colleagues have told me, affirm members in some ways but not others. You deserve to be affirmed for all of who you are. Look critically not just at what your religious community says, but what it does. And, if you are not supported, walk away.

Find another community if you are able. Sometimes, this means working to create one yourself.

One of the great gifts of the Queer community to our social arrangements is the affirmation that intentional community is good, right, and possible. In short, when it comes to community, Queer it.

Join and support political movements, especially those who use the techniques of nonviolent direct action. Call politicians, write them, write to your local paper, whether letters to the editor or opinion pieces, and go to marches and demonstrations carrying signs you have made yourself. Do this frequently.

Don't let people tell you nonviolent direct action "won't do any good." It is the only thing that ever has in human history.

Be Creative

Being human is being able to choose to be creative. In this terrible time, when so much of the rhetoric and the practices try to stomp on you and knock you for a loop, deliberately choosing to play is very helpful.

Make some art. If, like me, you have no talent drawing or painting, do it anyway. Finger paint, by the way, is terrific for expressing emotion. Or you can write a song or a fiction story. Some of you may know I have started writing murder mystery fiction. If music composition or story-writing does not appeal, create a play with some others and perform it, if only for yourselves.

Put on some music and dance as if no one is watching.

Dancing has been a crucial part of resistance movements for all of human history.

Celebrate

We must celebrate together for the joy of being human. I learned that from Mujerista theologian Ada María Isasi-Díaz. She once told me, "The problem with you gringas is you don't fiesta." So in memory of Ada,[19] let us fiesta like we mean it. Let's have fun together in our families, whether biological or of choice, in our communities or other groups. Fiesta is a direct insult to the abuser. The abuser does not want us to party as though we were free.

I like to think that's why Jesus and the disciples were criticized by the elites of their time for having a good time, eating and drinking together (Matt. 11:19). They were enjoying life and oppressors hate that in the oppressed.

Lament together, march together, and party together. And vote. That is subversion in my view.

Let's take back our lives.

NOTES

1. Susan Brooks Thistlethwaite, "2017 Imperative: Counter Trump's Political Philosophy of Abuse," *Huffington Post* (December 29, 2016). https://www.huffingtonpost.com/rev-dr-susan-brooks-thistlethwaite/2017-imperative-counter-t_b_13874456.html.
2. "What is Domestic Violence?" The National Domestic Violence Hotline. http://www.thehotline.org/is-this-abuse/abuse-defined/.
3. Jasmine C. Lee and Kevin Quealy, "The 487 People, Places and Things Donald Trump Has Insulted on Twitter: A Complete List," *The New York Times* (updated July 10, 2018). https://www.nytimes.com/interactive/2016/01/28/upshot/donald-trump-twitter-insults.html.
4. Daisy Grewel, "Do Trump tweets spur hate crimes?" *Salon* (July 5, 2018) https://www.salon.com/2018/07/05/do-trump-tweets-spur-hate-crimes_partner/.
5. Alison Kodjak and Susan Davis, "Trump Administration Move Imperils Pre-Existing Condition Protections," NPR (June 8, 2018). https://www.npr.org/2018/06/08/618263772/trump-administration-move-imperils-pre-existing-condition-protections.
6. Paul Bledsoe, "Moynihan was right: The GOP tax give-away will lead to safety net cuts," *The Hill* (January 3, 2018) http://thehill.com/opinion/finance/365905-moynihan-was-right-the-gop-tax-giveaway-will-lead-to-safety-net-cuts.
7. Russell Berman, "Will Trump Cut Medicare and Social Security?" *The Atlantic* (January 24, 2017). https://www.theatlantic.com/politics/archive/2017/01/will-trump-cut-medicare-and-social-security/514298/.
8. Andrew Rafferty, "Donald Trump has History of Contradictory Statements on Nuclear Weapons," NBC News (October 11, 2017). https://www.nbcnews.com/news/all/donald-trump-has-history-contradictory-statements-nuclear-weapons-n808466.
9. David Sanger, "Trump's Sense of Timing on Nuclear Threat Confounds Experts," *The New York Times* (July 24, 2018). https://www.nytimes.com/2018/07/24/us/politics/trump-nuclear-north-korea-iran-.html.
10. Glenn Kessler, Salvador Rizzo, and Meg Kelly, "President Trump has made 3001 false or misleading claims so far," *The Washington Post* (May 1, 2018). https://www.washingtonpost.com/news/fact-checker/wp/2018/05/01/president-trump-has-made-3001-false-or-misleading-claims-so-far/?noredirect=on&utm_term=.6497cbcaec36.
11. Lauren Duca, "Donald Trump is Gaslighting America," *Teen Vogue* (December 10, 2016). https://www.teenvogue.com/story/donald-trump-is-gaslighting-america.
12. Trump Putin: US president reverses remark on Russia meddling," BBC News (July 18, 2018). https://www.bbc.com/news/world-us-canada-44864739.
13. Tim Dickinson, "Inside the Decade-Long Russian Campaign to Infiltrate the NRA and Help Elect Trump," *RollingStone* (April 2, 2018). https://www.rollingstone.com/politics/politics-features/inside-the-decade-long-russian-campaign-to-infiltrate-the-nra-and-help-elect-trump-630054/.
14. Heather Timmons, "How the NRA's Money Forces Republicans to Fight Gun Control," *Quartz Media* (March 2, 2018). https://qz.com/1214787/how-the-nras-money-forces-republicans-to-fight-gun-control/.
15. "Papa! Papa! Audio of children stokes rage over Trump's family separation policy," CNBC (June 19, 2018). https://www.cnbc.com/2018/06/19/papa-papa-audio-of-children-stokes-rage-over-trumps-family-separation-policy.html.

16. "Protestors March Against Trump Immigration—As It Happened," *The Guardian* (June 30, 2018) https://www.theguardian.com/world/live/2018/jun/30/trump-immigration-family-separation-protest-live-updates.

17. Susan Brooks Thistlethwaite and Mary Potter Engel, *Lift Every Voice: Constructing Christian Theologies from the Underside* (Maryknoll: Orbis Press 1998). See Introduction.

18. Michelle Goldberg, "Of Course the Christian Right Supports Trump," *The New York Times* (January 26, 2018). https://www.nytimes.com/2018/01/26/opinion/trump-christian-right-values.html.

19. "In Memoriam: Ada María Isasi-Díaz," *Religious Studies News*. http://rsnonline.org/index19fb.html?option=com_content.

REFERENCES

Berman, Russell. "Will Trump Cut Medicare and Social Security?" *The Atlantic* (January 24, 2017). https://www.theatlantic.com/politics/archive/2017/01/will-trump-cut-medicare-and-social-security/514298/.

Bledsoe, Paul. "Moynihan was right: The GOP tax give-away will lead to safety net cuts." *The Hill* (January 3, 2018) http://thehill.com/opinion/finance/365905-moynihan-was-right-the-gop-tax-giveaway-will-lead-to-safety-net-cuts.

Dickinson, Tim. "Inside the Decade-Long Russian Campaign to Infiltrate the NRA and Help Elect Trump," *RollingStone* (April 2, 2018). https://www.rollingstone.com/politics/politics-features/inside-the-decade-long-russian-campaign-to-infiltrate-the-nra-and-help-elect-trump-630054/.

Duca, Lauren. "Donald Trump is Gaslighting America." *Teen Vogue*. https://www.teenvogue.com/story/donald-trump-is-gaslighting-america.

Goldberg, Michelle. "Of Course the Christian Right Supports Trump," *The New York Times* (January 26, 2018). https://www.nytimes.com/2018/01/26/opinion/trump-christian-right-values.html.

Grewel, Daisy. "Do Trump tweets spur hate crimes?" *Salon* (July 5, 2018). https://www.salon.com/2018/07/05/do-trump-tweets-spur-hate-crimes_partner/.

Kessler, Glenn, Salvador Rizzo, and Meg Kelly. "President Trump has made 3001 false or misleading claims so far." *The Washington Post* (May 1, 2018). https://www.washingtonpost.com/news/fact-checker/wp/2018/05/01/president-trump-has-made-3001-false-or-misleading-claims-so-far/?noredirect=on&utm_term=.6497cbcaec36.

Kodjak, Alison and Susan Davis. "Trump Administration Move Imperils Pre-Existing Condition Protections." *NPR* (June 8, 2018). https://www.npr.org/2018/06/08/618263772/trump-administration-move-imperils-pre-existing-condition-protections.

Lee, Jasmine C. and Kevin Quealy. "The 487 People, Places and Things Donald Trump Has Insulted on Twitter: A Complete List," *The New York Times* (November 21, 2018). https://www.nytimes.com/interactive/2016/01/28/upshot/donald-trump-twitter-insults.html.

"In Memoriam: Ada María Isasi-Díaz" *Religious Studies News*. http://rsnonline.org/index19fb.html?option=com_content.

"Papa! Papa! Audio of children stokes rage over Trump's family separation policy." CNBC (June 19, 2018). https://www.cnbc.com/2018/06/19/papa-papa-audio-of-children-stokes-rage-over-trumps-family-separation-policy.html.

"Protestors March Against Trump Immigration—As It Happened." *The Guardian* (June 30, 2018). https://www.theguardian.com/world/live/2018/jun/30/trump-immigration-family-separation-protest-live-updates.

Rafferty, Andrew. "Donald Trump has History of Contradictory Statements on Nuclear Weapons." NBCNews (October 11, 2017). https://www.nbcnews.com/news/all/donald-trump-has-history-contradictory-statements-nuclear-weapons-n808466.

Sanger, David. "Trump's Sense of Timing on Nuclear Threat Confounds Experts." *The New York Times* (July 24, 2018). https://www.nytimes.com/2018/07/24/us/politics/trump-nuclear-north-korea-iran-.html.

Thistlethwaite, Susan Brooks and Mary Potter Engel. *Lift Every Voice: Constructing Christian Theologies from the Underside*. Maryknoll: Orbis Press, 1998.

Thistlethwaite, Susan Brooks. "2017 Imperative: Counter Trump's Political Philosophy of Abuse." *Huffington Post* (December 29, 2016). https://www.huffingtonpost.com/rev-dr-susan-brooks-thistlethwaite/2017-imperative-counter-t_b_13874456.html.
Timmons, Heather. "How the NRA's Money Forces Republicans to Fight Gun Control," Quartz Media (March 2, 2018). https://qz.com/1214787/how-the-nras-money-forces-republicans-to-fight-gun-control/.
"Trump Putin: US president reverses remark on Russia meddling." BBC News (July 18, 2018). https://www.bbc.com/news/world-us-canada-44864739.
"What is Domestic Violence?" The National Domestic Violence Hotline. http://www.thehotline.org/is-this-abuse/abuse-defined/.

Chapter Two

A Womanist Perspective on the Election of Donald Trump

What Pastors Are Called to Do

Linda E. Thomas

When *Journal of Lutheran Ethics* editor, Dr. Carmelo Santos, invited me to pen an article to guide a pastor's preaching and actions in the midst of this current, turbulent situation since Donald J. Trump's inauguration on January 20, 2017–I was intrigued, even eager, to submit something. Yet I was also hesitant–I'm not Lutheran and I wondered if Lutherans would think that my voice is credible or worthy of being read. Then I thought to myself, "*Well, my Lutheran siblings often tell me,* 'you are a child of God,'" *then maybe I'll start here.*" So it is this singular theological claim I often hear among Lutherans, along with the notion of being a "sibling," that I will dwell for a portion of this essay. For as often as I hear it—and have continued to hear it this long year-and-a-half of Donald Trump's administration—and though I do believe these convicting words with all of my heart, soul, mind, and strength, still I cringe when I hear them, because I don't often experience an ethical response corresponding to the depth of meaning I personally attach to them.

Therefore, I issue a warning now. My aim in writing this piece is not to offend, but rather offer some insights about how these words are in fact an affront—not only to me but even to the integrity of the words themselves—when offered to vulnerable people who are directly and negatively impacted by the presidency of Donald Trump. I take this with even greater seriousness as a Methodist living and teaching among Lutherans, having been on faculty at the Lutheran School of Theology at Chicago since 2000, and thus, have been entrusted with educating and preparing women and men for ministerial leadership in the ELCA for 18 years—and as such my academic credentials and theological gifts for the ministry of teaching are a proven asset.

But just as teaching in this ELCA setting has been the joy of my life, there have also been struggles, struggles, which I will also share.

WHO AM I?

Let me introduce myself to you. I am a constructive theologian and anthropologist of African descent who comes to the task of understanding and analyzing the actions of the current White House administration from a hermeneutic of plurality. I work from my many contexts and thus I consider myself a multidisciplinary scholar. I approach this essay first from my social location. I'm a temporally able-bodied African American, an out-heterosexual woman, living in a country infused with patterns of behavior that force people to be pressed-down and constrained by a myriad of multisectorial societal structures. This inadvertent pressing-down is known as oppression, causing some to have a lived experience of not being able to breathe. And the Latin root of this word, "opprimere" meaning "pressed/pushed down," I find compelling.

I have a daughter who lives with asthma and often has trouble breathing. This is the case even though she takes medicine daily to control this disease, which still constricts her lungs and causes sharp pain. Even an abrupt change in the weather can trigger this—such as in the weeks following Donald Trump's election, when temperatures in Chicago dipped to below freezing and she had to be transported by ambulance from her school bus to the ER. Going to an ER is no-joke, as it fills me and my daughter with anxiety, disrupts our lives, and makes us wholly dependent upon medical professionals to help my daughter breathe again and equally dependent on a loving God who struggles to breathe as my daughter does and so, succors us, helps us cope, and find relief. So I believe living with oppression(s) is similar to having asthma. One's life is interrupted because an ascribed feature of one's body/self—causes a person to struggle to breathe/live—to struggle despite God's intention for all living creatures to have the breath of life.

Like the drop in temperature that sent my daughter and me to the ER, Donald Trump's presidency has been for us a dramatic shift in the life of this nation. Here at home and abroad, people believe the United States strives for the best for all its citizens and people. The office of the president of the United States is symbolically and structurally the most powerful office in the world. Though I do not believe that this office supersedes the Triune God's power, all the world knows of the destructive power that Trump and his cronies have recklessly unleashed upon the planet—targeting members of the LGBTQ community be they serving in the military or trying to buy a wedding cake, using executive orders to persecute our Muslim kindred both in this country and in other countries, not to mention draining our nations coffers for the sake of the superwealthy. And who can forget his twisted relationship to Vladimir Putin—so shockingly on display during Trump's recent meeting with him in Helsinki. Closer to home, his appointment of Senator Jeff Sessions as Attorney General has likewise made Bull Conner—a chief antagonist of the Civil Rights movement—seem a puppy for the damage he has done to civil liberties, defending a senatorial candidate accused of having molested teenage girls, removing safeguards put in place by the Obama administration to address police overreach, not to mention instituting the absolutely satanic policy of separating families that come to our southern border seeking asylum.

Harassment of racial-ethnic people, women, Muslims, and other vulnerable populations have seen a dramatic increase these last two-and-a-half years, as once-closeted racists openly express their vitriol in all manner of ways (most commonly seen by calling the police on black people for everything from selling water, to examining their own real estate property, even having beach front cook-outs). These victims have continued to be predominately black and brown people, but victims over all are almost always identities that are not white, heterosexual, able-bodied, and Christian. The nation's consistent uptick in hate crimes also confirms this, as what was once "merely" (violent) rhetoric during campaigns now has taken shape in political appointments, legislation, and his almost unceasing use of Twitter in order to directly attack his critics and rile up his base.

A WOMANIST RESPONSE TO TRUMP'S ELECTION

Since I am an African American woman committed to a liberation perspective, I call myself a "womanist"—using a term that Alice Walker coined in 1983.[1] Hence, understanding what a womanist is and what the term means is essential for understanding a womanist perspective of Trump's presidency.

A womanist such as myself is concerned about the vernacular, that is, what happens in everyday life to ordinary people. She is committed to dealing with concerns about food, shelter, and clothing, about health, life, and death. She is concerned about these things because they bring concord and manage difference. Thus, a womanist seeks solutions via grassroots and is committed to the notion that those historically silenced are indispensable to social change.

Further, as an anti-oppressionist discipline, womanism is against all forms of oppression and actively fights against them. A womanist is not limited to battling racism and sexism but also fights against homophobia/heterosexism, ableism, ageism (discrimination based on youth and age)—anything that thwarts the development and flourishing of the systemically oppressed. Womanism advances shared aspirations and seeks the best possible quality of life for all members of a community. Finally, womanism affirms the spirit. A womanist is fully cognizant and clearly articulates her relationship with "a spiritual/transcendent realm with which human life, living kind, and the material world are all intertwined."[2]

There are many ways a person's life can be blocked by overlapping oppressions that create death-dealing realities for those under multiple subjugations (e.g., transgender Muslim Latinxs living in poverty). Intersectionality demonstrates that multiple identities do not function autonomously, but rather transect and coalesce. My own intersectionality is being a black woman, juxtaposed with being an African American Christian woman ordained in the United Methodist Church. Adding to this list, I approach my work as an African American ordained Christian theologian in the womanist tradition. I am also an anthropologist called to love my neighbor as myself, and I must love myself first so I can love my neighbor properly. If I confess that all people are made in God's image; if every human being is a child of God—and therefore my sibling—it means that I have a familial obligation or a moral ethic to stand upon with my neighbor.

Hence, it perplexes me that Christians who support Donald Trump expect me to feel good when they make this theological pronouncement, I am a child/sibling of God. I know this already, because I have full agreement with it as a theological precept. However, I can love my sibling who is my neighbor living close by or far away because I love myself as one made in God's image well enough to ask, "what does it mean that our president does not view Mexicans, members of the LGBTQAI+ community, Muslims, people living with disabilities, women, and African Americans as fully human"; that he is committed to "Stop and Frisk" policies that buttresses the prison industrial complex as well as the elementary-school-to-prison pipeline for black and brown children; who has undone or tried to undo as much of President Obama's work as possible from health care reform, to guidelines for transgender students, and emissions standards; that he is a bald-faced liar who knowingly twists truth to suit his interests and bolster his bigoted base; that I live in fear for my Muslim neighbor's life and for my Mexican sibling's children. So I must say to Trump, *"Get your hands off my sister! Stop saying psychologically harmful things to children of immigrants and doing them long-term trauma by splitting up their families! Stop saying dangerous things that make grown men live with fear."*

I have and will continue to resist every single one of Trump's policies with every fiber in my body because he opposes life for my vulnerable siblings, children of God. Since I understand "sibling" to involve having a serious relational to another child of God—I ask you not to call me sibling if for you that word does not have my correspondingly responsible vernacular ethic. Don't say *"we all of us are children of God"* to make yourself feel better. I already know that I am child of God, which is the reason I fight oppression for myself and other vulnerable folks. When your self-interests mean my demise then I know that you view dimly those who endure intersectional oppressions, as I do. Our bright lights will never be dimmed, for their current runs straight from the living, Triune God.

THE TERROR OF LIVING IN A TRUMP ERA

The sage poet Maya Angelou had a saying that comes to mind whenever I see someone who behaves in a way that is not congruent with my values: "If people show you who they are, believe them."[3] So when listening to the news on television one evening during the 2016 presidential campaign, after I heard Donald Trump call president Obama "stupid," I walked over to the television, hands still wet and dripping from the dish water soap, and turned it off. For my values this six-letter word is a four-letter word and that particular six-letter word is not allowed in my house, especially because I am raising a daughter. Angelou's dictum applies here—but Donald Trump has shown this nation and the world over and over again exactly who he is and millions and millions in this country don't want to face the truth.

I now find myself postelection remembering the words of Heidegger, *"Only a god can save us."*[4] For me "a god" is the Triune God of our faith. What would make an African American womanist scholar quote Heidegger? I understand Heidegger's statement to be in a particular historical moment, and as I stand with Trump actively shredding my already deeply flawed government, flawed international relationships, and flawed reputation, I see parallels between our present moment and Nazi Germany. As in these postwar years, I hear people redeclaring these beautiful words that "the Holocaust" will never happen again. *"We will not allow it,"* they say, *"not on our watch"*—and I add myself to this chorus.

Let me respond by saying a couple of things. First, my point of departure, as a constructive womanist theologian and social and cultural anthropologist, is "from below." I examine culture and history through listening for those whose narrative is missing, if not erased. *Who are those that suffer macroaggresssions in micro-contexts?* Who are so off the map that we don't even notice that they are missing. Consequently, as a womanist I am deeply concerned about whose who are forever "invisible in plain sight," who are not noticed as missing by their peers. When these most vulnerable begin to say, *"I can't breathe." "I don't feel safe." "Something's wrong."*—then I know we are close to a crisis. Those who are marginalized during normal times are completely erased during a time of crisis, scapegoated by those in power.

This is dangerous and we must take their concerns with the utmost seriousness.

Second, Trump has long shown us who he is—first by his discourse during the 2016 campaign, and now his policy after only 18 months in office. His rhetoric has polarized the nation to the extent that even clear-thinking people shooed his words away, as though not calling him into question was allowed. And though some criticize him, our press continues to fall prey to the whims of a president who is a master of getting attention—and hence has consistently elevated his destructive discourse instead of setting boundaries and standards. For the media, "unbiased reporting" on Trump has meant reporting filth in order to sell copy or assuage our guilt for having chosen wrong over right. If the press cannot raise moral questions and concerns then isn't it time for those whose moral consciousness rises from sacred ground called to bring critical thinking and a rigorous editorial calculus as a consequence of the disaster of the last 18 months? When do those concerned about the common good bring a voice to an analysis that admits that harm was being done to the common good by the current president, especially because the elected leaders who make up the majority in the US Congress participates, colludes, and let's down the God they profess to believe?

As it was in Germany in 1933, Hitler's grand plan was parsed out little by little over a long period of time—the seeds of which he'd cultivated since 22 years of age. And it was all put in place so gradually no one noticed the buildup until it was too late.[5] I posit that this is happening in the United States now, as well.

I also know that while the Jewish Holocaust is the most referenced, it is not the only genocide that has occurred. Citizens of the United States do not regularly encounter Native Americans or know the history of their ancestors who dwelled on the land now called the United States of America, long before it was "discovered." Columbus and those who followed him, confiscated the land using nefarious methods over hundreds of years resulting in genocide of indigenous peoples. Citizens of the United States do not comprehend that the "land of the free and home of the brave" was stolen from aboriginal peoples slaughtered in numbers that equal extermination. Citizens do not know that what is now considered the United States was occupied by First-Nation people who were and are sovereign nations. Americans do not speak about the genocide of Native peoples because it is sacrilegious to even allude to their history. In addition, we would be remiss not to acknowledge the Armenian and Rwandan genocides as well as the torturous Middle-passage (MAAFA) an African genocide in the name of global capitalism and "progress." My point is, as a womanist it is simply insufficient to say "Never again!" when this has never really stopped happening. This too, we must admit.

WHAT PASTORS CAN PREACH

Pay attention when vulnerable people share concerns that are not noticed by the historically dominant culture. The dominant culture often minimizes these voices to their own detriment. Even more significantly, some historically "othered" people who work, live, and have their being in a historically dominant culture often "go along to get along" because it is difficult to express their full worth in unsafe environments. So as the "#MeToo" teaches us—we are called to not discount when children and even women cry out for help. This must not happen. And when brought to their attention, pastors must take a stand and speak out.

Pastors can also offer hope. Many African American pastors have had to weave a tapestry of Gospel-hope even as their flocks are persistently dismayed, disappointed, heartbroken, and angered. These preachers have always given sermons reminding their people of similar times in the history of this country when African Americans have had to "keep on keeping on," especially on the morning after death-dealing decisions have stifled our breath. Look at our history for confirmation. We came through the following, each an infamous illustration of our struggle:

- 1851—*Dred Scott v. Sanford.* The US Supreme Court rules that Dred Scott cannot sue for his freedom in a free state because he is still "property" in another state, a ruling that denied any possibility of citizenship for African Americans, imperiled fugitive slaves, and set abolitionists two steps back. The US Supreme Court hence legalized slavery in all the territories, exacerbating the sectional controversy and pushing the nation toward civil war. The ruling had only one precedent, where the Supreme Court declared an act of Congress unconstitutional, and handed an indisputable victory to slaveholding states.
- In the 1890s "the number of lynchings peaked in 1892, at 230, and continued at rates of over 100 murders per year. Southern states invented new measures to disfranchise black voters."[6]

Likewise, a ministerial leader must first do some intentional introspection to become self-aware of what the defining points of tension was for her or himself during this recent election, just as free African Americans in centuries past have had to do the same to ground their own hopes and actions.

For some it may have been the chanting of campaign slogans like "build that wall," calling opponents "stupid," or saying of a more-qualified presidential candidate, "she's a nasty woman"; for others, it may have been the shock of Trump's "locker room talk." For others, the tension may be that Trump is the first nominee/president-elect who did not disclose his income tax statements. For others, the tension is that he appointed a white supremacist, Steve Bannon, as chief strategist, and for others it is that he called violent, murderous white supremacists in Charlottesville "very fine people." Religious leaders must acknowledge and find power in the "straw that broke the camel's back," or as Reverend Frank Thomas said in a sermon on December 4, 2016—*we need to say that we are in mourning and then state what we have lost*—helping the wounded and angry to stay reflective, as opposed to reactive.

The next step is to understand (though not necessarily agree with) the reasons why so many people voted for Mr. Trump. What life experiences lead women and men to vote for him? Was it because of a perceived loss of status and racial privilege during the Obama presidency? Was it a reaction against being kicked to the curb by career politicians? Was it that people felt that they had lost their voice, money, and their lot in life seemed cursed?

To hear the perspectives from others who thought or voted differently than others as myself, we must develop the ability to take seriously the experiences and understand their positions. That takes some real work. Work that so many don't want to bother doing. It's easier to blame someone else for your challenges rather than working to understand the cause of the present situation, as well as actively endeavoring to grasp the perspectives of others that are different from our own. Believe it or not, we are called to "adapt one's mindset and behavior to bridge across differences,"[7] as well as pursue justice.

NOTES

1. Alice Walker, *In Search of My Mother's Garden* (New York: Harcourt Brace Jovanovich, 1983). See also my article "Womanist Theology and Epistemology in the Postmodern U.S. Context," in *Another World Is Possible*, Marjorie Lewis and Dwight N. Hopkins, eds. (London: Ashgate Publishers, 2009). There I acknowledge that Alice Walker used the term womanist in 1983 and Chikwenye Okonjo Ogunyemi used the term in 1985. See also Layli Phillips, *The Womanist Reader* (New York: Routledge, 2006).

2. Layli Phillips (New York: Routledge, 2006), xxiv.

3. "Words That Matter: Everyday Truths to Guide and Inspire," *O, The Oprah Magazine* (New York: Hearst Communications, 2010), 48.

4. Martin Heidegger, "Nur noch ein Gott kann uns retten," *Der Spiegel* 30 (Mai, 1976). 193–219. Trans. by W. Richardson as "Only a God Can Save Us," in *Heidegger: The Man and the Thinker*, edited by Thomas Sheehan (Chicago: Precedent, 1981), 45–67.

5. I wish to acknowledge and thank Paul Wilson for a conversation that helped crystalized my thinking about the events that led to the rise of Hitler and the seeming acquiescence to his demonic plans by the German and the world.

6. Rebecca Edwards, "1896—Racial and Religious Prejudice," 1896—the Presidential Campaign, Cartoons and Commentary (Vassar College, 2000), see http://projects.vassar.edu/1896/1896home.html.

7. Mitchell R. Hammer, Intercultural Developmental Plan, IDI® and the IDI Intercultural Development Plan® are registered Trademarks and Copyrighted (2007, 2011) by Mitchell R. Hammer, Ph.D., IDI, LLC, P.O. Box 1388 Berlin, Maryland 21811 USA.

REFERENCES

Ackerman, Spencer. "Obama Under Mounting Pressure to Disclose Russia's Role in the US Election." *The Guardian.* Wednesday, December 7, 2016.

Amar, Akhil Reed. "The Troubling Reason the Electoral College Exists." *Time Magazine,* November 8, 2016. Updated: November 10, 2016, 2:19 PM ET.

Editors of *O, The Oprah Magazine*. "Words that Matter: Everyday Truths to Guide and Inspire." New York: Hearst Communications, 2010.

Edwards, Rebecca. "1896—Racial and Religious Prejudice." *1896—the Presidential Campaign, Cartoons and Commentary.* Vassar College, 2000. http://projects.vassar.edu/1896/1896home.html.

Heidegger, Martin. "Nur noch ein Gott kann uns retten," *Der Spiegel* 30 (Mai, 1976): 193–219. Trans. by W. Richardson as "Only a God Can Save Us," in *Heidegger: The Man and the Thinker* (1981), ed. T. Sheehan, 45–67.

Glor, Jeff. "Trump on his meeting with Putin, U.S. intelligence and his response to critics." https://cbsnews.com/news/trump-putin-meeting-helsinki-russia-election-meddling-believes-us-intelligence-interview-transcript-today-2018-07-18/. Accessed July 24, 2018.

Gray, Rosie. "Trump Defends White-Nationalist Protestors: 'Some very fine people on both sides.'" https://theatlantic.com/politics/archive/2017/08/trump-defends-white-nationalist-protesters-some-very-fine-people-on-both-sides/537012/. Accessed July 24, 2018.

Kenneth, David. "What Happened to African Americans during 1877–1920?" The Classroom—Synonym.com. *www.synonym.com.*

Parker, Ashley, and David E. Sanger. "Donald Trump Calls on Russia to Find Hillary Clinton's Missing Emails." *The New York Times.* Wednesday, July 27, 2016.

Phillips, Layli, *The Womanist Reader*, New York: Routledge, 2006.

Chapter Three

Warriors of Compassion

*Coordinates on the
Compass of Compassion-Based Activism*

Frank Rogers

During the contentious elections for marriage equality in California, Leah Rosen moved, with her lesbian partner, to the rural central valley to serve as a temple rabbi. In addition to teaching Torah and leading Shabbat services, she started an LGBTQ advocacy center devoted to education and public witness. One day, as she was leaving the temple, she discovered a pamphlet on her car's windshield held in place by a stone large enough to shatter a plate-glass window. The pamphlet advertised an upcoming rally protesting marriage equality at the town-square intersection. Handwritten on the note were the words, "I dare you to stop us."

Leah knew who did it. The chairman of the caucus protesting marriage equality lived across the street from her. While she and her partner were unloading their moving van, he had gathered his grandchildren from his front yard then staked down placards condemning homosexuality. Every time she left the house, she felt his glare from the shadows within his living room window. The rock on her windshield, however, was the first act of outright intimidation.

As would anyone, Leah's instinctive reactions were outrage and fear. Part of her was furious, damned if she would back down, incensed enough to organize a counterdemonstration with blistering placards of her own declaring she could not be bullied. Part of her wanted to crawl away, ignore the threat and just swallow the indignity; after all, she still lived across from him, and reacting would only encourage him, or escalate his hostilities.

Trained in compassion-based practices of self-restoration and nonviolent social engagement, Leah refrained from acting out of her reactivity. Instead, she cultivated a grounded, contemplative presence and listened to the needs within her impulses. She recognized that she needed to stand strong in her personal identity and political commitments; yet she wanted to stand strong in a way that still invited relationship. She wanted to find a way to befriend her neighbor; to return hate with love and dignity; and perhaps, even, to win him over, not through rage and ridicule, but through empowered compassion.

So she got curious. She asked around and found out that he was a deacon in the Roman Catholic Church, and he had a passion for ministries supporting abused animals. Leah could appreciate that, serving on the board of a local animal shelter herself. She also found out that he had a source of pride, his homemade chili—the best in the central valley to hear him boast—which he showed off every summer at the annual parish festival.

That's when Leah got an idea.

On the day of the rally protesting marriage equality, Leah gathered some friends and staged a chili cook-off in the park across the street. They had music, balloons, booths for children, and a dozen pots of chili, all proceeds going to the local animal shelter. The energy was so contagious, and the chili so enticing, folks mobbed the park, ignoring altogether the handful of protesters at the rally. Before long, the protesters lost their steam and started packing up to dissemble. Leah took her cue and crossed the street toward them. She walked up to her neighbor, the ringleader, and said to him,

"Excuse me, I understand that you make a mean bowl of chili."

"The best in the central valley," he grumbled.

"Great," Leah replied, "you see, we're having a chili cook-off across the street, and I wonder if you'd be willing to be our honorary judge." The man was taken aback. "It's for a good cause," Leah encouraged, "all the proceeds are supporting abused animals." She gestured toward the other protesters. "Bring your friends," she continued. "Free chili for everyone."

The man could not resist. Before he knew it, he was across the street tasting chili. After sampling them all, he told Leah that none of them could hold a candle to his own. To which Leah suggested that they do it up right, design a chili cook-off together for the whole town, each of them drawing on their various networks to support it.

And that's what they did. They organized a veritable festival together, all the profits benefiting the animal shelter. It went so well, Leah suggested that her neighbor serve on the shelter's board. She offered him rides to the board meetings, which turned into stops for coffee along the way. And to the man's shock and dismay, after months of her indefatigable friendliness, he found himself actually liking this woman.

A year and a half went by before the gentleman worked up the gumption to ask Leah a personal question. "Tell me," he fumbled one day over coffee, "how long have you been a lesbian? And how do you really know? I mean, how does it work?"

Leah was curious if he had ever known anyone who was gay or lesbian. It turns out he had. His younger brother was gay, years ago. He came out to his family when he contracted AIDS, back when AIDS was a death sentence. The young man's family shunned him, as did his church, as did he, the older brother. The young man disappeared on the streets of San Francisco, and died alone.

Leah could see the shame and regret hidden within her friend. Moved, she offered him a gift. "In my tradition," she shared, "we say Kaddish for those who have passed away. It is a way of honoring their memory and hoping they have found the peace that eluded them on Earth. It would be my privilege if I could say Kaddish for your brother. If you want, we can do it together."

The man nodded. And the two of them, a conservative Roman Catholic deacon and a lesbian Jewish rabbi, gathered in a small town temple and honored the memory of a man who had died alone some twenty years earlier.

We are living in turbulent times. Violence and violation seem to permeate our world—shootings in our schools and concert venues, sexual assault in the workplace, abuse in our sacred institutions, the daily indignities suffered by virtue of one's race, gender, orientation, religion, immigration status, or political loyalties. To be sure, such turbulent times can activate all manner of emotions and impulses within us—outrage, fear, disgust, anxiety, feeling overwhelmed to the point of numbness, or powerless before the forces that threaten our hope for the kind of world we yearn to live within.

And in the midst of all the turbulence, both in our world and in our souls, people like Leah Rosen shine as beacons responding to violence and violation with compassion, courage, creativity, and a commitment to personal and social restoration. The Center for Engaged Compassion, where Leah Rosen trained, researches social activism that responds to conflict and violence with empowered compassion. Its programs integrate compassion-based communication skills, Internal Family Systems theory, restorative justice, conflict transformation, and nonviolent social action with the contemplative resources and practices of the world's spiritual traditions.[1] Its approach can be distilled into 12 core principles that inform and promote a compassion-based social activism.

1. *Violence is an affront to the moral fabric of society.* No one deserves to be abused or violated. No one deserves to be mistreated by virtue of their race or gender, their religion or political party, their income level or sexual orientation. No one deserves to be denied access to the resources on which our lives depend. No one deserves to have their houses of worship, their homes or schools, their night clubs or places

of business vandalized or terrorized. Violation is wrong, and should be prevented, confronted, and disrupted. And those victimized by violence should be protected—their healing tended, their dignity restored, and their freedom to flourish secured.

2. *Traditional "Flight or Fight" responses to violence are self-defeating.* Fleeing—in the form of ignoring violence, tolerating its indignities, dismissing its damage, or staying silent so as not to make it worse—only allows violence to continue unchecked while diminishing our humanity in the process. Fighting—retaliating in kind with either physical violence or emotional violence like shaming, berating, reviling, or ridiculing—only escalates violence, more firmly entrenching an adversary in the truth of their cause and perpetuating the cycle of mutual antagonism. As the famous maxim attributed to Gandhi observes, "A eye for an eye, a tooth for a tooth, only makes the world blind and toothless."

3. *Human beings have a core Self-essence within us, which can ground responses to violence that are empowered, wise, and compassionate.* Spiritual traditions recognize a core essence within us, calling it by various names—Buddha nature, imago dei, Christ consciousness, Soul, Atman, the inner "I," the Inner Light. Internal Family Systems, Jungian psychology, and mystics like Thomas Merton call it the true Self, a spiritual core of calm, clarity, courage, and compassion. When grounded in our Self-essence, we have access to bold, creative, strategic, even loving responses to violence and violation that both preserve our own dignity and treat our opponent with nonreactive care and curiosity. Leah Rosen accessed her Self-essence when, after relaxing her instinctive fight-or-flight reactivities, she settled into a space where she could be curious about her neighbor, open to his humanity, and be creative and resilient in the ways she engaged him.

4. *Human beings also have interior reactivities, all rooted in positive intentions.* As much as we all have a Self-essence, we also are often hijacked by interior movements—emotions, for example, like anger, disgust, or fear—that dislodge us from that grounded, empowered, compassionate essence. As the Compassion Practice, Internal Family Systems, and Nonviolent Communication reveal, these interior movements are all rooted in positive intentions. Our emotions and impulses are there for a reason. The spiritual invitation when hijacked is not to demonize our reactivities, nor even to try to suppress or manage them; rather, it is to befriend them, to listen to their cry. They are rooted in some essential life need that feels threatened in the moment—perhaps to feel safe, to feel valued, to have agency, to claim dignity. Extreme reactivities are rooted in deep wounds that ache for healing and care. In fact, our interior reactivities are pitch-perfect barometers of what

our souls need when confronted by violence. Leah's reactivities alerted her to the deep need to stand strong in her personal identity and her yearning to coexist peacefully with her neighbor.

5. *When we are activated by violence, our spiritual invitation is, first, to take the "U" turn and tend to our reactivities until we are restored into our grounded Self-essence.* Responding to violation out of fear or rage is not only counterproductive, it disregards and does violence to the cries within our own souls. Turning inward, or taking the "U" turn, invites us to cultivate a contemplative groundedness that is mindfully aware of our reactivities and listens to the deep needs hidden within them.[2] As Leah Rosen exemplifies, tending to these needs not only dissipates the intensity of our reactivities, it settles us into our Self-essence from which grounded, creative, and constructive responses to violence can be discerned.

6. *Once we are restored to our Self-essence, we can see our adversary with greater clarity.* When we are hijacked by our interior reactivities, we see our opponents through the obscuring lenses of our own fears and indignations. We see them merely as a threat, and we reduce them to one dimensional caricatures—a homophobic redneck, for example—we feel entitled to denigrate. Again, as Leah Rosen illustrates, when we ground ourselves in our Self-essence, we are able to see the other nonreactively, and be curious about them as full human beings. A man who loves animals emerges, with an endearing delight in his own culinary capacities. This opens the possibilities of treating him with kindness, even to the point of befriending him.

7. *Our adversary's offensive behavior is rooted in an interior cry within them aching to be heard.* The behaviors, emotions, and attitudes we find offensive make some sense within our adversary's experience. They are rooted in life-essential needs that feel threatened; fundamental values that feel at risk; primal wounds, impossibly painful, defended to the death but aching to be held. In essence, our adversaries are suffering. Their behavior is their cry fighting to be heard. The cry does not come out directly. It comes out in the form of destructive behavior or offensive attitudes. Hidden underneath, however, is their desperate plea—"I feel threatened; my life feels at stake; I am in pain. Please, someone, hear me." Leah Rosen's neighbor reveals this precisely. His behavior is violating; his homophobic attitudes are revolting. Yet they serve to protect him from a gut-wrenching terror—if he is wrong about homosexuality, his brother would have died alone for nothing. The shame would be unbearable. Better to rid the world, even violently if necessary, of anything that stings that still-bleeding wound.

8. *Our adversary's offensive behavior will continue until they feel heard and honored at the level of their deeper cry.* Shaming, ridiculing, attacking, cajoling, even outright debating our opponents only entrenches them more fully in the truth or righteousness of their positions. It reinforces their sense of victimization; it escalates their outrage at being discounted; and it mobilizes their resolve to fight even harder. This makes psychological sense. They are experiencing their deepest fears coming true. Their soul's cry is not being heard. And survival itself is at stake.

9. *Conversely, being heard can relax extreme attitudes and behaviors.* Offensive persons expect to be attacked, hated, feared, or dismissed. They do not expect to be befriended. When we are genuinely interested in them as human beings, seeking to understand what is at the heart of the matter for them, what is the source of their inflexible commitments, what is at stake within their passions, it has the potential of easing their rigidity. When we are not heard, we get louder. When someone cares enough to listen, we calm down. Curiosity softens defensiveness. We do not need to scream when someone is genuinely listening.

10. *Our adversaries are more than their offensive behaviors; they, too, have a Self-essence.* As much as we might like to believe that offensive people are incapable of goodness, such is not the case. However dimly, a true Self-essence pulsates within them like a pilot light of the soul. When their hardness feels safe enough to relax, they possess capacities of generosity, openness, kindness, and genuine connection. Leah Rosen's neighbor, a vitriolic persecutor of homosexuality, found himself praying alongside a lesbian friend and mourning the death of a dishonored brother.

11. *Compassion toward an adversary is possible without legitimating the violence of their behavior or agreeing with their viewpoints.* Recognizing that an offensive person is still human, and sensing the suffering hidden within their difficult behavior, opens the door for compassion. We can understand why a person has come to believe as they do; we can be moved by the painful circumstances that give rise to their actions. Such compassionate understanding, however, in no way condones nor minimizes violation and abuse. We must oppose violent behavior; educate the unenlightened; sequester the unrepentantly dangerous; safeguard the victimized; and empower the downtrodden. Compassion for the violator simply means that we refuse to dehumanize them in the process. We fight for justice with a backbone of boldness; and we hold our opponents with care.

12. *The goal of compassion-based activism is not simply stopping the offensive behavior, but winning our adversary over into right relation-*

ship. To be sure, activism seeks to curtail violation in all of its forms. Those who harm others—with words, behaviors, or public policies—must be stopped. However, the most effective and enduring transformation comes not from coercing the aggressor into submission. That only breeds a resentment that will smolder until a later eruption. Rather, compassion-based activism seeks to win over the hearts of our adversaries. It invites them, willingly, into right relationship by listening to their deepest concerns, finding points of connection, or simply believing in their humanity when no one else will. Leah Rosen found a way to dissuade a bigot from leaving stones on her windshield and discontinue his anti-gay rallies. She did it by making him a friend. This is our greatest spiritual power—transforming our enemy into a companion. After all, it is hard to demonize a person who holds you in your pain, and cries with you in your grief.

These 12 principles invite a compassion-based activism that fights for justice while loving our opponent. So what does this actually look like in practice? Compassion-based activism cannot be reduced to a list of specific actions. Any action can be done with a spirit of violence and contempt. A chili cook-off could become toxic with disgust, self-righteousness, and in-your-face hostility. Such emotional viciousness, even under the guise of nonviolence, is spiritually violent and mirrors the hatred we seek to resist.

Compassion-based activism, rather, is more defined by a set of qualities that comprise the spirit or energy with which any action can be performed. Instead of a list of actions to implement, then, we really need a compass to point in the direction toward which we might move. A compass is something we consult when we are lost or disoriented. It helps us get our bearings, the needle pointing due north. For the needle to move freely, the compass must be balanced, its magnetic forces held in an equilibrium. Eight coordinates circumscribe the compass of compassion-based activism, each one held in creative tension with another that must be balanced for the needle directing us to move freely. Taken as a whole, this compass orients us toward what compassion-based activism might look like in any situation of violence or violation.

1. Compassion-based activism embodies *empowered personal dignity*. James Lawson, a nonviolent activist with Martin Luther King, was leaving a café in the rural south during the civil rights movement when a passing motorcyclist spat into his face then pulled into a parking lot across the street. Rev. Lawson wiped the spit off his face with his handkerchief, walked over to the cyclist, and with dignified nonchalance, asked the cyclist for directions to a nearby town. The nonplussed motorcyclist knew of nothing else to do but give the man directions as if Lawson were his social equal.

Compassion-based activism is not passive before violation. It does not submit to its indignities, minimize its effects, nor retreat in cowering intimidation. Rather, it boldly stands up for one's personal dignity. It speaks truth to power, refuses to be shamed, and asserts one's worth before those who are dismissive or condescending. As Mahatma Gandhi taught, "The first principle of nonviolent action is that of noncooperation with everything humiliating."[3]

Sue Monk Kidd embodies this as well. She once popped into a drugstore where her 14-year-old daughter worked after school. She paused when she spied her daughter kneeling in the aisle stocking a bottom shelf. As she watched, two men walked up the aisle and stopped behind her daughter. One smirked to the other, "Now that's how I like a woman—on her knees." The other man chuckled as the daughter, hearing it all, dropped her head in humiliation.

Kidd knew, if she walked away in silence, her daughter's spirit could dim, condemning her to the interior posture, like too many women before her, of always being down on her knees before condescending men. Kidd was not going to let that happen.

She walked up to the two men and said, "I have something to say to you and I want you to hear it." The men stopped laughing. "This is my daughter. You may like to see her and other women on their knees, but we don't belong there. *We don't belong there!*"

The two men were dumbstruck. Then one said snidely, "Women." And the two walked away.

That night, back home, the daughter came to her mother's bedroom. "Mama," the daughter said, "about this afternoon in the drugstore. I just wanted to say, thanks."[4]

Compassion-based activism courageously embodies empowered personal dignity.

2. Empowered personal dignity is held in creative tension with an opposing magnetic force. Compassion-based activism also embodies *love for one's adversary*. In the same way that violence does not transform violence; hate does not transform hate. As King so memorably phrased it, "Darkness cannot drive out darkness; only light can do that. Hate cannot drive out hate; only love can do that."[5] Love is the transformative agent that can melt the heart of another. Cesar Chavez also knew this. When writing from jail to the farmowners exploiting the workers, Chavez underscored that his movement would resist with "every ounce of human endurance and spirit," yet they would resist not with dehumanizing violence, but with "love and compassion."[6] With King, he refused not only to shoot his opponents, he refused to hate them. Compassion-based activism recognizes the humanity of the other—they too have known suffering, they too have terrors and are fighting for their lives, they too have capacities for love, generosity and goodwill. As

Figure 3.1. The Compass of Compassion-Based Activism: First Pair of Compass Coordinates Image created by Frank Rogers

firmly as compassion-based activism fights for the dignity of the oppressed, it preserves the dignity of the oppressor as well. It refuses, not only to shoot them, but to humiliate them, denigrate them, dismiss them, hold them with contempt, or gloat over their demise. To paraphrase King again, "Let no one pull you so low as to make you hate them."[7] Compassion-based activism lives in this tension of standing up for justice while loving our adversary, even when they do not deserve it.

3. A second magnetic force balances the compass orienting compassion-based activism. On the one hand, compassion-based activism embodies a *universal inclusivity*. Spiritually grounded activists recognize that the compassion that inspires and sustains our work extends to all human beings. None are excluded from its embrace. Its loving, restorative energy is offered to the Republican and the Democrat, the peace activist and the NRA member, the terrorist and the terrified, the abuser and the abused. To be sure, we all have inclinations to demonize others as egregiously over the line and hopelessly irredeemable—that gang member is just a cold-blooded thug; that white supremacist is just a hardened bigot; that bully of a leader is just a power-hungry narcissist—then dismiss them as being beyond the reach of

civilized behavior. Compassion-based activism extends love to everyone. It embodies a radical inclusivity that refuses to place limits on those whom we will treat with dignity, compassion, and hope for restoration.

For many, this universal reach of activist love is rooted in a cosmic source. As King writes, "Whether we call it an unconscious process, an impersonal Brahman, or a Personal Being of matchless power and infinite love, there is a creative force in this universe that works to bring the disconnected aspects of reality into a harmonious whole."[8] Engaged Buddhists like Thich Nhat Hahn describe the web of interconnectedness in which all of us are one, each of us participating in one another's suffering and joy.[9] Jesus' nonviolent activism was rooted in a God whose infinite compassion extends to all like the sun that rises on the good and the evil, like the rain that falls on the just and the unjust.[10] However understood and described, compassion-based activism is aligned with a cosmic, universal energy that welcomes all persons into its care. As the bumper sticker succinctly puts it, "God bless the whole world. No exceptions."

4. This radical inclusivity is held in tension with another quality. Compassion-based activism also places *firm limits around violation*. As much as

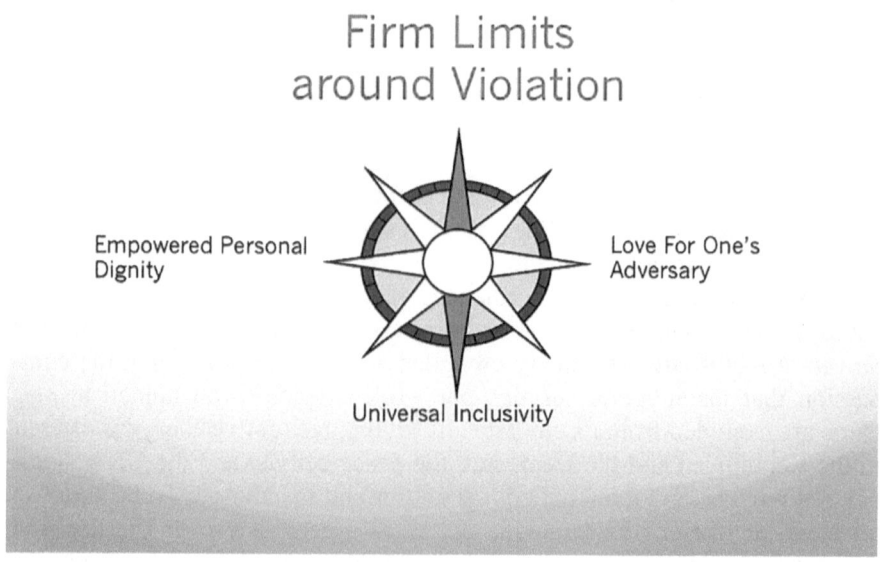

Figure 3.2. The Compass of Compassion-Based Activism: Second Pair of Compass Coordinates Image created by Frank Rogers

compassion-based activism extends love and dignity to all human beings, it does not allow violation to go unchecked. Compassion-based activism protects the vulnerable from abusive behavior, limits harm done by toxic people, draws firm boundaries around those who are dangerous, and sequesters those who are unrepentantly violent and violating. Compassion-based activism invites a radical reconciliation with even the most hardened perpetrator, but it recognizes that reconciliation has conditions. When a violation has occurred, relational restoration requires the offending party to acknowledge the offense, show remorse, make restitution, and commit to a rehabilitation that prevents future offenses. If the person refuses, say an abuser is recalcitrant or a terrorist remains violent, compassion-based activism stands firm. It does what is necessary to safeguard the endangered. And if that entails isolating the perpetrator from the human community, the activist complies and then, though relieved perhaps, grieves at the brutalities they must have endured to have become so calcified. When the Jews were liberated from Egypt, their captors dead in the Red Sea, the angels wanted to celebrate. But God intervened. "The work of my hands are drowning in the sea and you want to sing songs."[11] God's grief extends even to the suffering of the enemy.

5. Compassion-based activism is also *grounded in nonreactive presence.* Its responses to violence embody an inner stability even in the midst of challenge, conflict, or attack.

Nick, a friend of mine, once attended a peace vigil. After the invasion of Iraq, in the wake of 9/11, a Quaker group organized a silent witness for peace at a busy local intersection. When Nick, a longtime teacher of contemplative practice, arrived, a gentle elderly woman approached him to share the parameters. Her lifelong commitment to Quaker activism nurtured a radiant calm that informed the vigil's design. They gathered to create an oasis of peace within the fever of war. Nothing more. They offered a silent presence of care. Respect and courtesy would be extended to all. But no words were to be uttered. They would embody peace, not debate it. Peace speaks for itself.

She cautioned Nick that this could be difficult—people might gesture, honk their horns, shout out their dissent. Nick assured her that, as a teacher of contemplative practice, he knew how to be silent. He scrawled a sign, *Peace For Our Children* and took his place on the sidewalk.

Within moments, right in front of him, a pick-up truck stopped at a red light. The windows rolled down, talk radio blared from the speakers. The man inside fumed at the traffic, looked around, saw Nick, and spat out, "Your children would be dead if we lived in Iraq."

Nick, seasoned contemplative that he is, spat right back, "Your children will be dead if we keep bombing innocent people."

"Don't talk about my children!" the man shot back.

"Don't talk about mine!" Nick rejoined, "I want peace for them all!"

"*I'll show you peace!*"

"Show me! I'm right here!"

A gentle arm wrapped around my friend's shoulder. The elderly Quaker woman suggested they take a walk. As the light turned green, the truck pulled away. And the peace vigil settled, once more, into silence.

It can happen to us all. Even when well-intentioned, we get hijacked by fury, indignation, or self-righteous dismissiveness. This stands in stark contrast with the civil-rights college students integrating the lunch counters in Nashville. Though assaulted with epithets, burning cigarettes, thrown food, fists, and finally handcuffs, the Black students sat with poise, dignity, and nonviolent presence.[12] Compassion-based activism is nonreactive. We become reactive when we lose our grounding in the truth of what we know. The Black students in Nashville knew their truth—the truth of their dignity, the truth of their cause, the truth of their vision of a Beloved Community where their worth is God-given and their liberation is secured. And they knew it with such a steel spine of inner stability no thuggish brutality could knock them off their center.

6. This interior groundedness in the spine of one's truth is held in tension with another quality. Compassion-based activism embodies an *openness to*

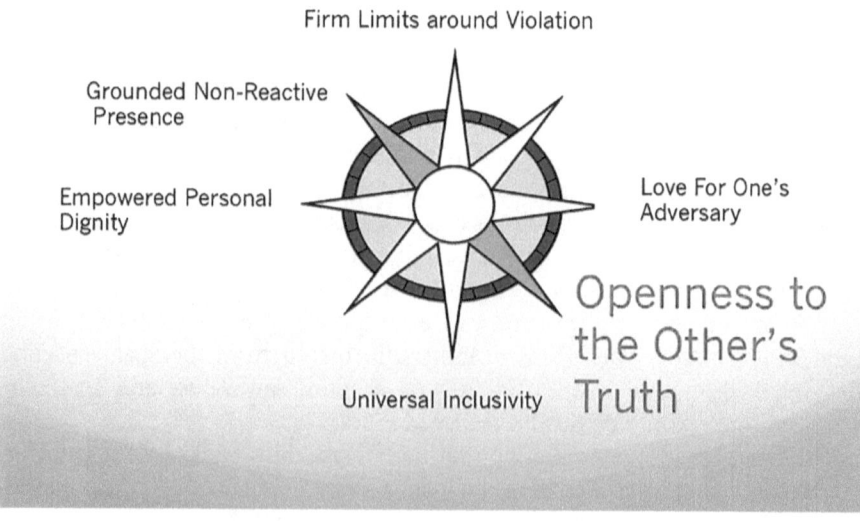

Figure 3.3. The Compass of Compassion-Based Activism: Third Pair of Compass Coordinates Image created by Frank Rogers

the other's truth. It recognizes that our adversaries are fighting for something that feels life-threatening to them. Their behaviors, passions, and ideologies are rooted in needs that feel essential to them, or sometimes, in suffering out of which their positions were forged. The compassion-based activist seeks to understand, with genuine openness, the truth within an adversary that informs their life posture.

In today's climate of vitriolic political polarization, this may be the most difficult and necessary invitation facing us. We need to cultivate spaces that are genuinely curious about the core concerns, the life experiences, the deep terrors that inform persons who embody positions, not only contrary to ours, but offensive to us. When people feel listened to, extreme positions relax, the heart of the matter can be revealed, and if common ground cannot be found, at least we can offer our adversary the gift of having been heard. Perhaps that will touch the buried pain that festers within their extremism.

Megan Phelps-Roper was literally the poster child for the Westboro Baptist Church. As a child, she held posters viciously condemning homosexuality at the funerals of gays and lesbians. As a young adult, she continued her campaign through social media. She expected people to vilify her in return, which only served to fuel her zeal. One small group, however, responded to her differently. They were genuinely curious about her. They asked her about her story, her experience growing up in her community, the concerns and values at the core of her viewpoints. Phelps-Roper grew curious in return. Who were these people who offered her such warmth and interest? She met them, stayed in their home, and, over time, could not reconcile her extreme beliefs with the humanity of the people befriending her. She renounced her virulent views, at the cost of being ostracized by her church and family. Now she writes and speaks about the power of dialogue and empathy when relating to extremists. She knows. Compassion-based activists, authentically open to the truth of her experience, de-radicalized her, and restored her to her humanity.

7. A final magnetic force orients the compass of compassion-based activism. Such activism embodies a *strategic focus on systemic violence*. No one is born a racist, a killer, a misogynist, a fundamentalist extremist. Violence is rooted in and perpetuated by a complex web of forces—family systems, cultural ideologies, institutional discriminations, political disparities, economic injustices, and generational trauma.[13] People engaged in violent behavior are themselves shaped by and enslaved to the social forces that give rise to violence in the first place. As King taught us, the enemy is racism, not the racist; poverty, not the ones robbing houses; terrorism, not the terrorist caught in the vast global forces that give rise to radicalization. Compassion-based activism involves strategic social analysis. It educates itself about the systemic causes of violence in our world. And it seeks both to free those captive to these systems, and to transform the systems themselves.[14]

8. Such rigorous systemic social analysis is balanced by a final quality. Self-led activism practices *imaginative social problem-solving*. So often, acts of violence polarize us into mutually unsatisfying fight-or-flight options. We are attacked, we either attack back or swallow it. A white supremacist demonstration happens in our town, we either stage a counterdemonstration escalating the tensions or we suffer it in seething silence. Compassion-based activism does not get boxed in by polarized, binary options. Rather, it is free, creative, imaginative, and playfully innovative. It sees violence as a problem-solving opportunity to brainstorm out-of-the-box possibilities that might defuse tensions, shift the power dynamics, and invite an alternative relationship between the parties involved. Leah Rosen thought out-of-the-box when she conceived of a chili cook-off to benefit abused animals.

The citizens of Wunsiedel, Germany were similarly creative.

Wunsiedel is where the Nazi officer Rudolf Hess was buried. For years, a group of neo-Nazis staged a fascist rally on Hess's birthday marching some two miles from the town-square to Hess's gravesite. The citizens knew that if they prohibited the rally it would only play into the neo-Nazis' image of being victimized, unable even to exercise free speech, inadvertently energiz-

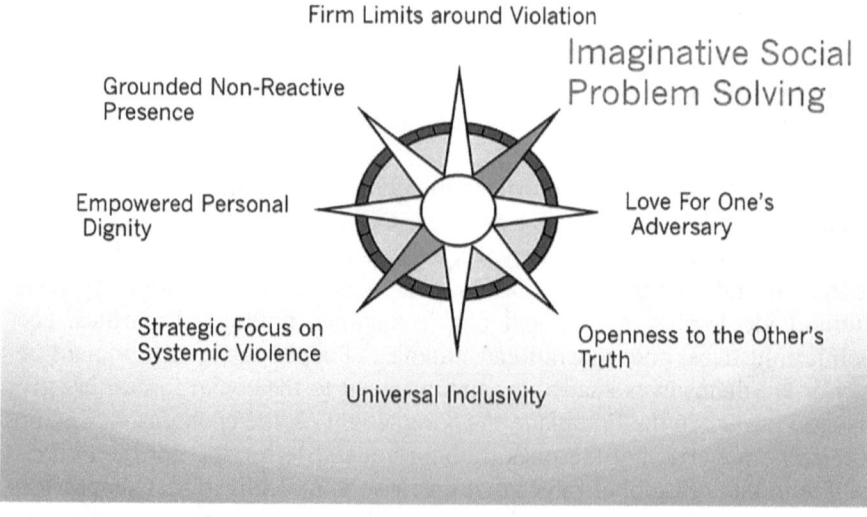

Figure 3.4. **The Compass of Compassion-Based Activism: Fourth Pair of Compass Coordinates Image created by Frank Rogers**

ing them all the more. Suffering it in silence was unacceptably excruciating. So they got creative. They turned the rally into a charity walk-a-thon. They gathered pledges from individuals and local businesses—for every meter a neo-Nazi walked, money would be donated to anti-fascist organizations. Suddenly, the dynamics were reversed. The citizens showed up to cheer the marchers on. They painted a starting line and finish line; they had aid stations to keep them going; they filled the route with signs informing the marchers of how much, so far, they had made for the cause and thanking them for their contributions.[15] This is imaginative social problem-solving at its best—creativity that shifts the power dynamics, dissolves the aggressor's momentum, and energizes the victimized.

These eight qualities comprise the coordinates on the compass of compassion-based activism. When we find ourselves in the midst of violence and violation, compassion-based activism invites us to seek that path that courageously embodies empowered personal dignity while extending a compassionate love for our adversary; that aligns with a cosmic universal inclusivity while firmly establishing limits around violation; that is calmly grounded in a truthful nonreactive presence while curiously open to our opponent's truth;

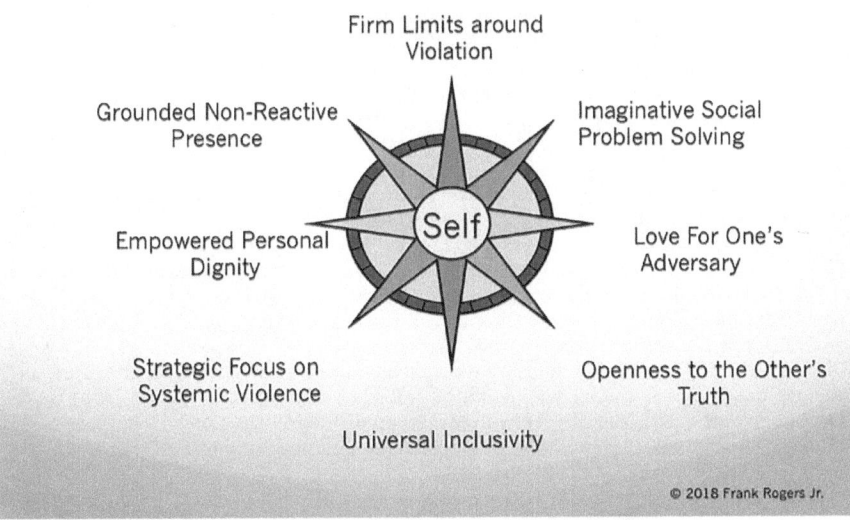

Figure 3.5. The Compass of Compassion-Based Activism Image created by Frank Rogers

and that strategically focuses on systemic violence while creatively engaging in imaginative social problem-solving.

And when we walk that path, we will find ourselves in good company. Leah Rosen, Megan Phelps-Roper, Sue Monk Kidd, Martin Luther King, Cesar Chavez, Mahatma Gandhi, James Lawson, along with unnamed peacemakers in segregated lunchrooms and Nazi birthplaces—these are the people showing us the way of compassion-based activism. They boldly fight violence and injustice, but they do so with weapons of love and grounded dignity, courage and creativity. They are warriors—warriors of compassion creating a world where war itself will one day be no more.

NOTES

1. http://www.centerforengagedcompassion.com. Influential resources include Frank Rogers *Practicing Compassion* (Nashville, TN: Fresh Air Books, 2015); Richard Schwartz *Internal Family Systems Therapy* (New York: The Guilford Press, 1995); Marshall Rosenberg *Nonviolent Communication: A Language of Life* (Encinitas, CA: Puddle Dancer Press, 2003); Howard Zehr *The Little Book of Restorative Justice* (New York: Good Books, 2014).

2. "U-turn" has been used in numerous contexts. I first heard it from Richard Schwartz, *You Are the One You've Been Waiting For* (Oak Park, IL: Trailheads Publications, 2008).

3. Quoted in Walter Wink *Engaging the Powers* (New York: Fortress Press, 1999), 177.

4. "That's How I Like to See a Woman" by Sue Monk Kidd—excerpted from *The Dance of the Dissident Daughter* (New York: HarperCollins, 1996), 7–10. Reprinted in Laura Slattery et al. (eds.), *Engage: Exploring Nonviolent Living* (Oakland, CA: Pace e Bene Press, 2005) 20–21.

5. Martin Luther King, *A Gift of Love: Sermons from Strength to Love and Other Preachings* (Boston: Beacon Press, 2012), 67.

6. "Letter from Delano" by Cesar Chavez—excerpted from *Christian Century* (Chicago: April 23, 1969. Reprinted in Laura Slattery et al. (eds.), *Engage: Exploring Nonviolent Living* (Oakland, CA: Pace e Bene Press, 2005), 127–128.

7. Martin Luther King, *Paul's Letter to American Christians* (Sermon, November 4, 1956).

8. Martin Luther King, "An Experiment in Love," in James Washington, ed. *A Testament of Hope* (San Francisco, CA: HarperSanFrancisco, 1986), 20.

9. See Sallie King, *Socially Engaged Buddhism* (Honolulu, HI: University of Hawaii Press, 2009).

10. Mt. 5:45. See Frank Rogers, *Compassion in Practice: The Way of Jesus* (Nashville, TN: Upper Room Books, 2016), 51–53.

11. Quoted in Elizabeth Johnson, *She Who Is* (New York: Crossroad, 1994) 260.

12. For footage, see "We Were Warriors," *A Force More Powerful*, directed by Steve York et al. (Princeton, NJ: Films for the Humanities and Sciences, 2000), DVD.

13. An excellent resource is Maria Cimperman, *Social Analysis for the 21st Century* (Maryknoll, NY: Orbis Books, 2015).

14. For her TED talk, see https://www.ted.com/talks/megan_phelps_roper_i_grew_up_in_the_westboro_baptist_church_here_s_why_i_left

15. Moises Velasquez-Manoff, "How to Make Fun of Nazis," *New York Times*, August 17, 2017, https://www.nytimes.com/2017/08/17/opinion/how-to-make-fun-of-nazis.html.

REFERENCE

Chavez, Cesar. "Letter from Delano." *Christian Century* (Chicago: April 23, 1969). Reprinted in Laura Slattery et al. (eds.), *Engage: Exploring Nonviolent Living*. Oakland: Pace e Bene Press, 2005.
Cimperman, Maria. *Social Analysis for the 21st Century*. Maryknoll: Orbis Books, 2015.
Johnson, Elizabeth. *She Who Is*. New York: Crossroad, 1994.
King, Martin Luther. "An Experiment in Love," in James Washington, ed. *A Testament of Hope*. San Francisco: HarperSanFrancisco, 1986.
King, Martin Luther. *A Gift of Love: Sermons from Strength to Love and Other Preachings*. Boston: Beacon Press, 2012.
King, Martin Luther. *Paul's Letter to American Christians*. Sermon, November 4, 1956.
King, Sallie. *Socially Engaged Buddhism*. Honolulu: University of Hawaii Press, 2009.
Monk Kidd, Sue. "That's How I Like to See a Woman," in *The Dance of the Dissident Daughter*. New York: HarperCollins, 1996. Reprinted in Laura Slattery et al. (eds.). *Engage: Exploring Nonviolent Living*. Oakland: Pace e Bene Press, 2005.
Phelps-Roper, Megan. TED talk, https://www.ted.com/talks/megan_phelps_roper_i_grew_up_in_the_westboro_baptist_church_here_s_why_i_left.
Rogers, Frank. *Compassion in Practice: The Way of Jesus*. Nashville: Upper Room Books, 2016.
Rogers, Frank. *Practicing Compassion*. Nashville: Fresh Air Books, 2015.
Rosenberg, Marshall. *Nonviolent Communication: A Language of Life*. Encinitas: Puddle Dancer Press, 2003.
Schwartz, Richard. *Internal Family Systems Therapy*. New York: The Guilford Press, 1995.
Schwartz, Richard. *You Are the One You've Been Waiting For*. Oak Park: Trailheads Publications, 2008.
Velasquez-Manoff, Moises. "How to Make Fun of Nazis." *New York Times* (August 17, 2017). https://www.nytimes.com/2017/08/17/opinion/how-to-make-fun-of-nazis.html.
Wink, Walter. *Engaging the Powers*. Minneapolis: Fortress Press, 1999.
York, Steve, et al. "We Were Warriors." *A Force More Powerful*. Princeton: Films for the Humanities and Sciences, 2000. DVD.
Zehr, Howard. *The Little Book of Restorative Justice*. New York: Good Books, 2014.

Chapter Four

Disrupting the Public Square

Prophetic Pastoral Care and Witness in Times of Trauma

Michelle A. Walsh

"Since the time that I came out here, it has been 6 minutes and 20 seconds. The shooter has ceased shooting, and will soon abandon his rifle, blend in with the students as they escape, and walk free for an hour before arrest. Fight for your lives before it's someone else's job."[1]

Where were you on March 24, 2018 when Emma González disrupted public expectations and comfort during the March for Our Lives event in Washington, D.C.? I suspect many of you reading this chapter, like myself, were otherwise occupied and did not watch her speech in full at the time, though you likely read about it later. I was traveling back from Chicago and first began to notice exclamations on my social media feeds. Later I read about it in news articles. A few days later, I sat down to view the actual video of her entire speech performance action, and I realized this was a much different experience than simply reading about it. Instead, my throat constricted as I experienced the full disruptive embodied power of Emma's fierce testimony and witness in the public square. I watched and listened as she strove to convey to the massive gathering what she and her friends had experienced and lost in just a few brief minutes, how their lives had been "forever altered" by the violent impact of the mass school shooting at her high school on Valentine's Day, February 14, 2018. "Everyone who was there understands," she said. Yet in that moment, and before a captive national media audience, Emma wanted to bring us viscerally with her to the day of the shooting. She was determined to force us to grasp and share in some, at least just some, of what they had experienced as a community. Her body, her dress, her words, her silence, her tears, and time itself, as she held the public stage and public cameras, became her tools. She did this both as a fellow survivor and ally to her community and lost loved ones and also as a warning to the audience before her in real time, in virtual time, and in the time yet to come. "Fight for your lives before it's someone else's job."

My throat constricted with both compassionate admiration and sad empathy. I experienced a familiar recognition that Emma the survivor was fighting back with all that was in her capacity to do. She conveyed her rage-filled silent wail in protest, determinedly wiping away any tears getting in her way, and, by doing so, she brought us collectively into her grief and angry resistance. We who count ourselves as survivors of violence and loss, myself included, can discover a fierceness through our different forms of resistance in the aftermath—we strive both to care for ourselves and others in this resistance, and we challenge those who would minimize, discard, or normalize our lived experiences as "not as bad as," "collateral damage," or "just the way things are." When we have the capacity to resist, we resist with all that is in us the dominant culture's belief that the world cannot be radically different.

Writing and research became my own path and practice of resistance to my lived experiences of the loss of multiple young people to violence in my former urban youth ministry. In my earliest research with fellow survivors in the aftermath of violent trauma, I came to call such performative public acts of witness, protest, and resistance a type of "prophetic pastoral care."[2] Such solitary acts and ongoing practices by survivors gave testimony to and warning about the personal and public impact of their lived experiences with the systemic structures of oppression. Through material and embodied expressions of advocacy and education in the public square, they also prioritized empathy, compassion, and solidarity with those most harmed by these oppressive structures. For the Abrahamic religions and in a Christian theological context (as well as across other religious traditions when drawing on their own cultural linguistic systems), these acts and practices become fruitful points of reflection for public theologies of activism and resistance, and we can trace the roots of such language and public theologies to developments during a similar period of historical social turbulence in the 1960s around the globe. As a survivor, I have learned from this history, as well as from the lived experiences and practices of my fellow survivors, and these necessarily impact my own theological understandings and practices when I attend to the lessons they convey rather than minimizing, ignoring, or discarding them.

HISTORICAL DEVELOPMENT OF PROPHETIC PASTORAL CARE THEOLOGY

As foremost a survivor of trauma, as well as a practical theologian who is trained as a clinical social worker and ordained as Unitarian Universalist clergy, I situate myself in a growing area of interdisciplinary contemporary studies that calls for the recognition of pastoral theology as public theology.[3] I do so out of a long and fierce search in my graduate school education for theological companions to my own lived experiences as a survivor of trauma. My search took me back to neglected or underestimated academic voices from the 1960s into the early 1980s[4] who explicitly explored a deeper intertwining of the pastoral and prophetic. Two major contemporary practical and pastoral theologians, Charles V. Gerkin and Larry Kent Graham, developed extensive practical theological frames for linking the pastoral and the prophetic in practical theology.[5] They became primary initial companions in my academic quest for language and theory. Their work serves as a significant ongoing contribution for those who would engage the field of public theologies of activism and resistance today, particularly for those of us writing openly as survivors.

Prophetic pastoral care involves practices that spiritually serve to heal and empower survivors in the aftermath of trauma and ongoing oppression. The prophetic dimension of such empowerment entails practices that also publicly call attention to the social conditions that create the groundwork for traumatic events and oppression to occur, with the intention of disrupting and transforming those social conditions toward a larger vision of peace and justice. Emma González engaged in this type of public disruption with the intent of transforming, or "transfiguring,"[6] her witnessing audience—and this also served as a form of empowerment for her and for her fellow survivors. We as her audience were transfixed and awakened to a new and different reality, and we became bonded in that moment to Emma and her community of fellow survivors. In my studies of other survivors in the aftermath of violence, they too found empowerment and forms of "healing" through types of public testimony and witness that involved embodied or material art practices—practices that also disrupted and "transfigured" the public square.[7] Certain questions then arose for me in these discoveries, and by implication for my fellow pastoral and public theologians, regarding the ongoing necessity for and implications of these public acts by survivors.

For example, in the aftermath of trauma, including violent trauma and ongoing oppression, do "healing" and growth actually *require* more than a focus on the individual by the pastoral caretaker? Does the pastoral caretaker *need* to understand the individual in a larger historical, social, cultural, and political context and then bring that perspective into the actual pastoral caretaking practices? Does sensitivity to this larger historical, social, cultural, and political context also impact our pastoral theologies, the questions we ask, and the use of sources and forms of pastoral care practice for the individual and the individual in community? Does the fullest form of pastoral care then include the need to engage in public policy advocacy to change systems on behalf of all individuals—and to be in alliance with those impacted individuals when doing so? If so, what might be practical examples of how this is done? As we draw on lessons of the past in developing public theologies of activism and resistance for our increasingly challenging and traumatic times today, my own fierce search found resonance in the social and political turbulence of the 1960s. There I discovered a brewing sociopolitical cultural zeitgeist fostering increased dialogue on these types of questions and on the relationship between the pastoral and the prophetic in Christian pastoral care in particular.[8]

Gerkin and Graham, both now deceased, were the first to elaborate systematically and theologically on the use of the phrase "prophetic pastoral care/practice" in answering yes to most of these questions.[9] However, it also is important to recognize that their work was connected to and built upon previous academic voices being raised as early as the 1960s. The earliest use of the phrase "prophetic pastoral care," for example, appears to be in 1966 by Wayne E. Oates[10] in a rarely referenced book, *Pastoral Counseling in Social Problems: Extremism, Race, Sex, Divorce*:

> Pastoral care cannot so easily be separated from the social context in which the counseling takes place. . . . Pastoral care involves the pastor in the social dilemmas of the neighborhood, community, city, county, state, nation. International situations and events that surround the pastor and his people affect the work of caring . . . The reciprocity between the pastoral caring and the prophetic confronting of responsibilities of the contemporary minister is the core concern of this book.[11]

Oates then goes on to elucidate "principles of prophetic pastoral care"[12] for reconciling the prophetic and pastoral tasks of a minister as two sides of the same coin. Gerkin acknowledged that Oates "wrote with deep conviction and great wisdom of the prophetic power of faithful pastoral care"[13] and referenced the above text by Oates. Oates also would be cited by Harvey Seifert and Howard J. Clinebell in their pivotal book, *Personal Growth and Social Change: A Guide for Ministers and Laymen as Change Agents*, influencing their understanding that: "Knowledge of counseling insights can make methods of social action more realistic and effective."[14] In other words, when a social activist is clinically informed, they also may be more effective in their social justice work. The effectiveness of pastoral and prophetic approaches were seen as mutually intertwined as early as the 1960s, a time as turbulent as our own.

THE PUBLIC THEOLOGICAL VALUE OF EMBODYING THE NARRATIVE ANEW

Building on Oates's earlier work among others, Charles V. Gerkin spoke as a Christian practical theologian[15] and argued that the Christian pastoral caretaker must "read the signs of the times."[16] If the caretaker desires to remain relevant in the contemporary situation, then attention must be paid to the shifting signs of a larger political and sociocultural context: "If we are to take seriously this living, historical, process-oriented understanding of what it means to live in and represent a tradition . . . [w]e will watch and listen for ways in which the emerging cultural issues of our time interrupt our accustomed ways of interpreting Christianity's sacred texts."[17] As the Christian pastoral caretaker encounters contemporary problems, the caretaker may turn to theological sources, such as Christian texts, in different ways for new narrative meanings in the practice of pastoral caretaking.

The texts continue to speak *prophetically* to the new situation, calling for an innovative response to the divine in the situation and challenging a group's (or an individual's) "common sense" of the situation with a new interpretation of the Christian text that better "fits" the cultural context.[18] Hence the narrative potential of the texts are multivalent and can actively shape a broader vision of possible responses and practices within the contemporary cultural situation. The Christian caretaker can draw upon the texts for narrative wisdom to challenge and expand norms and images held by *particular* groups or individuals who may be in conflict and thus develop a more foundationally held shared vision and unifying values. As an activist in the contemporary Poor Peoples' Campaign social justice movement, I witness them drawing on a similar narrative practice in their public theological approach to resistance work in our time.[19] I also witness contemporary immigration rights activists doing the same, with one particularly striking example being a church that put their nativity statues of the Holy Family in a cage in protest of migrant children being placed in cages at the US border.[20]

Later in the same text, Gerkin presents a "centrifugal model of Christian community"[21] and the location of the pastoral caretaker within this model:

> To embrace a centrifugal model of the Christian community will thus necessitate the valuing of movements of Christians out into the world away from the central locus of their community. . . . Involvement in the affairs of the world, rather than privacy of commitment away from the world, will be the expectation and invitation of such a community.[22]

The schema of the people of God then is inclusive not only of the faith community and individuals within that faith community in this model, it also is inclusive of all the communities in which those individuals participate, such as the larger human community, and includes other cultures and faiths as well as the physical and environmental world.[23] Public theologies of activism and resistance need a similar embrace of all communities, cultures, and faiths.

Gerkin argues that the prophetic placement of the pastor shifts and changes depending on the circumstance but always is responsive to the foundational *narrative image of Christian servanthood*. The Christian practical public theological narrative calls the pastor to minister not only to the congregation but also to the larger world as the pastor encounters the problems of the world in the microcosm of the congregation itself:

> The Christian community seen in the image of servanthood and nurturer of community is called out of its insular self-preoccupation into interaction and self-sacrificing engagement with all the problematic nooks and crannies of family living, including such contemporary front page issues as extra-familial child and infant care, family violence and child abuse, divorce and the fractured or reconstituted family, aging families, and family members who are no longer able to care for themselves, and the like.[24]

Thus Gerkin embraced a public prophetic dimension to pastoral care practices as the Christian texts and narrative are put into dialogue with the situation. The pastoral caretaker is not restricted to the Christian congregation but is called, if not actually propelled, outward into the world by the Christian vision of embodied servanthood to address the various wounds of the world as they are reflected in the wounds of the congregation as well. Narratives of other faith or secular traditions may find a similar prophetic call to public practices of activism and resistance in the context of their own lived experiences of those traditions.

THE PUBLIC THEOLOGICAL NEED FOR STRUCTURAL ANALYSIS IN DISRUPTION

Larry Kent Graham also would argue that "care of persons" is deeply intertwined with "care of world."[25] However, Graham was more explicitly interested in a *systemic analysis of structural power* as his primary approach, rather than solely the Christian narrative. In this approach to prophetic pastoral care, the pastoral caretaker needs to have an analysis of power and domination and to engage in practices that support the deconstruction of systemic institutionalized oppressions. Resonating even more fully than Gerkin for me from my own lived experiences, Graham drew liberally from his own lived experiences, interdisciplinary perspectives, process and feminist and liberation theologies, and sociopolitical terms and analysis. He particularly focused on a recognition of the forces of racism, sexism, colonialism, militarism, and ageism, among others. Later in his core text, *Care of Persons, Care of Worlds*, he coined a term, "demonic hegemony,"[26] for the forces which can result in profound suffering and evil in both individuals and the larger society.

Formed as a young adult in the politically turbulent 1960s, and entering doctoral studies in the 1970s, Graham sought to resist the "polarization"[27] of the individual clinical and social change perspectives. He allowed the "lived experiences" of his parishioners to challenge his theological thinking and ministerial practices:

> . . . I found that the increase of sexual and domestic violence among parishioners required a rethinking of our models. To care for persons in situations like these compelled me to address more fully the culture of violence in the structures of our society, which I realized were defining it. It became clear that the psyches of these injured and injuring persons were inextricably linked to the violent cultural patterns of our society. To respond to one required attention to the other. . . . The destiny of persons and the character of the world are intertwined. . . .[28]

Graham thus was explicit in a way that Gerkin was not that "the internalized and institutionalized culture of violence" must be addressed by pastoral caretakers and that this will require "a language of care that makes the concepts of power, values, and justice central in our thinking and practice."[29] Graham, like Gerkin, called for the linking of the pastoral and prophetic perspectives, but with an explicit understanding that *pastoral healing requires attention to the specific historical, political, and cultural structures of oppression in the society.*[30] "The prophets did not separate the personal from the public,"[31] an expanded vision of pastoral care was needed in which: "The classic pastoral care tasks of healing, sustaining, guiding, and reconciling are expanded to include prophetic efforts toward emancipatory liberation, justice-seeking, public advocacy, and ecological partnership."[32]

Contrasting his approach with Gerkin's, Graham wrote,

> . . . I am haunted by Gerkin's central emphasis upon selfhood, and his view that the self is an interpreter rather than a lover, justice-maker, and partner with nature. The moral dimensions of his model still seem to be ordered by a concern for individual self-realization and fulfillment of primary relationships. While the impact of contextual realities on individuals is highly emphasized in Gerkin's work, the reciprocal influence and social responsibility of individuals to their context is not developed.[33]

Graham's critique of Gerkin's hermeneutical approach parallels Barbara J. McClure's later critique of narrative therapy, that hermeneutical approaches tend to prioritize self-interpretations and self-meaning-making while neglecting the actual structural forces that may pose very real barriers to care of persons.[34] Hermeneutical approaches neglect the additional responsibility of the pastoral caretaker to address such structural forces in practice. I note here that both Graham and McClure are making larger distinctions than may be warranted of the visional power and practical role of narrative and hermeneutics in both the lives of individuals and of individuals in community over time, including for public theologies of activism and resistance.

For further example, the mere fact that both Gerkin and Graham come to language such as "prophetic pastoral care" signifies a reliance on a heritage of prophetic words, stories, *and* practices within the Jewish and Christian texts and traditions. Both are situated in larger Jewish and Christian narrative traditions that use the language of "prophet" and/or "pastor." Graham *relies* on a narrative vision of the prophet to "develop" his more nuanced focus on structural aspects of power and justice. Graham also underestimates Gerkin's focus on the "centrifugal model of Christian community" that highlights other narrative elements of the vision of the prophet in calling *all* to work toward dismantling structures of oppression, as also can be witnessed in my previous comments on current disruptive forms of contemporary activism.

It also is true that contemporary narrative therapy, as developed originally by Michael White and David Epston in the 1980s, was deeply influenced by poststructuralist analysis of power relations, particularly the work of Michel Foucault, that "storytelling rights are negotiated and distributed through the professional institution and its archives."[35] "The issues of power relations, structural inequalities, and ownership of the storytelling rights of personhood are central to the work of narrative therapy."[36] In contrast to McClure's concerns, narrative therapy is not necessarily grounded philosophically in the individual narrative, though larger sociocultural, political, and economic factors indeed may pressure individual pastoral care providers and therapists to focus primarily on the individual in practice.

For the purposes of this essay and its focus on prophetic pastoral care practices in the aftermath of violent trauma and ongoing oppression, I also note that Graham does not dismiss the experience of "self" but locates that experience and knowledge at the site of the body as "the primary basis for connecting with our worlds and for generating our sense of selfhood."[37] Graham speaks to the disruption of self that may occur when bodies are traumatized and to possible pastoral care healing practices for the body in the aftermath:

> A positive sense of self has its origin in a primal experience of physical well-being. Those whose bodies are abused early in childhood often develop truncated personalities and painfully dysfunctional orientations to their larger world. . . . Massage and bioenergetic therapies probably provide the most dramatic examples of how the psyche of persons can be accessed directly through the body. . . . The ministry of care is often challenged to respond to the spiritual and emotional dilemmas encountered by persons whose bodies are in

demise by illness, accident, or assault. The loss of the integrity and continuity of bodily life constitutes one of the most profound needs for care and empowerment....[38]

Such bodily disruption would include traumatic impact from a violent event as well, such as those Emma González's school community of fellow survivors experienced. Graham argued that a prophetic pastoral caretaker needs to take into account practices that help to heal the body for full liberation and empowerment to occur. If "survivors are experts" in their lived experiences, as I have argued based on my research,[39] then their embodied and material art practices, including those performed in the public square, become significant sources for theological development. In taking Emma's public testimony in Washington, D.C., at the March for Our Lives event seriously in this essay, I continue to lift up the prophetic pastoral care practices of survivors for "constructive practical theological"[40] reflection in the shaping of public theologies of activism and resistance. Attending carefully to the lived experiences of survivors, and those who serve or who are in relationship with them, can create points of reflection for testing and challenging theologies and practices, particularly public theologies and practices.

DISRUPTIVE POTENTIAL OF CONSTRUCTIVE PRACTICAL THEOLOGY FROM SURVIVORS

Emma held that public stage in a way that only the fierce embodied wisdom of survivors can—and that disruptive wisdom is needed for our times. James N. Poling became my final crucial ally in my doctoral studies for language and theory to support this wisdom. Constructive practical theology tests our various theological constructions and practices against the lived experiences of those about whom we may theologize. In my research and writing's focus on two lived religion case studies,[41] trauma survivors and the ecclesial or para-ecclesial ministries who serve them, were viewed as "primary theologians,"[42] providing the normative ground for reflection on all theologies of trauma. Their phenomenological experiences of the divine, spirituality, and healing were used to test for empirical "fit" with or "addition" or "challenge" to existing theological constructions and practices in the aftermath of violent trauma. Through such "testing," I pointed to how researchers may continue to expand our available constructive theologies of and practices in relationship to trauma, including untapped theological resources and practices. This also is true for public theologies of activism and resistance.

When confronted with traumatic experiences, how *does* a person or faith community grapple with the challenges of empirical reality? Can a person or faith community allow their tradition's beliefs and practices to be challenged by these new experiences and then reconstructed in the aftermath? Poling, who has devoted much of his pastoral and academic career to working with both survivors of violence and perpetrators of sexual and domestic violence, served as an additional companion ally for me. As a Christian faith practitioner, Poling allowed himself to be challenged by the experiences of the survivors and offenders he encountered in providing pastoral care—experiences that posed questions for his pre-existing classical Christian conception of God as both all-powerful and all-good, as well as for other Christian doctrines and practices. He named the methodology of his life's work "constructive practical theology" and summarized it as follows: "One of my assumptions is that normative claims of theology must always be tested within the crucible of everyday human life and faith."[43] The nature of this particular pastoral ministry led him to become more deeply committed to the prophetic work of social transformation and to witnessing to the multilayered web of oppressions that can hinder the work of both healing and social justice.

This method of taking those impacted by trauma and ongoing oppression seriously in their own practices for healing and empowerment—their prophetic pastoral care practices—means that public theologians also need to consider what they take seriously and give normative priority to as sources of their theologies. As a practical theologian, I took seriously the public practices of survivors in the aftermath of homicide, giving theological weight to a Mother's Day Walk for Peace with banners and memorial button pins and T-shirts as well as to the Peace Institute's specialized orders of funeral services that included pictures, letters to the slain loved one, and information for the community about trauma. I took this seriously and became curious about their public practices of testimony and witness, including disruptive practices, and I then attended to theories and theologies that fit or did not fit with their lived experiences, with the survivors' cultural linguistic "world/sense."[44] I allowed myself, even while being a fellow survivor carrying a different identity by race and class, to be challenged by their practices.

This is how, like Poling, I allowed my own "world/sense" to be disrupted by survivors who said that the language of "healing" is inadequate for them, which also led me on a new journey in taking theologies of disability more seriously in an attentive way than I had previously. This also is how I came to take seriously the street memorials that were created for those who had lost their lives to violence on the streets of Boston, as well as memorial buttons and pictures. These disruptive public practices led me on an interdisciplinary trail through cultural folklore studies and continuing bonds theory of grief work, as well as other psychological theories beyond the traditional sole use of psychoanalytic theory in religious studies and theology, such as liberation health theory, relational cultural theory, and internal family systems theory. Disruptive transformation/transfiguration breaks open the academic canon to new "world/sense," theories, and language.

CONCLUDING CHALLENGE

What would it mean for those of us who are public theologians of activism and resistance if we allowed ourselves to be transformed and transfigured by the public practices of survivors of trauma and ongoing oppression and to take seriously all of the forms of their testimony and witness in the public square, including that of Emma González? I suggest that it means we allow ourselves to be challenged by the disruption of our "world/sense" and to be opened by new possibilities and creative integrations—that we allow our moral imaginations and horizons of theologizing to be expanded by survivor testimonies and experiences. Public theologies of activism and resistance that remain attentive and open to the "mysterious, pulsing, vibrating, flowing process of spirit" are perhaps called to do no less as we witness to the uniquely troubling, and even apocalyptic, signs of our times and jointly forge new ways of prophetic pastoral care.[45]

NOTES

1. Quoted from the end of Emma González's speech and silent witness at the Washington, DC March for Our Lives, March 24, 2018. The full video can be viewed on-line, accessed June 4, 2018, https://www.theguardian.com/us-news/video/2018/mar/24/emma-gonzalezs-powerful-march-for-our-lives-speech-in-full-video. Throughout my references to Emma, I take responsibility for assuming the use of she/her/hers pronouns, though I do not know if she experiences these as her pronouns. I am aware that she identifies as bisexual and hence part of the LGBTQI community. See the following article, accessed June 6, 2018, https://www.cnn.com/2018/03/25/us/emma-gonzalez-what-you-need-to-know-trnd/index.html.

2. Michelle A. Walsh, "Prophetic Pastoral Care in the Aftermath of Trauma: Forging a Constructive Practical Theology of Organized Trauma Response Ministries." PhD diss., Boston University, 2014. ProQuest (AAT 3610856). See also Judith L. Herman, *Trauma and Recovery* (New York: BasicBooks, 1992) on the significance of trauma in cycles of attention and repression in public history.

3. For summaries of the movement of pastoral theology as public theology, see in particular Larry Kent Graham, "Pastoral Theology as Public Theology in Relation to the Clinic," *Journal of Pastoral Theology* (v. 10, 2000): 1–17; Bonnie J. Miller-McLemore, "Pastoral Theology and Public Theology: Developments in the U.S.," in *Pathways to the Public Square: Practical Theology in an Age of Pluralism*, eds. Elaine Graham and Anne Rowlands, 2003 (International Academy of Practical Theology: Manchester, LIT VERLAG: Munster, 2005), 95–105; and Bonnie J. Miller-McLemore, "Pastoral Theology as Public Theology: Revolutions in the 'Fourth Area,'" in *Dictionary of Pastoral Care and Counseling*, ed. Rodney J. Hunter (Nashville, TN: Abingdon Press, 1990/2005), 1370–1380. I also specifically am tracing the historical literature and use of the terms "prophetic pastoral care" rather than engaging the work of David Tracy on the various forms of public theology, though David Tracy's work also certainly plays a major role in the contemporary turn of pastoral theology toward public theology. See David Tracy, *The Analogical Imagination: Christian Theology and the Culture of Pluralism* (New York: The Crossroad Publishing Company, 1981).

4. See in particular Wayne E. Oates, *Pastoral Counseling in Social Problems: Extremism, Race, Sex, Divorce* (Philadelphia: Westminster Press, 1966); Harvey Seifert and Howard J. Clinebell, *Personal Growth and Social Change* (Philadelphia: Westminster Press, 1969); and Howard J. Clinebell, "Toward Envisioning the Future of Pastoral Counseling and AAPC," *Journal of Pastoral Care* (vol. 37, no. 3, 1983): 180–194. As men's public intellectual work

often overshadows that of women, special mention needs to be made of Howard Clinebell's intellectual partnership with his wife, Charlotte H. Clinebell, *Counseling for Liberation* (Philadelphia: Fortress Press, 1976). See also Harvey Seifert, "Prophetic/Pastoral Tension in Ministry," in *Dictionary of Pastoral Care and Counseling*, Rodney J. Hunter, ed., 963–966 (Nashville, TN: Abingdon Press, 1990/2005).

5. See in particular Charles V. Gerkin, *Prophetic Pastoral Practice: A Christian Vision of Life Together* (Nashville: Abingdon Press, 1991), and Larry Kent Graham, "Prophetic Pastoral Caretaking: A Psychosystemic Approach to Symptomatology," *Journal of Psychology and Christianity* (8, no. 1, 1989): 49–60. There are many streams that fed into the turn toward pastoral theology as public theology, including the claim of all theology as public theology—see again Tracy, *The Analogical Imagination*. But for the purposes of this essay, I particularly am interested in tracking the early dialogue partners who were using "pastoral and prophetic" language to expand theological frames for "pastoral" beyond the individual into larger communal and social frames of reference and transformation, hence "prophetic." This is an underexamined area in historical literature, particularly for those of us who need theological allies to our writing openly as survivors. See also Kathleen Greider, Gloria Johnson, and Kristen Leslie, "Three Decades of Women Writing for Our Lives," in *Feminist and Womanist Pastoral Theology*, eds. Bonnie Miller-McLemore and Brita Gill-Austern (Nashville, TN: Abingdon Press, 1999), 21–50, for a further overview of the role of feminists and womanists in shifting the paradigms for thinking of pastoral theology and care through the lens of community and context.

6. In a different book chapter essay, I began to use the Christian theological term "transfiguration" for the transformative impact of such practices on the public witnesses. See Michelle A. Walsh, "Taking Matters *Seriously*: Material Theopoetics in the Aftermath of Communal Violence," in *Post-Traumatic Public Theology*, eds. Stephanie N. Arel and Shelly Rambo (New York: Palgrave Macmillan, 2016), 241–265.

7. Ibid. See also Walsh, "Prophetic Pastoral Care Practices in the Aftermath of Trauma," and also Michelle A. Walsh, *Violent Trauma, Culture, and Power: An Interdisciplinary Exploration in Lived Religion* (New York: Palgrave Macmillan, 2017). I consciously put the word "healing" in quotation marks as some survivors rejected the language of "healing" in favor of the language of "learning to move again" after losing a child due to homicide. For survivor parents, the traditional metaphoric associations for the word "healing" as somehow "being whole again" without their child were highly problematic. New metaphors are needed.

8. I note too that the Christian tradition, of course, has not been the only religious tradition to grapple with these types of questions and issues, though I am focusing on the Christian tradition and Christian theologians in this particular essay. One additional interesting biographical book to examine that focuses on the global dimensions of religious reflection and activism during this period is by Robert H. King, *Thomas Merton and Thich Nhat Hanh: Engaged Spirituality in an Age of Globalization* (New York: The Continuum Publishing Group, Inc., 2003).

9. Gerkin, *Prophetic Pastoral Practice*; Graham, "Prophetic Pastoral Caretaking"; and Larry Kent Graham, "Care of Persons, Care of World: Discovering the Prophetic in Ministry to Suffering Persons," *Pastoral Psychology* (vol. 40, no. 1, 1991): 15–28.

10. Oates, *Pastoral Counseling in Social Problems*.

11. Ibid., 11–12.

12. Ibid., 18.

13. Gerkin, *Prophetic Pastoral Practice*, 81.

14. Siefert and Clinebell, *Personal Growth and Social Change*, 16.

15. See Charles V. Gerkin, *Crisis Experience in Modern Life* (Nashville: Abingdon Press, 1979) and Charles V. Gerkin, *The Living Human Document: Re-visioning Pastoral Counseling in a Hermeneutical Mode* (Nashville: Abingdon Press, 1984).

16. A classic reference from Matthew 16:1–3

17. Gerkin, *Prophetic Pastoral Practice*, 44.

18. Ibid., chapter 2.

19. Ibid., 63–64. One can see that such narrative wisdom need not be only religious in nature. There can be guiding secular or political narratives with deep historical roots as well

that can serve as a prophetic basis of call. The Rev. Dr. William J. Barber, II, one of the founders of the contemporary Poor Peoples' Campaign, is an exemplar of this practice as an orator when he finds common ground across both religious and secular narrative traditions to articulate a new moral narrative and vision. One masterful example was his speech at the 2016 Democratic National Convention, accessed July 4, 2018, https://www.youtube.com/watch?v=aw3PUghqlAA. See also Rev. Dr. William J. Barber, II, *The Third Reconstruction: Moral Mondays, Fusion Politics, and the Rise of a New Justice Movement* (Boston: Beacon Press, 2016).

20. Faith E. Pinho, "Church 'Detains' Jesus, Mary, Joseph to Protest Trump's Immigration Policy," *Religion News Service*, July 3, 2018, accessed July 4, 2018, https://religionnews.com/2018/07/03/indianapolis-church-cages-holy-family-in-immigration-protest/.

21. Ibid., 132–142.
22. Ibid., 133.
23. Ibid., Gerkin's Figure 2, 136.
24. Ibid., 139.

25. Larry Kent Graham, *Care of Persons, Care of Worlds: A Psychosystems Approach to Pastoral Care and Counseling* (Nashville, TN: Abingdon Press, 1992a) and Larry Kent Graham, "From Psyche to System," *Theology Today* (vol. 49, no. 3, 1992b): 320–332. See also Larry Kent Graham, "Toward a Social and Political Theory of Pastoral Care and Counseling," *Journal of Pastoral Psychotherapy* (v. 7, 1984–1985): 83–101.

26. Graham, 138. Graham first used the term "demonic hegemony" in "Prophetic Pastoral Caretaking: A Psychosystemic Approach to Symptomatology," *Journal of Psychology and Christianity* (8, no. 1, 1989): 49–60 (this before Gerkin's own 1991 use of "prophetic pastoral practice"). In his fuller book *Care of Persons, Care of Worlds*, Graham writes: "The concept of the demonic, as I am using it, refers to the 'principalities and powers,' or to the pervasive social and cultural conventions that distort our lives by elevating some partial good or truth into a dominant position from which all other good or truth is evaluated," ibid., 138. Graham consistently critiqued a theological anthropology that is individualistic in orientation rather than systemic, communal, and justice-seeking. He termed the model of care he critiqued: "the existential-anthropological model of care [which] puts the health and fulfillment of individual persons on center stage," ibid., 32.

27. Ibid., 12.
28. Ibid., 12–13.

29. Ibid., 18. The contemporary fruits of pastoral care approaches in which there is "a language of care that makes the concepts of power, values, and justice central in our thinking and practice" also might be seen in a recent book edited by Sheryl Kujawa-Holbrook and Karen Montagno, *Injustice and the Care of Souls: Taking Oppression Seriously in Pastoral Care* (Minneapolis: Fortress Press, 2009). Graham's work also was an influence on Carroll A. Watkins Ali, see her text *Survival and Liberation: Pastoral Theology in African American Context* (St. Louis, MO: Chalice Press, 1999). Yet as Barbara J. McClure also argues in *Moving Beyond Individualism in Pastoral Care and Counseling* (Eugene, OR: Cascade Books, 2010), the field of pastoral care and counseling remains institutionally constrained by many factors to keep the focus on the individual rather than transformation of the larger society.

30. To put this another way, power has many dimensions. Gerkin rightly calls attention to the power of normativity and the setting of standards within a culture and its institutions. Graham calls attention to other levels of power, including actual resources and decision-making power at institutional and cultural levels. The more any particular group is enabled to become dominant through access to resources, decision-making, and normative standard setting power, the more that group is positioned to define what "reality" is and what will be considered a problem and what not in any particular institution or sociocultural context. I am indebted to the work of what was formerly known as the Women's Theological Center in Boston, MA for my first exposure to this framing of a power analysis for anti-oppression work from the feminist tradition. See also Suzanne Pharr, "The Common Elements of Oppression," in *Homophobia: A Weapon of Sexism* (Inverness, CA: Chardon Press, 1988), 52–64.

31. Graham, *Care of Persons, Care of Worlds*, 19.
32. Ibid., 20.

33. Ibid., 36.
34. McClure, *Moving Beyond Individualism*.
35. Stephen Madigan, *Narrative Therapy* (American Psychological Association: Washington, D.C., 2011), 7.
36. Ibid., 21. See also Walsh, "Prophetic Pastoral Care in the Aftermath of Trauma" and Walsh, *Violent Trauma, Culture, and Power*. As I would discover in my case study with the Louis D. Brown Peace Institute, the power of storytelling and the giving of survivor testimony illustrated the usefulness of critical race theory as an additional social scientific theoretical tool for correlation to the prophetic empowerment of survivors, particularly in a community marginalized by race and class. See Lee Anne Bell, *Storytelling for Social Justice: Connecting Narrative and the Arts in Antiracist Teaching* (New York: Routledge, 2010).
37. Graham, *Care of Persons, Care of Worlds*, 73.
38. Ibid., 73–74.
39. Walsh, *Violent Trauma, Culture, and Power*.
40. The term "constructive practical theology" is attributable to the work of James N. Poling. See in particular *Rethinking Faith: A Constructive Practical Theology* (Minneapolis: Fortress Press, 2011).
41. See Walsh, "Prophetic Pastoral Care in the Aftermath of Trauma" and Walsh, *Violent Trauma, Culture, and Power*.
42. Mary Clark Moschella, "Ethnography," in *The Wiley-Blackwell Companion to Practical Theology*, 224–233, ed., Bonnie J. Miller-McLemore (Malden, MA: Blackwell Publishing Limited, 2012), 228. While Poling does not use the term "primary theologians," he does in fact treat survivor voices and experiences in that capacity in his works of constructive practical theology. Larry Kent Graham could be argued also to have engaged in a work of constructive practical theology when he was challenged by the experiences of his parishioners to rethink his own conceptions of pastoral care.
43. Poling, *Rethinking Faith*, 3.
44. "World/sense" is an alternative metaphor for "worldview" that I developed in *Violent Trauma, Culture, and Power*—one that was more fully embodied of the lived experiences of survivors as I witnessed them.
45. A tribute to the works of Catherine Keller, a primary dialogue partner for me in all forms of theology. See in particular *On the Mystery: Discerning Divinity in Process* (Minneapolis: Fortress Press, 2008).

REFERENCES

Ali, Carroll A. Watkins. *Survival and Liberation: Pastoral Theology in African American Context*. St. Louis, MO: Chalice Press, 1999.
Barber, II, Rev. Dr. William J. *The Third Reconstruction: Moral Mondays, Fusion Politics, and the Rise of a New Justice Movement*. Boston: Beacon Press, 2016.
Bell, Lee Anne. *Storytelling for Social Justice: Connecting Narrative and the Arts in Antiracist Teaching*. New York: Routledge, 2010.
Clinebell, Charlotte H. *Counseling for Liberation*. Philadelphia: Fortress Press, 1976.
Clinebell, Howard J. *Basic Types of Pastoral Care & Counseling*. Nashville: Abingdon Press, 1966/1984.
———. "Toward Envisioning the Future of Pastoral Counseling and AAPC." *Journal of Pastoral Care* (vol. 37, no. 3, 1983): 180–194.
Gerkin, Charles V. *Crisis Experience in Modern Life*. Nashville: Abingdon Press, 1979.
———. *An Introduction to Pastoral Care*. Nashville: Abingdon Press, 1997.
———. *The Living Human Document: Re-visioning Pastoral Counseling in a Hermeneutical Mode*. Nashville: Abingdon Press, 1984.
———. *Prophetic Pastoral Practice: A Christian Vision of Life Together*. Nashville: Abingdon Press, 1991.
Graham, Larry Kent. "Care of Persons, Care of World: Discovering the Prophetic in Ministry to Suffering Persons," *Pastoral Psychology* (vol. 40, no. 1, 1991): 15–28.

———. *Care of Persons, Care of Worlds: A Psychosystems Approach to Pastoral Care and Counseling*. Nashville, TN: Abingdon Press, 1992a.

———. "From Psyche to System," *Theology Today* (vol. 49, no. 3, 1992b): 320–332.

———. "Pastoral Theology as Public Theology in Relation to the Clinic," *Journal of Pastoral Theology* (v. 10, 2000): 1–17.

———. "Prophetic Pastoral Caretaking: A Psychosystemic Approach to Symptomatology," *Journal of Psychology and Christianity* (8, no. 1, 1989): 49–60.

———. "Toward a Social and Political Theory of Pastoral Care and Counseling," *Journal of Pastoral Psychotherapy* (v. 7, 1984-1985): 83–101.

Greider, Kathleen J., Gloria A. Johnson, and Kristen J. Leslie. "Three Decades of Women Writing for Our Lives." In *Feminist and Womanist Pastoral Theology*. Edited by Bonnie Miller-McLemore and Brita Gill-Austern, 21–50. Nashville, TN: Abingdon Press, 1999.

Herman, Judith L. *Trauma and Recovery*. New York: BasicBooks, 1992.

Keller, Catherine. *On The Mystery: Discerning Divinity in Process*. Minneapolis, MN: Fortress Press, 2008.

King, Robert H. *Thomas Merton and Thich Nhat Hanh: Engaged Spirituality in an Age of Globalization*. New York: The Continuum Publishing Group, Inc., 2003.

Kujawa-Holbrook, Sheryl A. and Karen B. Montagno, eds. 2009. *Injustice and the Care of Souls: Taking Oppression Seriously in Pastoral Care*. Minneapolis: Fortress Press.

Madigan, Stephen. *Narrative Therapy*. American Psychological Association: Washington, DC, 2011.

McClure, Barbara J. *Moving Beyond Individualism in Pastoral Care and Counseling: Reflections on Theory, Theology, and Practice*. Eugene, OR: Cascade Books, 2010.

Miller-McLemore, Bonnie J. "Pastoral Theology and Public Theology: Developments in the U.S." In *Pathways to the Public Square: Practical Theology in an Age of Pluralism*. Edited by Elaine Graham & Anne Rowlands, 95–105, 2003. International Academy of Practical Theology: Manchester, LIT VERLAG: Munster, 2005.

———. "Pastoral Theology as Public Theology: Revolutions in the 'Fourth Area.'" In *Dictionary of Pastoral Care and Counseling*. Edited by Rodney J. Hunter, 1370–1380. Nashville, TN: Abingdon Press, 1990/2005.

Moschella, Mary Clark. "Ethnography." In *The Wiley-Blackwell Companion to Practical Theology*. Edited by Bonnie J. Miller-McLemore, 224–233. Malden, MA: Blackwell Publishing Limited, 2012.

Oates, Wayne E. *Pastoral Counseling in Social Problems: Extremism, Race, Sex, Divorce*. Philadelphia: Westminster Press, 1966.

Pharr, Suzanne. "The Common Elements of Oppression." In *Homophobia: A Weapon of Sexism*. Inverness, CA: Chardon Press, 1988, 52–64.

Poling, James N. *Rethinking Faith: A Constructive Practical Theology*. Minneapolis: Fortress Press, 2011.

Seifert, Harvey and Howard J. Clinebell. *Personal Growth and Social Change*. Philadelphia: Westminster Press, 1969.

Seifert, Harvey. "Prophetic/Pastoral Tension in Ministry." In *Dictionary of Pastoral Care and Counseling*, Rodney J. Hunter, ed., 963–966. Nashville, TN: Abingdon Press, 1990/2005.

Tracy, David. *The Analogical Imagination: Christian Theology and the Culture of Pluralism*. New York: The Crossroad Publishing Company, 1981.

Walsh, Michelle A. "Prophetic Pastoral Care in the Aftermath of Trauma: Forging a Constructive Practical Theology of Organized Trauma Response Ministries." PhD diss., Boston University, 2014. ProQuest (AAT 3610856).

———. "Taking Matter *Seriously*: Material Theopoetics in the Aftermath of Communal Violence." In *Post-Traumatic Public Theology*. Edited by Shelly Rambo and Stephanie N. Arel. New York: Palgrave Macmillan, 2016.

———. *Violent Trauma, Culture, and Power: An Interdisciplinary Exploration in Lived Religion*. New York: Palgrave Macmillan, 2017.

Chapter Five

Protest and Resistance as the Liturgy of the People

Jennifer Baldwin

WHY PROTEST?

Gradually people gather as the appointed time draws near. Dressed in clothes fitting for the occasion, they mingle about waiting for one of the leaders to offer words of invitation. Songs are sung. Important texts are read. Invocations and supplications are made with hopes for a better future. Speeches of inspiration or discipline are offered. The gathered masses move together in response. Benedictions are spoken. And then the congregation departs—a bit changed by the experience. When people gather en mass around a shared value, commitment, or desire, there is opportunity for transformation. Transformation moves those present from isolation to community, from despair to hope, from powerlessness to agency, from silence to speech.

For those who regularly participate in the rhythms of shared religious life, the opening paragraph may feel like a general description of Christian life on any given Sunday. Communal religious practice always includes a structure that functions to hold the experience. For some traditions, the structure is clear, explicit, and named. For other traditions, the structure is covert, implicit, and fairly loose. Regardless of how readily identifiable the structure, it is always present providing a felt sense of familiarity and security. The structures of gatherings form our experience by guiding when we speak, are silent, stand, listen, reflect, kneel, sit, sing, pray or meditate, walk and in what direction, come together, and depart. The structures are what keep the experience from devolving into a cacophony of chaos. They are the spoken and unspoken rules or directions. The rules of social engagement are not only present in our religious gatherings; they direct the flow of life in our civic encounters—maintaining safety in our driving practices, guidelines in our professional norms, cohesion in social relationships, and a balanced order in our shared practices of governance. When we step out of the agreed upon social and civic norms, structures, or rules, we encounter social push back. If we engage in unsafe driving practices, we are issued a citation or angry honk. If we violate our professional norms, we may be subject to litigation or censure by our professional oversite boards. When we violate social norms, our friends rebuke or create distance in the relationship. And when our governance becomes out of order and functions to benefit the few by harming the many, we protest.

While the United States has a long history of protest action leading to national independence, voting rights, civil rights, and a host of specific causes and values, we are currently in an era of heightened protest and public resistance. Black Lives Matter, Standing Rock, Women's March, Families Belong Together, March for Our Lives, March for Science, multiple marches for teacher's wages, Pride, Unite the Right, protests against the Muslim Ban, social actions to defend the Affordable Care Act, and appeals to members of the US Senate regarding their vote on Supreme Court nominee Brett Kavanaugh are just a few of the most publically prominent protest demonstration movements in the last two years (2016–mid-2018). There are, of course, countless more local and regional protest demonstrations seeking to affect change related to everything from hospital closures to restaurant's choice to decline service.

Regardless of the strategies employed, public protest events are always accompanied by similar critiques from those viewing from the outside or those in opposition to the cause. Common challenges or criticisms of protests are that the action is ineffective, disruptive for bystanders, fail to have a unified message, are merely cathartic, and/or lack power to manifest change. From the perspective of those disengaged in protest and activism, these challenges have merit; they *are* cathartic, disruptive, distinct from and critical of those with direct power and responsibility . . . and intentionally so. Public protest is designed to disrupt established rhythms of life (i.e., strategies of walking in streets, blocking building entrances, sitting vigil in hallways). The disruption is the point. Resistance gatherings are intended to be cathartic by allowing masses of people to share and thus amplify a common voice. Activism is meant to draw focus to the actions of those in power when they stray from their duties as representatives of the people.

The power of protests is in communal, social, embodied mobilization of the people for the purpose of bringing light and attention to abuses of power in leadership, representation, or responsibility for the civic good. In the American context, protest is a public corrective to policies and governmental practices that promote harm rather than facilitate life, liberty, and the movement toward fulfillment.[1] As a corrective, protest proclaims "Enough!" This "enough" signals when government or corporate action is outside the bounds of the norms and values of society. It is a public admonition that things have gone too far. It communicates to those in power that their acts of commission or omission are in violation of the vision and will of the people. Just as the people in a representative democracy utilize their votes to install leaders into office, protests are the people's means of evaluating their leader's job performance in between elections. The voices and bodies of the people joining together in collective protest is powerful and effective as a counterweight to centralized governmental action. It is an intraterm evaluation of leadership and as such wields the power of public rebuke.

In order to understand collaborative public actions of protest and resistance, we must be clear on the function and structure of the actions. The overarching lens and argument of this chapter is that protests are a form of social liturgy. The first section will focus on liturgy as public work and service. As liturgy, protests are the work and service of the people in parallel to the service of representative leadership. Protests, activism, and resistance are the means through which society functions as a corrective to out of balance or misapplied leadership. As such, it is incumbent on the people to pay attention to the actions and rhetoric of elected leaders and provide oversite through the electoral process as well as public demonstrations in between electoral cycles. The liturgy of demonstrations is what keeps protests from deteriorating into anarchy. The second section illuminates the role of protests as social liturgy functioning as the visible resistance to systemic or governmental sins. In this capacity, protest activism nonviolently names the sins of social systems of oppression and the governmental choices that perpetuate systemic sin. The third section argues that protests are en mass performances of our shared values or social limits. They are embodied, collective, "choreographed," movements designed to evoke affect, reenact symbols of history, or communicate values.

LITURGY AS THE WORK OF THE PUBLIC

When most of us think about the word "liturgy," we either immediately think of the structure of Christian worship or we aren't entirely sure what the word means. If you were not formed within particular Christian traditions that forefront the liturgy of the Church in the life of the community and praxis of faith, the notion of liturgy may feel either foreign or confining. The Oxford English Living Dictionary offers two definitions. First, "a form or formulary according to which public religious worship, especially Christian worship, is conducted."[2] This is the definition that is most familiar to people who participate in Christian worship conducted with the guides of liturgical structure clearly present. The structure of liturgy includes a spoken and/or movement "script" that directs the flow and unfolding of the worship experience. The intention of the liturgy is to provide a form of consistency and familiarity with the rites and practices of the community of faith across time and geography. This first understanding of liturgy is explicitly and directly religious and limited to the religious sphere. The second definition, however, opens up the potential utility of the term "liturgy" for public and civic discourse. It is "(in ancient Greece) a public office or duty performed voluntarily by a rich Athenian."[3] On first glance, one may be a bit confounded; what do these two contexts have to do with one another? Etymologically, "liturgy" is the combination of "leitos" meaning "public" and "-ergos" meaning "working or service." Most directly and simply, "liturgy" means "public work" or "public service."

When translated to the religious sphere, liturgy via communal worship is the religious work of the people or congregation. In context of religious faith and praxis, it is the public work of the community of faith to gather in worship. Worship is not a spectator event; it is the active service of the community through the guidance of the clergy or spiritual leader. Worship is the work and offering of the community. Within the civic realm, it either designates acts of voluntary service to the society by those with abundant resources, as in ancient Athenian society, or, in contemporary society, acts of embodied work or service by the populous. In what ways do persons enact public works or public service? How do we gather together in our work as a society rather than as individuals? What happens when we utilize the lens of the work or religious worship in order to see and identify our civic work and service as a public?

Primarily, religious worship is a communal and fully embodied performance (i.e., "the action or process of carrying out or accomplishing an action, task, or function"[4]) of relationality with the divine and community. It is the gathering of the people for the purpose of expressing fidelity to God and each other through embodied actions that build relationship, mend ruptures, and express gratitude. In the context of Christian worship, these actions are facilitated by the structure of the gathering of the community, invitation, communal songs, prayers of thanksgiving, supplication, or repentance, offering of forgiveness, reading of sacred texts, homily or sermon for reflection, offering of gifts, rituals of remembrance or transformation, and benediction. Each component of the worship gathering invites the participant to join in one voice with the community in expressing the joys, challenges, failures, resources, and transitions of human life and to offer appropriate response to God. Honesty in the reality of our lived experiences as individuals or as a community invites us into communion with others who also struggle and rejoice in the human experience. As a community work, liturgy generates space for the ritual processes that support us through significant life transitions, including births, deaths, coming of age, and significant relationship commitments. It is the gathering of the community in the rituals of baptism, funerals, confirmation, weddings, ordinations, etc., that lend strength and resiliency to individuals in times of uncertainty and transition. Religious worship utilizes particular communal and embodied practices to increase relational connection among human beings and between humanity and God or the divine. These relational connections enrich our lives in good times and sustain us in times of struggle, grief, or trauma.

The liturgy of worship provides a particular form (gathering, readings, etc.) and function (as holder of ritual space); it also has a purpose. In surveying noted scholars of liturgical studies Alexander Schmemann and J. J. von Allmen, Nicholas Wolterstorff highlights two key purposes: community actualization and "recapitulation of the history of salvation, it is the epiphany of the church, and it is the end and future of the world."[5] From Schmemann Wolterstorff notes, "the church *actualizes* herself in her enactment of the liturgy . . . it has something to do with understanding liturgy as consisting not of liturgical texts but as a way of doing something."[6] It is the *way* in which communities church (read "church" as a verb rather than a noun) that is formative. Religious (or civic) communities are not actualized and come into the fullness of their being through spectating the actions of leaders or in the products of their labor; it is through active participation—through the work of the people. What the people do and how they do it will always provide a more honest reflection of the values and priorities of the community than their formal documents. Mirroring Schmemann's notion of actualization, von Allmen identifies the epiphany of the church as "by its worship the Church becomes itself, becomes conscious of itself, and confesses itself as a distinct entity (42)."[7] In between the re/membering of the history of the community and the eschatology of who the community can become is the space in which the community comes into conscious awareness of its being, identity, and confession. This movement occurs via the liturgy of worship.

What happens when we dare to extrapolate the significance of worship for the formation of religious communities (the first definition of liturgy) into civic spaces or secular community gatherings and action thus harkening to the second definition? What if communal gatherings in which people joined together in streets, congressional offices, parks, or governmental sites functioned as a form of social actualization? What if society actualizes itself in the enactment of civil engagements including the actions of protest and civil resistance? If protests are a form of civil "worship" and follow a similar pattern of vocal, communal, embodied performance, then the ways in which protests occur illuminate something about participants shared understanding of national history, hope for the future of society, and emergence of a shared conscious awareness of being, identity, and, consequent, confession. How we protest forms who we are as a people. What and why we protest points to our shared values and limits. Public protests and resistance actions remind us of our nation's history replete with periods of both shame and honor. Movements like Black Lives Matter and Unite the Right (in their diametrically opposing origins, intentions, and goals) remind us that the consequences of slavery and Jim Crow laws continue to course though society. A courageous accounting of our national history both reminds us of our shortcomings as well as recalls the aspirations that reveal and call forth the best in us. Communal and embodied movement and action demands that we are consciously aware of who we are, what we stand for, and clarity of our vision of how to form a more perfect union that committed to life, liberty, and movement towards fulfillment for all persons endowed with these inalienable rights by our Creator. And, it is through our protests that society "becomes itself, becomes conscious of itself, and confesses itself as a distinct entity"—for better or worse.

PROTEST AS VISIBLE RESISTANCE TO SYSTEMIC OR GOVERNMENTAL SINS

Protest, resistance, and activism holds a special role in American society. From our fight for independence and national founding, protests have emerged as fuel for social change. Breaking through the calcification of the status quo with a vital energy for a more free and authentic life, protests signal change and transition. They are often a rising up of a population who has been oppressed, marginalized, or abused; the manifestation of a people yearning to be free. Across our national history from the Boston Tea Party to our current explosion of protest, public demonstrations emerge as visible manifestation of previously obscured suffering. Suffering that prompts protest can either be personal and direct by those who endure the harm (Ferguson Unrest and Standing Rock) or outrage on behalf of those who suffer and are silenced (Families Belong Together). In either case, mass protests are nearly always a response to trauma, suffering, or harm inflicted by governmental forces or representatives. Protests are the visible resistance by the people to systemic or governmental abuses of power or sin.[8]

Dirk Lange, in his text *Trauma Recalled: Liturgy, Disruption, and Theology*, helpfully highlights the roots and embodiment of liturgy in an event (concrete historical occurrence), beginning (communal catalyst), memory (narration), and repetition or disruption (embodied action/memorializing).[9] These four elements give rise to communal embodied liturgies in the church or in the streets. Within the Christian framework, the event is of the crucifixion of Jesus, the beginning is the gathering of the disciples or Pentecost, memory refers to sacred texts and traditions, and repetition or disruption is encountered in ritual practices that either repeat or disrupt the narrative. Within the civic arena, the composition of liturgy as the work of society is *visible* in public square, discourse, and view (in real time or virtual). Events can include the killing of unarmed persons or censorship of research data; beginnings are the growing awareness of the event through social or mainstream media; memory incorporates the histories of dismissal, harm, or oppression that contribute to the event; and repetition or disruption often manifests in activism or protest. In each instance, protest is ignited by an actual event that is deemed unacceptable enough to warrant a public response and rebuke.

While the notion of "liberal snowflakes" or "social justice warriors" (as a pejorative term) as cultural terms may be fairly new, the call for public response and responsibility to unjust social structures is not. Human beings have long held an impulse toward justice (as conceived from the particularity of context and lived experience). The desire for justice emerges from the central emotion of righteous anger. When we perceive injustice, we experience anger as an activating force to motivate change and restore justice. Of course, anger can, and often, goes awry and moves toward destruction or harm. Nevertheless, productive anger can function to motivate change, call those engaging in unjust practices to accountability, and bring sinful abuses of relational power (between persons or between social structures and individual/communities) to light.

There is a tendency within prominent protestant traditions to personalize and individualize Christian faith—to emphasize one's personal relationship with Jesus over the community as the people of faith. This tendency makes sense within the context of the United States which holds strong national stories of "the self-made man" or the pioneers conquering the Wild West. However, we lose significant resources of actualization, agency, and mobilization when we emphasize individual faith and responsibility and gloss over social faith and responsibility. Walter Rauschenbusch, a Baptist pastor and theologian writing at the opening turn of the 20th century, rightly and skillfully called the Christian community of his era to account and action by advocating for the church to fully engage with society. Rauschenbusch's understanding of the need for Christianity to forefront the role of society emerged from his experiences of the consequences of the Gilded Age (1870–1990) which produced poor working conditions, child labor, and illiteracy and motivated the Social Gospel Movement (1880–1925). For Christian leaders of that era, the cost of the societal neglect of its vulnerable citizenry was unconscionably high and demanded attention. In a nation that purported to hold the life and teaching of Jesus in high regard, the presence of significant suffering, maltreatment, and unnecessarily imposed limitations on human sustenance is antithetical to the ministry of Jesus. Rauschenbusch and others astutely noted that many of the constraints that produced suffering en mass were social and governmental imbalances, greed, and sin. Additionally, these social ills were not and are not merely a feature of a particular era—they endure and manifest across time.

Social and governmental sins are fundamentally abuses of relational power that are enshrined in the economic, political, legal, and social structures. They manifest in unjust distribution of access to basic survival needs (affordable housing, reasonable access to healthful foods, appropriate safety and protection, clean air and water, mental and physical health, etc.), laws designed to increase social inequity for the benefit of those who make the laws and their compatriots, and inconsistencies in how laws are employed, adjudicated, and violations are punished. When the structures that order society are out of balance and shift in a manner that crushes some in order to advance others, they become manifestations of Rauschenbusch's "Kingdom of Evil" and no longer reflect or promote the "Kingdom of God." The Kingdom of Evil persists through the ages and was manifest in the crucifixion of Jesus. Rauschenbusch "enumerate[s] six sins, all of a public nature, which combined to kill Jesus. He bore their crushing attack in his body and soul. . . . In so far as the personal sins of men have contributed to the existence of these public sins, he came into collision with the totality of evil in mankind."[10] The six social sins are (1) Religious bigotry, (2) Graft/political corruption and political power, (3) corruption of justice, (4) mob spirit/mob action, (5) militarism, and (6) class contempt.[11] These are sins perpetrated through social power and under the direction of persons and institutions of social leadership.

As a brief expansion, religious bigotry not only relates to oppression on the basis of religious practice and community affiliation; it also includes the joining of religious leaders and organizations in consenting to, cosigning, and promoting the sacredization of social injustice. Rauschenbusch writes, "It takes religion to put a steel edge on social intolerance. Religious bigotry has been one of the permanent evils of mankind, the cause of untold social division, bitterness, persecution, and religious wars."[12] The second sin, graft and political power, recognizes the presence—covertly or overtly—of an ever-present subgroup of society with access to paths of leadership.

> There is always an oligarchy, wherever you look; monarchial and republican forms of government are both protective devices for the-group-that-controls-things. This group is the universal government. For every oligarchy political power is convertible into financial income and social influence, thus satisfying the powerful double instinct for money and for power.[13]

In our contemporary, awareness of this in-group shows up in anger, resentment, and rhetoric about "the elite" or "establishment." The corruption of justice points to the perversion of legal and judicial systems in which those in power make laws or appoint judges who pass a litmus test or confirm loyalty to party, ideology, or a particular benefactor. Additionally, Rauschenbusch notes that "Even if the judge is wholly free from bias, the law itself in all countries, presumably, is on the side of property.... [Furthermore], Our own legislatures rarely contain any spokesman of the class which needs a voice most of all."[14]

The fourth social sin is the presence of mob spirit and action. "The mob spirit is the social spirit gone mad." The social spirit can be a powerful force for justice and health; however the important distinction between productive protest and mob gatherings is whether or not there is an intention of violence—of any form including physical, psychological, economic, etc. When

> the social group then escapes from the control of its wiser and fairer habits, and is lashed into action by primitive passions.... Rarely are mobs wholly spontaneous; usually there is leadership to fanaticize the masses. At this point this sin connects with the sins of selfish leadership.... So it was in the case of Jesus. The mob shouted for the physical force.... There was "patriotism" in this choice.[15]

The sin of militarism is not limited to the structures of official military but also includes civil systems that enact the orders of the state—especially in carrying out executions (by bullet, injection, protective guidelines, suicide, or disease) of those deemed a threat, undesired, or a scapegoat of those with social power. The sixth sin addresses the impact of economic sin and income inequality. "Parasitic incomes produce class differences; class differences create class pride and class contempt.... They are a direct negation of solidarity and love. They substitute a semi-human, semi-ethical relation for full human fraternity."[16]

These six social sins combined to accomplish the crucifixion of Jesus and continue to perpetuate "crucifixion" of those with less social, economic, political, legal, or civic power.[17] When political self-interest determines governance, economic inequality generates class contempt, religious leaders justify and bless manifestations of social intolerance under the guise of civility or piety, due process is disposed, and those in power are donned with military might and (nearly unquestioned) oversight of communities, communal social action can devolve into mob action that is ruled out of power, fear, and self-interest. However, when the sins of social systems and government are seen with courageous clarity and we are able to claim our "wiser and fairer habits" the social spirit can manifest in protests for justice, decency, and health. Protests, resistance, and activism led by the social spirits of wisdom, integrity, compassion, and justice can reinstate into our social forefront the mandate of Jesus to care for the "least of these" (Matthew 25:40).

Chapter 5

PROTEST AS MASS PERFOMANCE OF SHARED VALUES OR SOCIAL LIMITS

If the Kingdom of Evil is marked by the six social sins and functions to maintain power among the few at the cost of significant harm and suffering by the many, what are the features of the Kingdom of God. While Rauschenbusch discusses features of the Kingdom of God, he does not offer a direct inversion of the social sins marking the Kingdom of Evil. Nevertheless, such an exercise is useful for mapping religious or theological dimensions of social protests and activism. What are social virtues as counter to social sins? (1) Religious acceptance that provides protection against social intolerance and balms for the wounds inflicted by bigotry. (2) Just use of political power-power with focused intention on behalf of and for the people. (3) Fostering and promotion of the integrity of justice in which justices are aware of their own biases and utilize their power of adjudication to continue the crafting of social structures of health and wholeness. (4) The presence of social spirit/social action in which wisdom and compassion both motivate and temper (as appropriate) public demonstrations. (5) The civic cultivation of options for promoting and preserving safety by means other than violence (actual or threatened). In following the wisdom of the prophet Isaiah, "And they shall beat their swords into plowshares, and their spears into pruninghooks: nation shall not lift up sword against nation, neither shall they learn war any more" (Isaiah 2:4). (6) The intentional manifestation and maintenance of economic justice which includes livable wages, access to basic human needs (housing, food, preservation of "good enough" attachments between children and parents, water, education, medical and mental health care, etc.) and opportunities to acquire skills and practice a trade or profession. These six social virtues signal the health and prosperity of a nation that is wise and mature in its civic life. When we, as a nation, fail to demonstrate these virtues, the social spirit rises to action to advocate for our shared values or decry the violation of our shared social limits.

Protest movements are a manifestation and mobilization of the social spirit and reveal or reflect who we are as a people. Protest, as social liturgy or our civic public work, is a kind of en mass ritual dance that is scripted, structured, and purposeful movement of bodies—individual and the body politic. They are embodied, collective, "choreographed," movements designed to evoke affect, reenact symbols of history, or communicate values. As such, protests are physical mobilizations of bodies within the civil body. Writing on the intersections of politics and dance, Randy Martin writes, mobilization—what moving bodies accomplish through movement—"is . . . to indicate the practical dynamic between production and product. Here, production is what dancing assembles as a capacity for movement, and the product is not the aesthetic effect of the dance but the materialized identity accomplished through the performance of movement."[18] Production, in the realm of protest movements, points to the liturgy of the action—its words, songs, signs, body postures, body movements, etc. Will "the people" march? Lay down symbolizing deaths? Collect shoes to draw connections between people killed or harmed by governmental policies? The product is the formation of who we are as a people. Harkening to the first section, it is the social action of protest and resistance through which we as a society "becomes itself, becomes conscious of itself, and confesses itself as a distinct entity." Public political mobilizations of the social spirit reflect the values and limits of the populace both in what occurs in the actions of protest and as the actual constituting of the public identity in the performance of protest. It moves us from theory to praxis, from ideology to identity. We are who we are through performance of our social action.

Protest and resistance movements often function as a counterbalance to performativity of populist leaders: Trump's inauguration—Women's March, the travel ban—protests at airports, "no tolerance" police at the border—Families Belong Together, and increased militarization of police and unjust deaths of people of color—Black Lives Matter. In his analysis of populism as a political performance style (as an alternative option to an ideology, platform, or party), Benjamin Moffitt states that populism as a "Political style can be understood as *the repertoires of embodied, symbolically mediated performance made to audiences that are used to create and navigate the fields of power that comprise the political, stretching from the domain of government through to everyday life* (original emphasis)."[19] Noting the performativity of populism as a strategy to acquire political power is an important shift for our understanding of protest as social liturgy enacted by the people to reclaim political power when it is being used destructively or against the will of the populous. Populism, as a political performance style, and protest, as the performance of the people, function to maintain the balance of power. When institutions of political power fail to maintain order and health, protests are the people's mechanism for stepping in and motivating course correction in between election opportunities. In the context of the United States, when the people discern that one of the three branches of government (executive, legislative, and judicial) is running unchecked by the other two and the press (the unofficial fourth branch of government) is unable to contain the overreach, protests emerge as the fifth branch (the people).

Moffitt's analysis of populism is exceedingly relevant and helpful for understanding the surge of protest and activism movements during the Trump administration. He notes that populism as a political style has three distinct characteristics: appeals to "the People" versus "the Elite," displays of "bad manners" by the populist leader, and the generation or capitalizing of "crisis, breakdown, and threat." Each of these three dimensions of the political performance style of populism is intentional, strategic, and aimed to consolidate political power or to distract from abuses of political power. The generation of political tribalism that segments the populous into "us versus them" prompts intranational divisions and amplifies feelings of competition, scarcity, and apprehension thus allowing the populist actor to frame themselves as the hero or savior. The performance of "bad manners" or behavior unappealing to "the elite" (however that group is cast) signal the leaders as "one of us" and not "one of them." These two features ultimately set the groundwork for the third: the presence of crisis, breakdown, or threat.

> Populism gets its impetus from the perception of crisis, breakdown or threat (Taggart 2000), and at the same time aims to induce crisis through dramatization and performance. This in turn leads to the demand to act decisively and immediately. Crises are often related to the breakdown between citizens and their representatives, but can also be related to immigration, economic difficulties, perceived injustice, military threat, social change or other issues.[20]

Threats and crisis solidify power and tribalism while also providing public distractions from matters that are perhaps more central but less publically enticing—akin to a thief setting a controllable fire in the backyard and drawing the resident's attention to the crisis in the back so that no one notices the home being robbed.

Public protests are the work of the people to counter the actions of the populist leader seeking to incite crisis or structural breakdowns. As embodied, communal movements of the social spirit, protests are a form of civic "dance" as well as social liturgy. "Dance" in its most general form is the intentional bodily movement of one or more persons for the purpose of expression, connection, or communication. Dance, as a general category, opens up lenses of analysis and reflection on communal movement practices. When placed in conversation with politics, generally, and populism more specifically, the significance of crisis and movement opens up. Martin writes,

> Dance generates a sense of being in the midst of a crisis, a break, a rupture, even a loss and a prospect at the same time; thus while dancing may appear to be a series of stops and starts, for the dancer, next steps are already in motion, already passing from one (im)balance to the next. . . . When applied to political life, the idea of crisis suggests a series of unconnected moves, each of which is prompted by a thought and a decision, rather than something continuous in itself and capable of going beyond itself.[21]

The lens provided by dance theory provides a space of intention and centeredness in the midst of crisis, breakdowns, and/or threats. As Martin highlights, embodied, communal movement practices provide a sense of grounded identity and being in the midst of the seeming chaos of populist generated threats. The space generated by and for the dancer in the midst of the dance, is akin to the role of identity generation, awareness, and articulation through the liturgy of the Church that points us to and connects us with something beyond. Additionally, dance takes within itself motion, (im)balance, and continuity in the face of apparent rupture—thereby cultivating spaces for subversive opposition to abuses of political power.

Dance; Liturgy; Protest—embodied, communal, formative. Movements that inherently accomplish a task. When we gather to dance, worship, or protest, what are we coming to know about ourself and what are we completing? Ultimately, these practices in their inter-/intra-personal, congregational, and civic incarnations (respectively) generate the embodied space and resources to move into our identity more fully. Performances of embodied communal movements on dance floors, in houses of worship, and in the streets indicate who we are as a people, what we value, what we are unwilling to accept, and who we refuse to become. "[L]iturgical theology aims, first of all, not at self-examination by the church of its liturgy but at self-understanding by the church of the theology implicit and explicit in its liturgy."[22] As we engage in movements of protest, we also must cultivate curiosity and adopt intentionality about what we are implicitly and explicitly revealing and communicating. If our embodied, communal movements both reveal and form our identity, we must take care in how we are formed.

The intention of this chapter has been to introduce a new way of considering the work and function of protests, activism, and resistance movements through the lens of liturgical studies—with assists from dance studies. When presented with surges in social and public activism, it is essential to access the harm inflicted or the violated boundary that is generating the movement. Human beings don't generally expend energy on protest actions unless such action is required for justice or survival. Consequently, protest actions always have an intention, function, and goal. Likewise, the action of embodied, communal, public protest is often a goal in itself as a performance of social values and/or limits. Why protest? Protests generate and reveal who we are. They show us what we will stand for and what we will let slide past. They tell us who is included; who is worth protecting; how we will comport ourselves in the face of crisis, threat, or trauma. They show us what truths we do accept as self-evident and what rights we have as children of God. Will we create and advocate for a more perfect union with rights, liberty, and justice for ALL?

NOTES

1. I intentionally shift the language of "pursuit of happiness" to "movement towards fulfillment" in an effort to counter the cultural trend towards consumption and entertainment. "Hap-

piness," in our current era, tends to designate an experience of joy or pleasure that is often fleeting and requires a nearly addictive like pursuit to regain requiring ever extravagant means. "Pursuit of happiness" can be a destructive and often frenetic position that damages potential for sustainable fulfillment. As a counter, I offer "movement towards fulfillment" as an alternative. Fulfillment recognizes the sustainable satisfaction of "enough." It is attainable, stabile, and productive.

2. Liturgy, *Oxford English Living Dictionary*, https://en.oxforddictionaries.com/definition/liturgy (Accessed July 1, 2018).

3. Ibid.

4. Performance, *Oxford English Living Dictionary*, https://en.oxforddictionaries.com/definition/liturgy (Accessed July 1, 2018).

5. Nicholas Wolterstorff, 9f.

6. Ibid.

7. As quoted in Ibid., 10.

8. For more on the relationship between trauma and a theology of sin as abuses of relational power, please refer to Jennifer Baldwin, *Trauma Sensitive Theology: Thinking Theologically in the Era of Trauma* (Eugene: Cascade Press, 2018).

9. Dirk Lange, *Trauma Recalled: Liturgy, Disruption, and Theology* (Minneapolis: Fortress Press, 2010), 2.

10. Walter Rauschenbusch, *A Theology for the Social Gospel*, Macmillan Co., 1917, reprint (Louisville: Westminster John Knox Press, 1997), 248.

11. Ibid., 248f.

12. Ibid., 249.

13. Ibid., 251.

14. Ibid., 253.

15. Ibid., 254–255.

16. Ibid., 257, 256.

17. Ibid., 248f.

18. Randy Martin, *Critical Moves: Dance Studies in Theory and Politics* (Durham: Duke University Press, 1998), 4.

19. Benjamin Moffitt, *The Global Rise of Populism: Performance, Political Style, and Representation* (Stanford: Stanford University Press, 2016), 38.

20. Ibid., 45.

21. Martin, 1.

22. Wolterstorff, 3.

REFERENCES

Baldwin, Jennifer. *Trauma Sensitive Theology: Thinking Theologically in the Era of Trauma*, Eugene: Cascade Books, 2018.

Lange, Dirk. *Trauma Recalled: Liturgy, Disruption, and Theology*, Minneapolis: Fortress Press, 2010.

Martin, Randy. *Critical Moves: Dance Studies in Theory and Politics*, Durham: Duke University Press, 1998.

Moffitt, Benjamin. *The Global Rise of Populism: Performance, Political Style, and Representation,* Stanford: Stanford University Press, 2016.

Rauschenbusch, Walter. *A Theology for the Social Gospel*, Macmillan Co., 1917, reprint Louisville: Westminster John Knox Press, 1997.

Wolterstorff, Nicholas. *The God We Worship: An Exploration of Liturgical Theology*, Grand Rapids: Eerdmans Publishing Co., 2015.

II

Cultural Resourcing for Activism

Chapter Six

"Because I'm Your Mother, That's Why"

Scientific Authority and the March for Science

Lisa Stenmark

When I was a kid I often rebelled at bedtime—I had many strategies for delaying the inevitable, most of them familiar to parents (and children). I would negotiate (5 more minutes!), I would sneak into the hallway outside the living room where I could see the TV (and where my parents would find me after I fell asleep), I would demand a reason, "I'm not sleepy! I don't want to go to bed! Why do I need to go to bed?!" My mother responded (like most mothers, perhaps), "Because I am your mother, that's why." And that ended it, because there was no appeal. This is authority—it compels action or belief without the need for force or persuasion. There were good reasons for me to go to bed, and for doing the other things that my parents told me to do, even when I didn't want to—like eating my vegetables, not drinking water out of the gutter, or running into the street. I was a child and left to my own devices I likely would have sat up every night eating candy until sometime after the test pattern came on. There were—and are—a lot of good reasons for going to be early. But that's not why I did it. I did it because she was my mother. That's why.

On April 22, 2017, hundreds of thousands of people around the world participated in a March for Science and a movement was born to, in the words of the organization's Web site, defend science against "an alarming trend toward discrediting scientific consensus and restricting scientific discovery."[1] Signs at the March declared "Science is the Solution," "There is no Alternative to a Fact," "Just the facts ma'am," "Science is Real," and a quote from Neil de Grasse Tyson, "The good thing about science is it is true whether you believe it or not."[2] These signs urge us to accept what "science" tells us because it is only about facts and it is uniquely able to describe the world as it really is. In a previous paper I addressed the singular notion of "truth" produced by science (and science alone) and, while I affirmed the importance of defending truth claims in public, I also described the risks posed by truth claims in general, and for science in particular.[3] I argued that a defense of rational, scientific truth was no more (or less) important than a defense of other kinds of truths. While the March for Science is good, because it encourages community discussion of science and is intentional about diversity and inclusivity (going so far as to provide specific ways to accomplish this), it is not sufficient because what it advocates is more akin to a lecture than a discussion and its understanding of diversity was not broad enough. We need more than a diverse group of scientists speaking *to* the public and any successful defense of science should include an exchange of culturally and epistemically diverse perspectives.

In that previous paper, I touched on the subject of authority, although I did not have time to explore it sufficiently, and it is to authority that I now turn. The underlying idea behind the defense of science is not only that "science" is a unique and superior form of knowledge, but that the public (nonscientists) should accept scientific facts *because* they have been produced by science and scientists: like my mother, their justification comes down to "Because we're science, that's why!"[4] And we largely do accept it: on the weekend of the second March for Science (in April 2018) I was at a conference made up mostly of academics in the humanities. At several points we touched on the issue of climate change and the overwhelming attitude toward those who doubted the reality of global warming—"climate deniers"—was negative. I pressed my colleagues: "But why do *you* believe that global warming is happening?" They cited "overwhelming evidence," the consensus of scientists, etc. But, when I asked what the evidence was, people got vague. The believed in global warming "Because it's science, that's why!"

My point is not that global warming is fake or that scientists are untrustworthy. My point is what is going on in the March is far more complicated than the need to just accept the "facts" of science. Science defenders are not defending "facts," they are defending the authority of scientific institutions to determine what those facts are. I believe global warming is happening, and I think it is caused by human activities, but not because of "facts," but because, by and large, I trust the institutions of science. Those who doubt that global warming is real do not, at least on this issue. For them, "Because we're science, that's why!" is not sufficient.

In this paper I will begin with a brief discussion of authority, distinguishing between executive, epistemic, moral, and instructional authority. I will then argue that the strategy employed by the March for defending science is counterproductive because defenders of scientific authority base their defense on epistemic authority, but challenges to scientific authority have more to do with institutional authority and most often occur in those instances where the epistemic authority of science encroaches on other areas, including moral authority. Because science defenders ignore these other dimensions, they actually undermine the authority of science. I conclude by arguing that instead of asserting the epistemic authority of science, we need to focus on much more public engagement with science. Building on the work of Linda Zerilli, I argue that this means more than educating the public about science but promoting an exchange of perception as a way to turn science into "public truths," which are truths that make demands on us.

AUTHORITY: WHAT IT IS

In public life, as in private, authority is that which compels action or belief without the need for force or persuasion.[5] Obviously, this does not mean that authority is not persuasive or coercive; merely that authority is sufficiently forceful and persuasive in and of itself. In fact, the need for outside force or persuasion is the clearest indicator that authority has been weakened or lost altogether. If I have to convince you to believe what I say or do what I ask, it means I lack authority, if only in this instance or at this time. In the words of Hannah Arendt, "where force is used, authority itself has failed, where arguments are used, authority is left in abeyance."[6] It is only when "Because I am your mother, that's why" or "Because I am president, that's why" is sufficient that authority remains intact. If the response is "So what?!" or "I don't care," authority has vanished. There are other options, of course. Parents may rely on force or even violence (physically placing the child in her bed or a spanking), threats ("If you don't go to bed, you can't go to the party tomorrow!"), bargaining ("You can stay up for half an hour, if you promise to go to bed without complaining"), and even appeals to reason ("If you don't get enough sleep you'll get sick"). Any of these might get the child into bed (eventually), but none is authority in and of itself. In each case, authority has been replaced by something else, a different kind of authority (e.g., reason or mutual agreement) or the force of violence and coercion. Only when a child accepts "because I am your mother," as sufficient is the authority of "motherness" intact. In public, the same options exist and if the authority of (for example) the state is challenged, the state can use threats and punishment, justify existing laws, or negotiate a change. In each of these cases, the original authority has been replaced with something else.

The ability to compel action—to *have* authority—is different from the ability to compel belief—to *be an* authority. While both are compulsive, it is important not to confuse *executive authority*, the ability to compel action, with *epistemic authority*, the ability to compel belief. When we conflate executive and epistemic authority we may start to believe that if we have authority it means we are more knowledgeable (we aren't), or that if we have epistemic authority people have to believe us (they don't). As a teacher, I can use my executive authority to confer grades as a way to make my students say (or write) what I want, but I can't make them believe it. "Not to listen to someone who has appropriate knowledge may be foolish or imprudent; but no one has the right either to be heard or to be believed simply because of his real or purported knowledge."[7] While being an epistemic authority does not guarantee that my statements are true, merely reliable, when it becomes conflated with executive authority, it is easy to drift from "you can trust what I say because I am an authority" to "what I say is true because I am an authority." Part of the danger of conflating executive and epistemic authority is that executive authority is self-fulfilling—executive authority can be arbitrary or capricious, but it is never "wrong," as Richard Nixon famously pointed out when he told David Frost, "when the president does it, that means it is not illegal."[8] But, executive authority does not extend out into the world and it cannot change reality, or public opinion, as Nixon found out. So, being an authority does not guarantee the truth of a statement because, unlike executive authority, epistemic authority is ultimately dependent on whatever it is that is known—no matter how much epistemic authority an engineer has, the reality of gravity can cause a bridge to fall.

There is a third kind of authority, moral authority, which *can* be thought of as a kind of epistemic authority—knowing how to live well—but moral authority is more than knowing how to live well, it comes from actually living well and it is embodied in a life. Again, it is important to distinguish moral authority from other kinds of authority—knowing how to live well is no guarantee that one will live well, nor does moral authority confer the ability to force others to live a certain way.

Each of these forms of authority has a kind of individual or internal dimension: we accept authority (often without thinking) because we feel compelled to do so. Epistemic authority exerts force through our senses—we see, hear or taste and are compelled to believe—or through the force of reason, while moral authority exerts its force on a kind of moral sense. The force of moral authority is narrative because something about the way an individual, or community, lives in the world is compelling. Moral authority has a force because we desire to live well and loses its force if we have no desire for the life that embodies it. Even executive authority has an internal dimension, reflected in the idea that some people have a "forceful personality" and we feel compelled to acquiesce to their demands. But each form of authority also has what we could think of as an external dimension as well, an institutional dimension which reinforces authority over time and over generations. This dimension helps explain the force of authority absent this personal compulsion—we don't need to personally see the evidence, or the embodiment of an idea, to accept that it is true.

The weight of repeated acquiescence exerts its own force: institutional authority feels like an external reality, outside of human choosing, that exerts a force on us as real as gravity.[9] In the Western tradition, this experience is expressed in the idea of an Absolute that exists outside of human culture and control—as well as human limitations—that can be the basis for our judgments and actions. But, while the experience of institutional authority *feels* like something over which we have no choice, we do have a choice, because *all* authority requires a kind of acquiescence, even if it is only tacit. We *can* refuse to obey a command or believe what an authority tells us—and when we refuse to recognize it, authority ceases to exist. There are consequences: the consequences for rejecting executive authority might be threats or violence, while the consequences for accepting epistemic authority is something more like the force of reality. But, although there are consequences, authority has still been rejected.

This need for constant (if tacit) approval and acceptance means that, while we may experience authority as fixed or given, it is actually quite fluid. Arendt refers to this ongoing process of approval as the relationship between authority and tradition, in which each generation accepts, rejects, and revises authority. Institutional authority is the embodiment of this relationship, and it may combine different forms of authority—executive, epistemic, and moral.

Different forms of authority can conflict—we may be commanded to do something (executive authority) that violates our ethical beliefs (moral authority). There may also be conflicts between different authoritative institutions—e.g., conflicts between institutions associated with "religion" and "science." There can also be conflicts between institutional authority and what I have called internal authority—the "sell by date" on the milk versus what my nose tells me. When these conflicts arise, we may choose one authority over another, or revise (or reject) both, but when institutional authority is treated as though it were absolute and unchanging, then responses to these conflicts are limited. Continuing to insist on institutional authority once it is questioned or there are cracks in the façade—"Pay no attention to the man behind the curtain!"—can either lead to absolutism or authoritarianism, or it will undermine all authority. The ideal is a constant augmenting, which gives institutional authority its longevity and its sense of stability as each generation has the opportunity to consider authority, to contribute to it, and to pass it on.

To illustrate what I mean, we can go back to the example of parental authority. As a child gets older she gains more experience, learns new things in school, and sees people living lives that are different from hers, which may cause her to question what her parents have told her. This is a natural process, but it is why parents are so concerned about what their children learn in school, or see on television, etc. "Because I am your mother" might work for a while, but insisting on rigid acceptance is likely to lead to the loss of all parental authority. On the other hand, when parents allow their authority to be revised and augmented, it lasts. In my case, "because I am your mother" continues to influence my life and actions, but not because I blindly accept what my mother told me. Her authority is different than what it was when I was a child and she wanted me to go to bed—although it turns out she was right about that!—but she continues to have authority, 10 years after her death, because I have reflected upon her counsel (much of it passed on from her mother, and so on), rejected some of it, accepted some of it, and in the process of adapting and then adopting what she has given me, I have made it mine, a tradition that I will pass on. This is not only true of parental authority, it describes the process of how I have made intellectual, moral, and other authorities mine as well.

Institutionalized authority in its various forms is necessary for human collectivities; without them there could be no community, and certainly no complex communities. Institutionalized authority provides stability, continuity, and permanence to society, making coordinated action possible, allowing us to pass on knowledge from generation to generation and providing a sense of *who* we are, not just what we do and believe. This continuity is an essential part of a stable world, and is necessary for healthy public discourse. Its loss "is tantamount to the loss of the groundwork of the world."[10] But too much reliance on authority also undermines public judgment, because it is "always associated with inequality of some kind,"[11] and can make citizens become accustomed to accepting what they are told without thinking. To understand authority as something that must be accepted without change turns authority into a tool of domination, an absolute that undermines judgment. Thus, authority presents something of a paradox: we need it to live a life in community and to exercise public judgment, yet it can also threaten community and undermine public judgment.

AUTHORITY AND THE MARCH FOR SCIENCE

Those who March for Science, along with other science boosters, urge the public to accept the truth claims of science. This appeal to epistemic authority is justified by the assertion that science is "just about the facts," because science and scientists are, or should be, above politics and are thus able to provide unique access to the world as it really is—"So Bad Even Introverts Are Here."[12] They further support the epistemic authority of science by claiming a variety of real-world benefits: "Got plague? Me Neither. Thanks Science!"[13] and "No Science, No Beer!"[14] It is worth noting that this "reality" is the old external Absolute of the Western Tradition, an unchanging foundation of decision-making that is unsullied by human limitations.[15] It is doubly tempting in an American context because it resembles Scottish Common Sense Realism, which had a profound influence on both the Founders and on the public's perception of science. This is an understanding of science as primarily empirical—based on our experience of the world—with scientists simply making observations and collecting data based on careful experiments. This view was influential because it was a very democratic view of science—anyone could perform experiments and make observations, so that no one had to rely on outside authority but could instead rely on the authority of their own senses.[16] This respect for the authority of science as something based in the "real world" and the compulsion of our senses still exists, contrary to the kind of widespread disregard for science implied by the March for Science. The public continues to believe that science can solve problems—both general and specific—and even those who "oppose science," hold scientific authority in such regard that they oppose science by claiming to *be* science.[17] There are, of course, disagreements about particular scientific claims, but not because they were "generated through a scientific way of knowing."[18]

Clearly, the issue is not epistemic authority. At least one conflict arises because the epistemic authority of science is not based in the "reality" of the world as most people *experience* it and, contrary to Scottish Common Sense Realism, it never has been. Modern science has always relied on instruments not available to everyone, which means trusting in the senses of the scientist, and not our own. Moreover, contemporary science increasingly focuses on aggregation of data, and probabilities, none of which can be compelling in the same way that, for example, the movement of planets or the existence of microbes can be compelling if you have the instruments to look at them. The real issue is not the epistemic authority of science, but institutional authority—who is or is not a scientist, who can say what is and is not a scientific "fact," what counts as data, and how that data will be judged. Many scientific truths, such as natural selection or global warming, are not compellingly true in and of themselves and must rely on the institutional authority of science. If that authority were intact, then science would establish the "fact" of global warming, which people would generally accept as true, and public debate would center on the best way to respond. It doesn't work that way because the institutional authority of science has been challenged—often by other institutional authorities, and often for political, economic, or other reasons. To the extent that supporters of science ignore the institutional dimension and insist that the authority of science is "facts" or "reality," they distort the issue and further undermine the institutional authority of science when the claims of science often contradict our individual experience and our senses.

I suspect that everyone reading this has disagreed with a scientific claim at one point or another, but this does not mean an across-the-board rejection of scientific authority—unless one thinks that authority must be unchallenged and unchanged. Disagreement likely occurs because the claim contradicts something I already believe (a belief that was likely shaped by science), my experience, or other institutional authority. For example, I have been reading that new research challenges studies that show that women's periods will sync when they live in close proximity. I have so far disregarded this new research. The reason for my "science denial" is that I believe I have personally experienced this on multiple occasions and, while I *may* be wrong, I am not going to change my mind until I see more data, a good explanation for why the old data was wrong, and an explanation for what I have experienced—this is Kuhn's paradigm shift in miniature. The same dynamic is at play in other cases of "science denial," as when people reject the claim of global warming because the winter had been so cold.

One need not accept a couple of decades of scholarship that reveal the ways that science is socially constructed to accept that the authority of science is a lot more complicated than "just the facts." Science is an institution, and scientists have institutional interest, and when the institutions of science push against the authority of our senses or the authority of other institutions, there is going to be resistance. In particular those institutions whose power and profit are threatened by scientific claims are going to exploit any conflict with our senses to further undermine the authority of science. Claims about global warming threaten powerful institutions (like the fossil fuel industry), who successfully undermine the authority of scientific institutions because global warming is *not demonstrably true* outside of our reliance on the institutions of science. These scientific facts have no compulsion, at least until the force of reality—and catastrophic climate change—compels agreement.

The problems with scientific authority do not merely arise because of conflicts with the authority of our senses or with other institutions. That's because some science supporters engage in a kind of epistemic overreach that gives science credit for every human advancement, even beer, while simultaneously denigrating other forms of knowledge: "Science, It's Like Magic but Real."[19] Moreover, defenders conflate the epistemic authority of science with executive authority, so that having epistemic authority—the ability to produce a scientific fact—becomes executive, authority, and "science proves" becomes a command to believe a certain thing or, more accurately act a certain way. The March for Science is not really about getting people to *believe* the claims of science, it is about getting them to act a certain way: to fund science and respond to scientific claims.

They also extend the epistemic authority of science into areas of moral concern. John Evans makes a strong case that resistance to science is not about the epistemic authority of science or the ability of science to produce genuine knowledge about the world, but about its moral implications. People push back against scientific claims because they overstep the boundary of moral authority, and this is not just perception. Looking at conflicts between scientists and religious ethicists in the area of biomedical science in the 1950s and 60s, Evans found no instances in which the *fact claims* of science were challenged and arguments on both sides could not be "distinguished in terms of their rationality, their reliance on dogma, or in terms of other features central to the stereotyped contrast between religious and scientific styles of thought." At issue were the moral implications of scientific activity.[20] As a more recent case in point, several religious groups were sharply opposed to Proposition 71 in California, an initiative to provide three billion dollars for embryonic stem cell research.[21] Supporters of the initiative relied on the epistemic authority of real-world applications—it would "save lives"—and ignoring moral claims of opponents (as well as their own moral claims), framed the issue as one between those who wanted to "defend scientists' right to continue their search for *truth*" and those who wanted to impede progress based on outmoded beliefs. No one was challenging the epistemic authority of science, or the veracity of scientific statements about stem cells, they were challenging its moral authority—opponents did not want to live the life that science promised, at least in some cases, and did not find it compelling.

THE ALTERNATIVE: MAKING TRUTH PUBLIC

Faced with a loss of authority, it is tempting to try to retain or regain that authority by reasserting it: "Because I'm your mother, that's why" or, "Because its science! That's why." The discussion so far suggests that this is not going to work, largely because science is about a lot more than epistemic authority. To the extent that science defenders ignore the executive, institutional, and moral dimensions of scientific authority, they undermine the very authority they are trying to protect. It is worth noting that this loss of authority is not unique to science, it is part of a broader loss of authority that is characteristic of modern, plural democracies (and which the authority of science was supposed to mitigate). As Arendt noted, this loss of authority creates a crisis in the modern world—and she was well aware of the dangers posed by this loss of authority—but it also presents an opportunity. Just as a challenge to parental authority is the first step to becoming a reasoning adult, so too is the loss of authority in public an opportunity to reestablish and reinvigorate a more robust public space.

From the perspective of public life, the question is not how to establish what is "in fact" true nor is it a question of whether science can make reliable claims about the world as it "really" is. These are epistemological questions and, while they are legitimate concerns for philosophers and scientists, what the public needs from science is not merely to establish absolute facts. Instead, what the public needs is for science, and other authoritative institutions, to provide generally reliable facts that we can all *agree on* and *act on*. When scientists leave the lab and their claims enter into the public realm, the concern for public life is not truth per se, but whether we are in a position to do anything about what we believe to be true, and thus we are no longer talking about epistemology or "truth," but something more like what Linda Zerilli calls "public truth,"[22] or a truth that makes demands on us. And this is really what the March is about as well because the concern is not just that the public should believe what science says, but that we should respond to what we hear. The Marchers want those truths to make demands on us.

There is insufficient space here to fully develop Zerilli's understanding of public truth or political objectivity, and how these relate to the question of scientific authority. But it is significant to note that too much emphasis on authority or truth that comes from outside of the public, political space undermines the public space because a robust public needs more than a defense of objective truth, it needs people who can make political judgments. Insisting that we simply accept the truth claims of science undermines judgment because it suggests we do not need to judge. Suggesting that we can (and should) make those decisions outside the give and take of public discourse can "lead us to lose track of our own part or voice as democratic citizens in deciding what will and what will not belong to the common world."[23] The authority of science is an institutional authority, which requires more than educating people about already formed ideas, as occurs in the kind of "town hall" meeting proposed by the March, where scientists come in and "educate: the public about the newest scientific research."[24] The facts of science do not emerge outside of public discourse—public discourse is "the very condition of their formation, articulation and circulation in a broader process of critical thinking and judging" and is the process by which "facts come to have some truth for us in a politically significant sense."[25] Zerilli's position reinforces my argument that the solution is not better science education, or making people more aware of scientific discoveries—although these are good things and should be part of the process of public deliberation—because we need to do more than determine what is "true." The public engagement with science is an augmenting of the authority of science, "a democratic world-building practice that creates and sustains human freedom and the common space in which shared objects of judgment can appear in the first place."[26] This is not going to be an easy process—and the loss of shared authority *is* a threat—but it's also an opportunity to reengage people. The March for Science doesn't do that. But through a more open exchange with a greater variety of perspectives—it could.

NOTES

1. This was the language used on the original March for Science website, "Our Mission" as of October 23, 2017. The language on the website has since changed, although as of this writing it is still being used on some of the affiliate websites.
2. See, e.g.: Stephen Shankland, "Nerds with Words: Signs from Silicon Valley March for Science," *CNET* (4/22/17), https://www.cnet.com/pictures/signs-from-the-march-for-science-in-silicon-valley/15/; *Politico Staff*, "21 of the Best March for Science Protest Signs," *Politico* (4/22/17), https://www.politico.com/gallery/2017/04/22/march-for-science-best-protest-signs-photos-002423?slide=0.
3. Lisa Stenmark, "Modern Political Lies: Science and Religion in a Post-Truth World," in *Navigating Post-Truth and Alternative Facts: Religion and Science as Political Theology*, edited by Jennifer Baldwin (Lanham, MD: Lexington Press, 2018).
4. As with all authority, there is an inherent inequality: we should accept science because scientists know better. This is not an anomaly, scientists, "almost universally" believe that the general public is "inadequately informed" about science and that opposition to science is based on "scientific illiteracy." They view the public as "non-rational and unsystematic in their thinking," relying on anecdotes, emotion, and self-interest. John H. Evans, *Morals Not Knowledge: Recasting the Contemporary U.S. Conflict Between Religion and Science* (Oakland: University of California Press, 2018), Ch 2. Scientists want engagement with the public, but see it as imparting information, not dialogue.
5. For a much more developed discussion of authority, see Lisa L. Stenmark *Religion, Science and Democracy: A Disputational Friendship* (Lanham, MD: Lexington Press, 2013).
6. Hannah Arendt, "What Is Authority? " in *Between Past and Future: Eight Exercises in Political Thought* (New York: Penguin Books, 1968), 93.
7. DeGeorge, *Nature and Limits of Authority*, 59.
8. Nixon went on to clarify, correctly, "If the president, for example, approves something because of the national security, or in this case because of a threat to internal peace and order of significant magnitude, then the president's decision in that instance is one that enables those who carry it out, to carry it out without violating a law." These interviews are available online, and an edited transcript is available in *The Guardian*, https://www.theguardian.com/theguardian/2007/sep/07/greatinterviews1.
9. While there is not room to explore this here, this strikes me as similar to what Foucault was getting at with the idea of discursive power.
10. Arendt, "What Is Authority," 95.
11. Richard Sennet, *Authority* (New York: W.W. Norton, 1980), 10; E. D. Watt, *Authority* (New York: St. Martin's Press, 1982), 47.
12. Akshat, "Best Protest Signs."
13. *Politico* Staff, "Best March for Science Protest Signs." This sign showed up in multiple places, with multiple diseases, including polio and rubella.
14. Ibid. This sign also showed up in multiple locations, including one that took credit not only for beer, but also wine, coffee and clean water. Given the number of these signs, along with its promotion in T-shirts, this appears to be one of the "official" signs.
15. Lisa Stenmark, "Storytelling and Wicked Problems: Myths of the Absolute and Climate Change," *Zygon*, vol. 50, no. 4, December 2015, 922–36.
16. Walter H. Conser, Jr., "Baconianism," in *Science and Religion: A Historical Introduction*. Edited by Gary B. Ferngren. Baltimore, MD: Johns Hopkins University Press (2002): 193–195.
17. Evans, chs 5. The Discovery Institute, a conservative think tank that supports ID does so "to improve science education." Supporters of ID still claim that it is not religion, and is supported by scientific evidence. Evans, Ch 5.
18. Evans, ch 6.
19. Akshat, "Best Protest Signs"; *Politico* Staff, "Best March for Science Protest Signs." Considering that beer has been around for over 5,000 years, and thus predates modern science by at least that long, it's a bit of an overreach—the sign could more accurately say "No Iran, No Beer" or "No Monks, No Beer."

20. Evans, ch 4.
21. A summary of the initiative, along with arguments and rebuttals is available at: http://vigarchive.sos.ca.gov/2004/general/propositions/prop71-title.htm.
22. Zerilli, *A Democratic Theory of Judgment* (Chicago: University of Chicago Press, 2016), 3.
23. Ibid.
24. March for Science website, https://www.marchforscience.com.
25. Zerilli, *Democratic Theory of Judgment*, 68.
26. Ibid., xiii

REFERENCES

Arendt, Hannah. "Lying in Politics." In *Crises of the Republic*. 1–47. New York: Harcourt Brace Jovanovich, 1972.
——. "Truth and Politics." In *Between Past and Future: Eight Exercises in Political Thought*, 227–264. New York: Penguin Books, 1968.
——. "What Is Authority?" In *Between Past and Future: Eight Exercises in Political Thought*, 91–141. New York: Penguin Books, 1968.
Akshat, Rathi. "The Best Protest Signs from Around the World at the March for Science," *Quartz*. 4/22/17. https://qz.com/966436/march-for-science-the-best-signs-from-protests-around-the-globe/.
Besley, John C. and Matthew Nisbet. "How Scientists View the Public, the Media and the Political Process," *Public Understanding of Science* 22, no. 6 (2011): 647.
Conser, Walter H., Jr. "Baconianism." *In Science and Religion: A Historical Introduction*, edited by Gary B. Ferngren, 193–195. Baltimore, MD: Johns Hopkins University Press, 2002.
DeGeorge, Richard T. *The Nature and Limits of Authority*. Lawrence, KS: University Press of Kansas, 1985.
Evans, John H. *Morals Not Knowledge: Recasting the Contemporary U.S. Conflict Between Religion and Science*. Oakland: University of California Press, 2018. Online doi:https://doi.org/10.1525/luminos.47.
March for Science. https://www.marchforscience.com.
Politico Staff. "21 of the Best March for Science Protest Signs." *Politico*. April 22, 2017. https://www.politico.com/gallery/2017/04/22/march-for-science-best-protest-signs-photos-002423?slide=0.
Sennet, Richard. *Authority*. New York: W.W. Norton, 1980.
Shankland, Stephen. "Nerds with Words: Signs from Silicon Valley March for Science," *CNET*. April 22, 2017. https://www.cnet.com/pictures/signs-from-the-march-for-science-in-silicon-valley/15/.
Stenmark, Lisa. "Modern Political Lies: Science and Religion in a Post-Truth World." In *Navigating Post-Truth and Alternative Facts: Religion and Science as Political Theology*, edited by Jennifer Baldwin. Lanham, MD: Lexington Press, 2018.
——. *Religion, Science and Democracy: A Disputational Friendship*. Lanham, MD: Lexington Press, 2013.
——. "Storytelling and Wicked Problems: Myths of the Absolute and Climate Change," *Zygon,* vol. 50, no. 4, December 2015, 922–36.
Watt, E. D. *Authority*. New York: St. Martin's Press, 1982.
Zerilli, Linda. "Truth and Politics." In *Truth and Democracy*, edited by Jeremy Wilkins and Andrew Norris, 54–75. Philadelphia, University of Pennsylvania Press, 2012.
——. *A Democratic Theory of Judgment*. Chicago: University of Chicago Press, 2016.
——. "Toward a Feminist Theory of Judgment." *Signs: Journal of Women in Culture and Society.* vol. 34, no 2, 2008.
——. "Toward a Democratic Theory of Judgment." In *Judgment and Action: Fragments Toward a History*, edited by Vivasvan Soni and Thomas Pfau, 191–222. Evanston, IL: Northwestern University Press, 2018.

Chapter Seven

Black Theology and Hip-Hop Theology

Theologies of Activism and Resistance

Willie Hudson

Black theology and Hip-hop theology and their relationship to inner-city spiritual development, particularly regarding black and brown youth, are important to understand and study. This chapter will address various socio-theological realities and how Black theology and Hip-hop theology help mediate those complexities to shape spiritual development in the inner-city context. An important motif that surfaces includes the experiences of racist social, political, judicial, economic, and theological complexities that arrest spiritual development within the inner-city. This chapter highlights and argues that Black theology and Hip-hop theology, more than any other theology, are crucial for inner-city spirituality because no other praxis seems sufficiently sophisticated for the complexities of their cultural environment. When Black theology utilizes Hip-hop theology through the black and brown experience, a salvific rhetoric might clearly be personalized from an oppressive perspective. There is value when theology is understood and lived on the level of the hearer. God must become *real* in one's life, which can happen because of theologically demanding an end to the oppressive complexities that hinder this reality. Therefore, the goal of this chapter is to solidify the relationship of Black theology and Hip-hop theology in the space between activism and resistance.

To better understand a definition of Black theology as utilized in this study, a concept developed by James Cone will become the foundation for consideration:

> Black Theology is a theology of black liberation. It seeks to plumb the black condition in the light of God's revelation in Jesus Christ, so that the black

community can see that the gospel is commensurate with the achievement of black humanity. Black Theology is a theology of "blackness." It is the affirmation of black humanity that emancipates black people from white racism, thus providing authentic freedom for both white and black people. It affirms the humanity of white people in that it says No to the encroachment of white oppression.[1]

Black theology must draw upon the scriptures to construct a social gospel that makes God central to both those who speak the language of the streets and the language of the church, while understanding that Hip-hop theology is a countercultural, subversive vehicle through which disaffected black and brown youth can engage the resources of biblical faith and Christian tradition. Hip-hop has been both an empowering and debilitating phenomenon for Black youth culture. Hip-hop is empowering because it creates a sense of pride, resistance, and victory in the face of adversity. Hip-hop embraces a style in fashion, language, attitude, and business. It opened the creative doors for its members to express their inner-most feelings. Hip-hop gives its generation a voice and a sense of community.

So, what is hip-hop? What is the difference between hip-hop and Hip-hop theology? Christian rap is but one area of the "rap" genres; however, this genre is set aside (sanctified) for God. This is a very important point to this discussion; the main difference between hip-hop and Hip-hop theology is that hip-hop makes no room for Christ; Hip-hop theology evangelized with music makes only those rap lyrics that deal with Christ. Additionally, hip-hop in its original design—during the 1970s—was designed for healing, restoration, and communication. It was a common vehicle for black and brown young adults to come together . . . not apart.

Socially, hip-hop has been attributed as a 'black" movement. For many people, pastors included, the word hip-hop produces some of the most negative vile perceptions of young black and brown youth. . . . God's babies. For these people, the word hip-hop suggests music that contains cursing and music videos that depict graphic sexual behavior, violence, gangs, drugs, an unabridged focus on money, cars, oversized rims, jewelry, saggy pants, and tattoos. For them, hip-hop suggests a culture gone wrong; a culture absent of God and the moral character that emulates evil rather than holiness, a culture not able to be redeemed. But this is not hip-hop; this is not what God intended for this culture.

In most cases, hip-hop and all the negative connotations associated with it are in fact, reflections of an American reaction to issues that have always been a problem with youth, no matter what generation it happens to affect. These issues continue to plague generations of young people as they grow into adulthood and leave unresolved fragmented emotions that hinder them from productive maturity. These issues include racism, violence, drugs, alcohol, loneliness, inadequate education, abandonment, lack of security, finance, self-esteem, broken homes, and families. It is the negative implications of hip-hop that has consistently impacted the growth of this culture within the church. Otis Moss III in an article entitled, *Real Big: The Hip-Hop Pastor as Post-Modern Prophet* also speaks to this language of societal injustices through hip-hop:

> Hip-hop uses language and technology to entertain, critique, and define the urban centers from which it originates. Hip hop is a means for young black men and women to define their reality. It gives value to their world, which has been defined by white culture as having no value. It may not always be positive or Afrocentric, but hip-hop points to the problems in society that many black people have refused to address. The hip-hop community recognizes the contradiction of urban existence and the fallacy of the American dream founded upon a system that exploits people of color.[2]

The studies of Black theology and Hip-hop theology are broad concepts with limited academic investigation and even less theological consideration when studied in respect to their value for spiritual formation. Scholars of religion like Gordon Lynch, Anthony B. Pinn, Nancy T. Ammerman, and others represent intellectual inquiry into nontraditional social and cultural practices like hip-hop. Yet, however, there has been meager attention to hip-hop's effect on spiritual formation. Monica Miller's work, *Religion and Hip-Hop* argues that there may not be something religious in hip-hop and that as scholars, trying to find something religious about the cultural practices of hip-hop is what theologians are trained to do; however, in that endeavor, she has found that the religious content sought is elusive, and that theologians should in fact be rethinking what is called religious. In his work, *Terror and Triumph: The Nature of Black Religion*, Anthony B. Pinn argues that the dehumanization and black objectification of the slavery period were the very factors that called forth the response known as black religion. Daniel Hodge's work, *The Soul of Hip-Hop: Rims, Timbs and a Cultural Theology* argues how hip-hop addresses and challenges the institutional church to bring a higher involvement with God to this generation.

Scholarship on black theology is a little more available, however, as the church continues its current socially complacent theological involvement, its roots in black thought and experience becomes "forgetful." *For My People: Black Theology and the Black Church* by James Cone calls for unification of Black theology and the Black church to bridge the adversities of racism. *Introducing Black Theology of Liberation* by Dwight Hopkins addresses the principles of black theology and the challenges black theologians face in ministry and their respective communities but falls short of any mentions as to the effects of Hip-hop theology on those challenges. *The Hip-Hop Generation: Young Blacks and the Crisis in African-American Culture* by Bakari

Kitwana examines how hop-hop youth today see social political troubles and how a new empowerment of this examination opens a door to a new strategy of resolution, however, there is no mention of how this new strategy is rooted in black biblical history.

While in the space between cries of "Black Lives Matter," "No Justice, No Peace," "I Can't Breathe," "I am Trayvon," "I am Mike Brown," there are juxtaposed shouts of "Law and Order," "Make America Great Again," and "Just say no." Each cry and shout express a critical, silent, and deadly war cry that goes unidentified, or at best, misidentified by its combatants. Additionally, it should be observed that the cries and shouts mentioned above postdate similar war themes. It was Martin Luther King Jr. who shouted, "Free at last, free at last." The cry, "I am a man," spoke to the basic rights violated by Memphis black sanitation workers (1968) against unacceptable working conditions. As a war cry, these banshee screams, or mottos encapsulates the beliefs and ambitions that spurs on encouragement during engagements to unnerve the enemy and rally its own soldiers with hope, purpose, and fearlessness.

Spiritual warfare is a violent state of destruction, trauma, bloodshed, and psychological stress complicated by an end of death. The effects of *spiritual* warfare upon the human psyche complicates the lives of those who must survive in the war zone of their mind. This is especially overexaggerated in young minds. Youth will learn more by what they see than by what they hear; *spiritual* warfare is a visual teacher of a perceived false power. Gangs, police officers, and parents begin to look like the same combatants fighting in Beirut, Afghanistan, or Palestine. Youth in the inner-city are exposed to death at a young age. To others, the distance between survival and death is a high wire walk along the tight rope of traumatic experience. Denyse Hicks-Ray argues, "A child exposed to gang warfare or domestic violence is likely to be hyper aroused. It also decreases a person's ability to pay attention. Children with PTSD are often misdiagnosed with learning disabilities or attention deficit/hyperactivity disorder (ADHD) because they're too fearful to pay attention in school."[3]

The War on Crime (Drugs) and the War on Poverty are two declared wars upon the demographic of the inner-city designating it as the battlefield. Racial profiling has identified the "enemy" and legislative strategies legitimized the killing of victims, justification for collateral damage, and the taking of prisoners that give rise to the present carceral state. Religion has trained young adults how to go to church, but not how to go to war (spiritually). There is a declared and undeclared war on the black and brown youth of inner-cities. These wars have legitimized the taking of inner-city prisoners and confining them in prison plantations as the "new slave." The declared war is the War on Drugs policy of 1973 and the continued undeclared war takes place in the media and its attack on the inner-city. In his work *Dear White America: A Letter to a New Minority* Tim Wise states,

> More evidence of modern-day racial bias manifests in the criminal justice system. Back in 1964, about two-thirds of all those incarcerated in this country were white, while one-third were persons of color. By the mid-1990s those numbers had reversed, so that now, two-thirds of persons locked up are black and brown while only a third are white. This shift was not the result of a change in who commits crime, but rather stemmed mostly from the disproportionate concentration of justice system resources in communities of color, especially due to the so-called War on Drugs. Although whites comprise roughly 70 percent of all drug users and are every bit as likely as people of color to use drugs, nine in ten people locked up each year for a possession offense are people of color.[4]

The explosion of incarceration oppression was not an instantaneous occurrence, but in fact, has been developing for quite a few years. The ages of those who fall to this system are from within the hip-hop generation. It imprisons many young men at a point in their lives where they are transitioning from boyhood into manhood. Bakari Kitwana states, "Most of the defendants were hip-hop 'generationers,' ranging from twenty-one to forty-one years old."[5] Additionally, Kitwana cites another study which documents the population incarcerated in US state and federal prisons and local jails has climbed from fewer than 200,000 in 1965 to nearly 2 million now. According to the Bureau of Justice, approximately 50 percent of federal and state prisoners are African American.[6] Kitwana continues with statistics which reflect the damage done to hip-hop: "These statistics reveal that race is clearly a factor. Approximately 1 million Black men are currently under some form of correctional supervision. And the hip-hop generation is suffering the greatest casualties; approximately one-third of all Black males age 20–29 are incarcerated, or on probation, or on parole."[7]

To outline the dimensions of this *spiritual* war, two things were important: First identify the enemy and second determine the battleground. Additionally, to make these two things clear in the eyes of America, network television news media was deployed. David Jerigan and Lori Dorfman conducted a study of network television news from 1990 through 1991 and found that a predictable "us against them" frame was used in the news stories, with "us" being white, suburban America, and "them" being black Americans and a few corrupted whites.[8] Presently, the image of the black "criminal" is perpetuated with images of saggy pants, certain colors, black men with hoodies, tattoos, and bald heads, identifying them as the "enemy." The "enemy" is centered in what is referred to as the "ghetto." A ghetto is a space where members of a minority group live especially because of social, legal, or economic pressure. Furthermore, it is a place of conferred social inferiority and limited opportunity. Michelle Alexander states, "Thus it is here, in the poverty stricken, racially segregated ghettos, where the War on Poverty has been abandoned and factories have disappeared, that the drug war has been waged with the greatest ferocity."[9]

The rhetorical voice of the Civil Rights Movement falls upon deaf ears of this hip-hop generation. This generation feels that the Civil Rights Movement is outdated with no relevant knowledge of the way "things are" today. Despite their apprehension that the Civil Rights Movement is in a state of antiquity, the black and brown experience has not changed. The black and brown experience is overcrowded ghettos, public housing, overpolicing of black males, guns, crime, gangs, poor education, unemployment, and drugs. Black theology is how to make some sense of purposeful victory through this type of experience when it seems that God has turned His back. James Cone remarks, "The black experience is catching the spirit of blackness and loving it. It is hearing black preachers speak of God's love despite the filthy ghetto, and black congregations responding Amen, which means that they realize that ghetto existence is not the result of divine decree but of white humanity."[10] The goal, therefore, is for Black theology to recognize God's presence in the events that affect the black and brown community. How is Black theology to accomplish this revelation? Who will preach the gospel so what is heard can be believed by those young souls who have lost confidence in God?

A new rhetoric of Black theology finds the hungry ears of youth of the inner-city, both black and brown. The true nature of the street must be matched with the culture of the community. The ghettos and barrios of the city live by a different set of rules. No one church can change the landscape of injustice, oppression, and poverty. No one church can heal the wounds of the American sin of racism and injustice; no one church can expect to bring salvation and deliverance to those with no hope; it will take the church; one body, one bride of Christ, one blood and one cross. A youthful theological activist and resistance mindset demands a different form of rhetoric. This new rhetoric must match the anger and intensity of its source: the street. If they are to hear, they must be listening; otherwise, faith cannot come (Romans 10:17, KJV). The passion of Jesus Christ must be experienced in the passion of the language that speaks to the black and brown experience. Traditional Christianity has not spoken with the passion necessary to quench the fiery darts of black and brown suffering. James Cone explains, "Black Theology is survival theology, it must speak with a passion consistent with the depths of the wounds of the oppressed. American theology identifies theology as a dispassionate analysis of "the tradition," unrelated to the sufferings of the oppressed."[11] This new hermeneutic must be preached with a combination of the toughness of a serpent and the softness of a dove, a tough mind and a tender heart that includes the militancy of Malcolm X and the hope of Martin L. King Jr.

The church should be ashamed and appalled the old Jim Crow system of oppression, injustice, and racism has resurrected itself in a penal system disguised in the raiment of American justice. The outward cry of the Civil Rights Movement, "Free at Last, Free at Last," becomes muted by the resistant shouts of the New Jim Crow, "Law and Order, Law and Order." But there is another voice shouting across the yawning gaping abyss of the search for freedom and equality, and that voice is the next generation of worshippers who are shouting with a loud voice, "No Justice, No Peace; Know Justice, Know Peace," and this voice must speak in the rhetoric of Black theology. Life, liberty, and the pursuit of happiness becomes a lie in the face of constitutional truths. All people are created equally, but not all people stay equal. The egalitarianism of the will of the people becomes unbalanced on the scales of justice. For many sons and daughters, their God-given privilege for the protection of their innocence falls upon the parent. Their innocence, trust, faith, and dignity should not be a pawn in the political process or a "matter of fact" consequence of adult misjudgment. The history of the United States and the subsequent future of children should be two paths that have the same destination; life, liberty, and the pursuit of happiness. If there is abridged freedom, prolonged suffering, oppression of the poor, and abuse of power by the affluent upon the poor, there must be liberation theology; if these conditions exist in the synthesis of freedom and oppression in the inner-city, Black theology has a distinguished character of antithesis.

Different theologies teach us different understandings about God, but that understanding must be contextualized to the listening ear of the hearer. As particular attention focuses on the inner-city, traditional Christianity that professes turning the other cheek is not effective or useful for spiritual formation. Mixing faith conversation with the militancy of Malcolm X and the hope of Martin L. King Jr. will bring hope and identity with Christ and will show youth a God who cares for His poor, oppressed, and disenfranchised people. This identification cannot be done easily outside the rhetoric of Black theology in the inner-city. Since hip-hop is an international language of youth, the combination of Black theology and Hip-hop theology will assist youth to learn how to love God with all their heart, all their souls, all their mind, and all their strength (Mark 12:30, KJV).

The next generations of hip-hoppers are seeing the society, the church, and themselves through a different lens, and they seek spirituality that speaks directly to them. Their voice is not speaking through the theology of orthodox Christianity because they believe traditional Christianity has betrayed them with complacency and silence. Black theology, like Hip-hop theology, is not a black thing, but, in fact, is a God thing, and when the oppression of black and brown people becomes a matter of the past, the oppression of all oppressed people passes. When injustice for black and brown people is not the color of their skin, the injustice for all people will be de-colored.

Britannica defines guerilla warfare as the type of warfare fought by irregulars in fast-moving, small scale actions against orthodox military and police forces and, on occasion, against rival insurgence forces, either independently or in conjunction with a larger political-military strategy. Although the use of the term *guerilla warfare* may bring some immediate backlash, it must be remembered that guerilla warfare is not new to American history. During the Civil War there were at least six guerilla fighters. Of these guerilla fighters, four were confederate leaders/generals; John McNeil, William Quantrill, William T. Anderson, and John Mosby. Additionally, two were union leaders/generals; James H. Lane and Charles Jennison.[12] It should be noted that guerilla fighters involved in such a war all share the same ideology: liberation and freedom from oppression when political resolution seemed to fail. Are Gangstas the urban guerilla fighter? Dr. Ebony Utley offers a study that examines how the "gangsta" of the inner-cities, despite oppressive conditions, still make God their prominent focus. Utley argues that when rap emerged as a response to the deteriorating social conditions of the inner-city, the presence of God became a more prominent theme. When rap embraces religion in response to the social conditions of the time, the result is a complex incorporation of traditional and nontraditional religious beliefs and practices.[13]

Michael Eric Dyson in his work, *Holler If You Hear Me: Searching for Tupac Shakur*, reveals Tupac as a prophet while much of society sees him as a thug or gangsta. Dyson makes this claim, "The gangsta's God—or the thug's theology—is intimately linked to his beliefs about how society operates and who is in control. For many thugs, 'God is the great accomplice to a violent lifestyle."[14] To the gangsta, traditional Christianity does not communicate with the power of deliverance and redemption. The language of the preacher is not the experience on the street. The church experience is not a valid expression of this oppression, but rap settles the mind and provides an avenue of expression absent in the Civil Rights ideology. James Cone explains what black revolutionaries see as the traditional church weakness, "Reacting to the ungodly behavior of white churches and the timid, Uncle Tom approach of black churches, many black militants have no time for God and the deadly prattle about loving your enemies and turning the other cheek."[15]

Gangsters do not wear the robes of sanctimonious procedure nor do they resemble the pretentious representations of pastoral status. If an examination of biblical leaders is considered, it can be determined that David, a shepherd, did not look like a king. Moses, a felon, did not look like a deliverer. The Apostle Paul as a Christian hater and killer did not look like an apostle. Jesus, our savior, did not look like a sacrifice. Surely, baggy pants, turned ball caps, twisted braids, untied shoes, and oversized clothes are not something that God would consider useful for His purposes. These are broken vessels and cannot bring any honor to God or the church . . . right? What looks irrational to us, God will use for His glory.

In most traditional old generation homes in the inner-city, there is usually a picture of Christ. In this picture, Jesus is envisioned with blond hair, blue eyes, and white skin. This has been the iconic representation of Jesus for many years. But to the mindset of a gangster, this portrayal of Jesus is unrelatable and foreign and represents a form of betrayal considering the oppression of poor people by "religion." Daniel White Hodge in his work *The Soul of Hip-Hop: Rims, Timbs and a Cultural Theology* made the following statement:

> For Hip-Hoppers, such portraits of Jesus have been used as tools in the church's attempt to control and maintain status quo. So why would any true Hip-Hopper want to join a religion like that? Instead, Hip-Hoppers imagine a different Jesus; not some blond-haired, blue eyed, White embodiment of perfection but rather a Black Jesuz. Black Jesuz is multiracial. Black Jesuz understands the pain and misery of the inner-city. Black Jesuz does not always answer prayers when we want him to, and yet Black Jesuz can relate to the poor, downtrodden and set-aside.[16]

The intentional misspelling of Jesus with a *z* rather than an *s* is significant. It indicates a break from the traditional and adds a degree of "ownership" or "claim" to a Jesus that belongs to this generation. There is no disrespect intended with this spelling, however any perceived disrespect cannot be any greater than the associated disrespect that dares to color the Son of Man as white.

As a society, ask what are they supposed to do? What is the language to be used to heal and connect with their struggles? Both socially and theologically, a new rhetoric must be employed to communicate to this generation with words they understand and practice in their lives. What do the hip-hop generation think about religion? The methodology that has always been used to teach about God is not the way it must continue. If the Church continues to teach as it has always taught, then it is not new; it is a habit. The bible teaches that old wine should not be put in new wine skins. Black theology speaks to a hip-hop generation because it lends its rhetoric to youth who do not have the patience for the standard method of theology. There is a weakness and slave undercurrent in the "waiting for the promise-land" mindset. Black thought must be fed the knowledge of God through the rhetoric of Black theology. In the language of the street, it can be better stated this way, "If you ain't been there and done that, you can't tell me how to do that." This is what the rhetoric of Black theology can provide. In one of his most disputed and respected books, James Cone makes the following statement: "We cannot afford to do theology unrelated to human existence. Our theology must emerge consciously from an investigation of the socio-religious experience of black people, as that experience is reflected in black stories of God's dealings with black people in the struggle for freedom."[17]

With Black theology being the theme of this chapter, and the emphasis placed on liberation, Garth Baker-Fletcher's *Xodus: An African American Male Journey* argues that, "A kind of revolution is happening, described by rappers with a back-burner beat of hip-hop rhythm, moving the minds, bodies, and feet of the masses away from the control of the system toward a new place."[18] This revolution did not have its beginnings in today's culture, but begin prophetically with slavery and now is at a spatial time in history where fulfillment is imminent. Clearly, while the subjects of racism, mass incarceration, injustice, inequality in education, crime, poverty, unemployment, and other sociopolitical problems are being calmly discussed elsewhere, there has to be a rhetoric that expresses the anger and frustration that inner-city youth feel over their continuing encounters with Jim Crow policies.

The typical religious answers of "let's pray," or "in the world, but not of it," or just the silence of cooperation and apathy is not sufficient for a generation considered as Civil Rights Movement drop-outs. Black theology is not enough by itself. Although it offers a rich interpretation of God, bible, black history, and experience, it falls short in speaking the language of a generation robbed of its history. It fails by itself to respond to the psychological needs of youth who are struggling with oppressive circumstances. Michelle Alexander confirms, "A new civil rights movement cannot be organized around the relics of the earlier system of control if it is to address meaningfully the racial realities of our time. Any racial justice movement, to be successful, must vigorously challenge the public consensus that underlies the prevailing system of control."[19] The social barriers that were present during the civil rights movement have not been removed, but have in fact been refocused and re-strengthened into an upgraded form of oppression. These barriers are not only noticeable on social levels but are also seen in the church.

Most young hip-hoppers are faced with life changing choices that demand survival take priority over salvation. They must make a daily decision between the profane and the sacred, life and death. This leaves no time for an irrelevant gospel. Black theology is a teaching. It teaches young people how and why to worship God. It is a method of communication, a method of evangelism that can be realized in the inner-city context because people can recognize *who* they are and *whose* they are. This is the symbiotic relationship between Hip-hop theology and Black theology. Hip-hop theology teaches young people how to praise God as to what He has done through their relationship with Him. The expression of that union is in the power of the music and its ability to produce and/or reconcile the religious experience with identity through rap, the universal language of hip-hop.

Hip-hop theology has a platform of activism: rap. Inherent to the nature of rap, there is a duality in which hip-hoppers must take cognizance of what is happening in this form of expression. There is a bitter line between the sacred and profane in which identity can be lost or at best confused in the inner-city context. Herein is the dilemma of the rap lyric: it has the power to celebrate a consciousness of black respectability or lend itself to a consciousness of anti-social pathology. The prophetic voices of the civil rights era are silent in the age of the new prophetic voices of this hip-hop generation. The old nihilistic prophetic voices that spoke from generations past have no "game" in the reality of where hip-hoppers are now.

Black theology and Hip-hop theology found each other in the oppressive consciousness of those who believed that freedom is found in Jesus Christ. Black theology teaches about the other worldliness of earthy atrocities as Hip-hop theology articulates that language. Many people who are black, brown, and poor do not have a "champion" who speaks on their behalf. Now, through the efforts of this chapter, Black theology is joined to a voice (rap) and the voice is joined to a purpose (theology). Who can "pray" when it seems the entire world is against you and every day is just another day in the hood that forces everyone to survive like animals. With this marriage, there is now a bridge between the sacred and profane, and there is not an all-or-nothing conversion necessary to realize Jesus; in fact, as young people come to faith through Black theology utilizing the voice of Hip-hop theology, *Jesuz* can be found and experienced. Martin Luther King Jr. stated, "As long as the mind is enslaved, the body can never be free. Psychological freedom, a firm sense of self-esteem, is the most powerful weapon against the long night of physical slavery."[20]

The challenge is clear; theologians are charged to break the fall of racist sin and fulfill the mandate of righteous dominion over its power by the grace of God. A theological task awaits those with a firm conviction that powers and principalities in high places will not circumvent God in His redeeming work of the Cross of Jesus. From his work, *A Testament of Hope: The Essential Writings and Speeches*, Martin Luther King Jr., states, "There comes a time when one must take a position that is neither safe, nor politic, nor popular, but he must take it because conscience tells him it is right."[21] The three-fold foci of this chapter are Black theology, Hip-hop theology, and their conjoint working together to combat America's deadliest sin: racism. Black theology offers a political agenda for a theological revelation to flow through the prophetic voices of Hip-hop theology. Racism and injustice have been so much a part of the inner-city it has become a way of life like a neighbor that lives next door. Black theology is a means to keep the focus of oppression on the minds of those who are oppressed and to bring black radical faith in line with history and theology. Hip-hop theology provides the communicative means to defuse the time-bomb that is ticking away in the inner-city. Traditional Christian rhetoric does not convey this freedom effectively; neither can it academically explain present-day enslavement to the extent that black and brown young people experience it.

NOTES

1. James Cone, *A Black Theology of Liberation: Twentieth Anniversary Edition* (Maryknoll: Orbis Books, 2010), 152.
2. Otis Moss III, "Real Big: The Hip Hop Pastor as Postmodern Prophet," *The Gospel Remix: Reaching the Hip Hop Generation* ed. Ralph C. Watkins (Valley Forge: Judson Press, 2007), 114.
3. Denyse Hicks-Ray, *The Pain Didn't Start Here: Trauma and Violence in the African American Community* (Atlanta, Georgia: TSA Communications, 2004), 20.
4. Tim Wise, *Dear White America: Letter to a New Minority* (San Francisco: City Lights Books, 2012), 35.
5. Bakari Kitwana, *The Hip Hop Generation: Young Blacks and the Crisis in African-American Culture* (New York: Basic Civitas Books, 2002), 52.
6. Ibid., 53.
7. Ibid., 54.
8. David Jerigan and Lori Dorfman, "Visualizing America's Drug Problems: An Ethnographic Content Analysis of Illegal Drug Stories on the Nightly News," *Contemporary Drug Problems* 23 (1996): 169, 188.
9. Michelle Alexander, *A New Jim Crow: Mass Incarceration in the Age of Colorblindness* (New York: The New Press, 2012), 100.
10. Cone, *A Black Theology of Liberation*, 25.
11. Ibid., 18.
12. Evan Andrews, "6 Civil War Guerilla Leaders" [Article, September 4, 2012] (History.com History Stories) available from https://www.history.com/news/6-civil-war-guerilla-leaders, accessed May 28, 2018.
13. Ebony A. Utley, PhD, *Rap and Religion: Understanding the Gangsta's God* (Westport: Praeger Publishing, 2012), Kindle Book.
14. Michael Eric Dyson, *Holler If You Hear Me: Searching for Tupac Shakur* (New York: Basic Civitas Books, 2001), 211.
15. James Cone, *A Black Theology of Liberation: Twentieth Anniversary Edition* (Maryknoll: Orbis Publishing, 2010), 57.
16. Daniel White Hodge, *The Soul of Hip-Hop: Rims, Timbs and a Cultural Theology* (Downers Grove: Intervarsity Press, 2010), 126–127.
17. James Cone, *Black Theology and Black Power*, 5th ed. (Maryknoll: Orbis Books, 1997), 15.
18. Garth Baker-Fletcher, *Xodus: An African American Male Journey* (Minneapolis: Fortress Press, 1996), 175.
19. Michelle Alexander, *The New Jim Crow: Mass Incarceration in the Age of Colorblindness* (New York: The New Press, 2012), 223.
20. Martin Luther King Jr., *Where Do We Go from Here?* A speech delivered at the 11th Annual SCLC Convention in Atlanta, Georgia, August 16, 1967.
21. Martin Luther King Jr., *A Testament of Hope: The Essential Writings and Speeches* (New York: Harper One Publishing, 2003).

REFERENCES

Alexander, Michelle. *A New Jim Crow: Mass Incarceration in the Age of Colorblindness*. New York: The New Press, 2012.

Andrews, Evan. "6 Civil War Guerilla Leaders" [Article, September 4, 2012] (History.com History Stories) available from https://www.history.com/news/6-civil-war-guerilla-leaders, accessed May 28, 2018.

Baker-Fletcher, Garth. *Xodus: An African American Male Journey.* Minneapolis: Fortress Press, 1996.

Cone, James. *A Black Theology of Liberation: Twentieth Anniversary Edition.* Maryknoll, New York: Orbis Books, 2010.

———. *Black Theology and Black Power,* 5th ed. Maryknoll, New York: Orbis books, 1997.

Dyson, Michael Eric. *Holler If You Hear Me: Searching for Tupac Shakur* New York: Basic Civitas Books, 2001.

Hicks-Ray, Denyse. *The Pain Didn't Start Here: Trauma and Violence in the African American Community.* Atlanta, Georgia: TSA Communications, 2004.

Hodge, Daniel, White. *The Soul of Hip-Hop: Rims, Timbs and a Cultural Theology.* Downers Grove: Intervarsity Press, 2010.

Jerigan, David and Lori Dorfman, "Visualizing America's Drug Problems: An Ethnographic Content Analysis of Illegal Drug Stories on the Nightly News," *Contemporary Drug Problems* 23 (1996).

King, Martin Luther Jr., *A Testament of Hope: The Essential Writings and Speeches.* New York: Harper One Publishing, 2003.

———. *Where Do We Go from Here?* A speech delivered at the 11th Annual SCLC Convention in Atlanta, Georgia, August 16, 1967.

Kitwana, Bakari. *The Hip Hop Generation: Young Blacks and the Crisis in African-American Culture.* New York: Basic Civitas Books, 2002.

Moss, Otis III. "Real Big: The Hip Hop Pastor as Postmodern Prophet," *The Gospel Remix: Reaching the Hip Hop Generation,* ed. Ralph C. Watkins. Valley Forge, Pennsylvania: Judson Press, 2007.

Utley, Ebony A., *Rap and Religion: Understanding the Gangsta's God.* Westport: Praeger Publishing, 2012.

Wise, Tim. *Dear White America: Letter to a New Minority.* San Francisco: City Lights Books, 2012.

Chapter Eight

"Saint Hillary," On Unserious Activism

Tony Hoshaw

UNSERIOUS DESIRE

Gay men tend to feel passionately about Hillary Clinton. In 2014, Amy Chozick wrote a piece for the *New York Times*, "Hillary Clinton's Gay Rights Evolution."[1] Chozick observes that to "a generation of younger gay men in particular, Mrs. Clinton's appeal extends to a more *primal* connection" (emphasis added). That "primal connection" has something to do with the fact that, after being knocked down in a bruising 2008 primary battle with then Senator Obama, Hillary managed to get back on her feet. "'We get her like we get our moms,' said Fred Sainz, a spokesman for the Human Rights Campaign. . . . 'We've seen the travails she's been through and the fact that she's not just a survivor but a conqueror.'"

In a 2015 piece, again for the *New York Times*, Chozick cites none other than historian George Chauncey Jr.[2] While Chauncey does not observe much interest in Clinton among his (young) students, he seems to think that the "resonance of the long-suffering woman with older gay men, in particular, cannot be underestimated," and he "pointed to Judy Garland, her tortured relationship with men, her alcohol addiction and the heartbreak felt in her songs." "That really resonated with gay men," according to Chauncey, "in a period when they did face a lot of anguish themselves, because there was such widespread hostility and discrimination. . . . We can laugh at it, but these were really powerful anthems for gay men, and there is something really powerful about that connection."

"Of course," Chozick remarks, "gay life is incredibly diverse, and the *cliché* of the strong woman with diva appeal does not speak to everyone" (emphasis added). And, of course, such diva appeal does not "cancel out more substantive concerns about Mrs. Clinton's policy positions." In fact, Hillary's diva appeal must be handled with great care, *at least by Hillary's gay devotees*. Chozick remarks, in parentheses, "(It could also offend some voters, if not delicately managed)."

Putting aside for the moment the incredible diversity of gay life, it is an incontestable truth that Hillary is a gay icon. She is among the women that gay men tend to identify with—for example, Judy Garland, Joan Crawford, Patti LaBelle, Beyoncé, and Lady Gaga. And her gay appeal has to do, as Chozick aptly puts it, with a "primal connection"; it is about something other than "substantive concerns about [Hillary's] policy positions." The relationship between the serious stuff of politics (i.e., policy positions) and a "primal connection" with a political figure like Hillary is what seems to baffle and disturb people.

Take another example, again from 2015. "Despite a less than perfect record on gay rights," writes Alex Seitz-Wald, in an article for *MSNBC*, "Hillary Clinton's complex relationship with her LGBT base," Clinton has long been popular among many in the LBGT community, and *for reasons that go beyond politics*" (emphasis added).[3] Seitz-Wald's story features a gay string quartet called Well Strung. Their video, "Chelsea's Mom," a play on Fountains of Wayne's 2003, "Stacey's Mom" went viral during the Summer of 2015 and caught the attention of the Clinton campaign.[4] "We kind of grew up with Clintons. She's not just this far away political figure, being a mother and caring for the nation in that way," said Well Strung violinist Chris Merchant.

Seitz-Wald argues that Clinton's gay appeal "seems to transcend politics for many in the LGBT community," and that idea is precisely what perplexes gay media personality Mike Signorile, who, according to Seitz-Wald, is "exasperated by gay Clinton fans he sees as being 'seduced by a superficial message.'" Signorile seems to have changed his tune since 1999; he is apparently no longer willing to even entertain the possibility that "what Washington needs right now . . . is a stylish and gritty Hollywood-style 'battle-ax' . . . an industrious Joan Crawford for the new millennium. . . ."[5] No, according to Signorile, "[Hillary] is being very vague still as to what she is going to do as president, except for those platitudes of showing gay couples in a video and supporting marriage after everybody else did. . . ." He continues, "And I don't think there's anything . . . except for her speech to the U.N. General Assembly in Geneva, that she can point to as a real leader in LGBT issues."

These articles highlight the tendency to confuse or to blur the distinction between the *actual* Hillary Clinton, the candidate, and her policy positions, and "Hillary" as a "superficial" image or as an aesthetic figure. Hillary's gay appeal has everything to with "Hillary" as an *aesthetic figure*, a figure that necessarily refers to the actual Hillary Clinton—but is not essentially about her, who she is *"really."* That is to say that gay male identification with Hillary is not an expression of identity-based gay politics; it is a manifestation of *gay subculture*. Hence it has to do with the idea that "gay is something you do," with the idea that gayness is "not a state or condition," but rather a "mode of perception, an attitude, an ethos: in short, a practice."[6]

Returning to Chozick's description of gay life as "incredibly diverse," homosexuality as a practice, rather than as "a state or condition," is actually something *anyone* can do. In fact, not all gay men participate in gay subculture (sad but true). What, however, is "it," gayness as a social practice—or, as I am contending here, gayness as a mode of resistance? "It" is the politics of the superficial, the politics of style or camp politics. Given that we do not take style seriously, it is not surprising that gay identification with Hillary is consistently described as "beyond politics." Gay identification with "Hillary" (a manifestation of gay desire) is an expression of resistance to the politics of seriousness, to the horrors of that kind of political desire that is uncompromising and that gets conflated with the way things are or must be, with nature and/or the natural.

HAIRSTORY

To understand what "Hillary" signifies, what it means to identify with "Hillary" as an aesthetic figure or as a style one can try on and how identifying with her is an act of gay resistance to the politics of seriousness, we may consult Well Strung's music video, "Chelsea's Mom." In this context, I cannot do justice to Well Strung's brilliant articulation of Hillary's gay appeal. I enthusiastically refer you to the video itself. The key to interpreting the song is, in my view, Hillary's hair. "She rocked the bobs and the highlights/Yea we loved her hair," Well Strung sings. It is Hillary's hair (and I will focus on "the bobs" below) that helps us make sense of the logic that holds the song together, namely that Hillary is "sexy and strong" or, better yet, conventional and defiant. As David M. Halperin argues, "A hairstyle *is* about something. It has to be about something. If is not about anything, it's not a hairstyle—it's just hair (Or perhaps it's bad hair . . .)."[7] What, then, is Hillary's hair about?

On March 8, 2017, Hillary gave a speech for International Women's Day. Her speech was well received, as her message to resist resonated with her supporters and others. Yet what seemed equally interesting, generating passionate responses, was her new bob.[8] Even the negative reviews of Hillary's hairstyle point to the simple fact that people continue to feel *passionately* about (Hillary's) hair. But why?

Hillary's own hairstylist, John Barrett, may help us understand what hair does politically and culturally. We have only to consult his 2016 book, *Hair*.[9] Barret argues:

> There's beauty in the luster of a woman's hair. . . . But there is also artifice. A part of her, and yet not her in the way hands and lips undeniably are, her mane lies in that interstitial space between adornment and essence, between authenticity and artifice. That's what drew me to hair as a boy in Ireland: the chimerical quality, the ability it had not just to define, but to create a person.[10]

Barrett clearly thinks hair should be understood in its own right. Hair is not like lips or hands. Hair is less attached to our bodies; it possesses a "chimerical quality." Relatedly, notice the proximity of beauty to artifice (or style) in Barrett's quote above. While he seems to think hair is beautiful in itself, how it is arranged seems related to and equally important for hair's beauty.

As a child, Barrett sat in Mass admiring the clothing and hairstyles of the Church women. The women looked "all the same expect one lady, with her bold, bleached hair, her unending eyelashes."[11] That singular woman's (hair)style inspired the young Barrett to ask, "How could someone be so beautiful?"[12] The woman, Barrett observes, worked in a bakery, "but she commanded our attention."[13] The boy Barrett seemed to think (hair)style was the thing itself. It told you everything you needed to know about the woman: she is beautiful *and* different.[14]

Significantly, Barrett reminds us that hairstyles have a history. For example, "[t]he bobs of the Roaring Twenties allowed women the unthinkable—an edge of masculinity."[15] In the 1920s, the bob was understood rather one-dimensionally, it seems, in the key of feminine rebellion (what I think Barrett means to convey by "an edge of masculinity"). "Today," Barrett thinks, "it is the flexibility of hair, that there is no norm, which defines us."[16] Nowadays, or so the story goes, women move seamlessly between long and short hair. "Uniformity is the enemy."[17] And yet Hillary, who "cares less about her hair than most people," according to Barrett, keeps returning to the bob.[18]

Lynn Yaeger, who writes the "Introduction" to Barrett's *Hair*, agrees with Martin Luther, "The hair is the richest ornament of women."[19] According to Yaeger, "Hair can define a social movement. . . . It can thrill and inspire us, fill us with longing and envy, stun and surprise us."[20] Yaeger asks a rather provocative question: "Can it be an accident that so many creative women, so many women in the arts, are drawn to extreme bobs?"[21]

History has a way of repeating itself, and Yaeger notes that the prevalence of the extreme bob is being challenged by long(er) hairstyles. "If bobbed hair had the power to disrupt, to upend traditional notions of appropriateness and gentility, long locks were indicators of unbridled naturalness and its louche cousin, rampant sensuality."[22] Significantly, there is nothing extreme about

Hillary. It should not surprise us that she avoided, as far as I can tell, the extreme bob (e.g., the bobs of Louise Brooks or Rei Kawakubo[23]). At one time, however, she did wear long hair.

Returning to the 1990s, Shawn J. Parry-Giles situates us within the cultural and political dynamic of hair relative to Hillary's career.[24] She observes that when Bill Clinton's campaign tried to make Hillary more appealing to voters in 1992, they *cut* her hair. "When introducing a story captioned 'Campaign Makeover,' . . . Tom Brokaw," Parry-Giles observes, "offered the following assessment that reinforced Clinton's outspokenness and overexposure, 'The political image makers are hard at it this year. They worried Hillary Clinton was coming off too bright, too outspoken, too upfront. So, they asked her to warm up a bit.'" How did they accomplish that? "In evidencing the makeover, Andrew Mitchell charged that Clinton had 'a new, softer hair do.'"[25] And that new, softer do happened to be a shoulder-length bob.

The need to "soften" Hillary was the consequence of two remarkable moments in two press-related events between the end of January and mid-March 1992. The first moment occurred in a *60 Minutes* interview, given by both Bill and Hillary in the midst of the Gennifer Flowers controversy. In that interview Hillary declared, "You know, I'm not sitting here, some little woman standing by my man like Tammy Wynette."[26] In the second moment, a response to an allegation that Governor Clinton channeled government money to Hillary's law firm, Hillary remarked, "I suppose I could have stayed home and baked cookies and had teas, but what I decided to do was to fulfill my profession, which I entered before my husband was in public life."

The impact of those lines, expressing what we may call, borrowing a phrase of Lynn Yaeger, Hillary's "tonsorial audacity," managed to frame Hillary's career. The Wynette line conveyed Hillary's independence relative to her marriage. The cookies and teas line conveyed her independence relative to traditional family values.[27] Both performances contributed to an impossible rhetorical situation for Hillary: if Hillary was a (radical) feminist, she was a fake woman.

The shoulder-length bob was intended to change that. And maybe that has something to do with why *we* identify with Hillary. That is, while the shoulder-length bob was an attempt to soften Hillary by way of a conventionally feminine hairstyle, it also signified a way out of conventionality. *If you know hair*, you know Hillary's shoulder-length bob signifies rebelliousness (i.e., an "edge of masculinity") *in addition to* conventionality (i.e., it is not too short or severe). Her stylist in 1992 either knew absolutely nothing about hair's social meaning or knew absolutely everything about it. I think her stylist knew everything about hair's social significance, and so Hillary's hair became her: a figure at once totally acceptable (she did, in fact, stand by her man . . . and continues to) and totally unacceptable, abject or even monstrous (she is bitchy, but she is no one's bitch).

UNSERIOUS POLITICS

An axiom of gay subcultural studies is that what gay subculture signifies is inseparable from the figure figuring it. Hillary is a figure of gay subculture. Thus to identify with Hillary is to identify with a specific mode of life or practice. In other words, gay desire, defined here as both conventional and defiant, is inseparable from gay politics, a politics, in this case, of hair. Or so I will now argue.

Hillary's 2016 campaign returned us to the 1990s (and beyond) in, I think, an unexpected way. Ruby Cramer brings out the surprising dimension of Hillary's 2016 campaign by succinctly identifying a few talking points of that campaign: "Hillary wants to talk with you about love and kindness."[28] Cramer reminds us that for Hillary those themes go all the way back to her infamous 1969 student commencement address. Hillary was the first student to make such an address at Wellesley College.[29]

Significantly, Hillary was *mocked* for raising similar kinds of topics as worthy of serious political discussion in 1993. Cramer points to a speech Hillary gave at the University of Texas: "'We need a new politics of meaning,' she tells the crowd. 'We need a new ethos of individual responsibility and caring . . . a society that fills us up again and makes us feel that we are part of something bigger than ourselves.'" For these comments, Hillary was framed as a saint.

The cover of *The New York Times Magazine* on May 23, 1993 says it all: Hillary is dressed in a flawless white dress; her hair is perfectly structured and pulled back. She is framed by a white backdrop and is standing just beneath the magazine's title, in pink lettering, and an announcement of Allan Bloom's "Death of Eros" in teal. Hillary is the feminine image of the politics she supposedly represents: "The Politics of Virtue."

Cramer observes that inside the magazine, opposite the title of the article, "Saint Hillary," was included an image of Hillary explicitly portrayed as a saint (appropriately in the image of Saint Joan of Arc), complete with a shoulder-length bob and holding a sword.[30] *None of this was a compliment.* According to Cramer, the author of "Saint Hillary," Michael Kelly, interpreted some of Hillary's ideas over literally and others as "easy, moralistic preaching couched in the gauzy and gushy wrappings of New Age jargon."[31]

Significantly, saint was not the only way Hillary was understood between January and May 1993. Consider the cover of *Spy Magazine*, February 1993. Hillary is portrayed as a dominatrix, complete with long hair, in the Oval Office.[32] Next to her image is printed the question, "What Hillary Problem?"

The problem is, of course, Hillary is not baking cookies and giving teas. *Spy Magazine* did not approve. According to Amber Jamieson and Adam Gabbatt, journalists for the *The Guardian*, *Spy Magazine* columnist Barbara Amiel asserted that "[t]he first lady has emasculated America." Amiel apparently went on to muse, "I guess that is what radical feminists always wanted to do, but when the Bobbitt syndrome hits the only superpower left in the world, it's not only the Mr. Bobbitts who are in pain. We all are." The reference, in case we missed it, is to Lorena Bobbitt. In 1993 she became infamous for cutting off her husband's penis.[33]

The image of Hillary as a saint, a saint in the image of Saint Joan of Arc, wearing a shoulder-length bob brings both cover images of Hillary together. Michael Kelly asserts, "While an encompassing compassion is the routine mode of public existence for every First Lady, there are two great differences in the case of Mrs. Clinton: She is serious and she has power."[34] "Saint Hillary" is a conventional woman (i.e., she is like every First Lady) and she is defiant, a monstrosity relative to the masculinist protocols of the phallus (i.e., "[s]he is serious and has power"). Hillary is ladylike, indeed—and she wields a sword.

Fast-forward to 2015. Hillary is in the midst of her second bid for president: "The language is simpler now," Cramer remarks, "[t]here's no 'mutuality of respect' or 'politics of meaning.' There has been no big speech, and the press hasn't come calling. It's nothing abstract or long-winded. It's just a simple aside on the trail—a few words about love and kindness." A few words that were mentioned just after the Charleston, South Carolina, shootings (Hillary had just been in Charleston), where nine people were gunned down in a bible study at Emanuel African Methodist Episcopal Church: "I know it's not usual for somebody running for president to say what we need more of in this country is love and kindness. But that's exactly what we need more of."[35] Hillary is still speaking . . . about love and kindness. Hillary continues to take seriously what the vast majority of masculinist (male and female) US politicians think is unserious, namely love and kindness as *political* concepts.

Speaking of love as a political concept, Michel Foucault argued:

> Imagining a sexual act that does not conform to the law or to nature, that's not what upsets people. But that individuals might begin to love each other, that's the problem. That goes against the grain of social institutions. . . . The institutional regulations cannot approve such . . . relations: relations that produce a short circuit and introduce love where there ought to be law, regularity, and custom.[36]

While Hillary does not signify a love that in some sense replaces or stands in the place where there once was "law, regularity, and custom," as gay desire is

UNSERIOUS THEOLOGY

Attention to the gay tendency to identify with maternal figures like Hillary alerts us to feminine identifications in biblical literature.[37] In the Gospel of Matthew, Jesus is declared to be of Mary, of the Spirit (Matthew 1:16, 20). In the Greek text, it is especially clear that Mary and the Spirit are aligned—and they are aligned with a tradition of conventional (mothers) and abject (erotically disreputable) feminine figures. The Spirit is a figure of Mary.

Mary's abjection is *amplified* by the genealogy, wherein she is linked to other (*erotically*) disreputable women: Tamar, Rahab, Ruth, and the wife of Uriah (Matthew 1:3, 5, 6). In his *An Ethic of Queer Sex: Principles and Improvisations*, Jennings helpfully situates Mary within a politics of prostitution or outlaw desire.[38] "In this line of remarkable women (which concludes with Mary)," Jennings writes, "there is a strange priority given to women who are sexually disreputable . . ." (100). What makes Tamar, Rahab, Ruth, and the wife of Uriah "sexually disreputable"?

Tamar is unwilling to let the men in her life shirk their responsibility to her, even if that means she must play the role of a prostitute (Genesis 38). Rahab is, like many sex-workers, wise and seems to grasp how the upcoming "street skirmish" is going to go. She shrewdly takes sides in the battle, saving her entire family from destruction (Joshua 2:1–22, 6:1–27). Ruth, furthermore, refuses to abandon another woman for the sake of her own security in the arms of another man and takes the sexual initiative (Ruth 1:16–17, 3). Finally, Bathsheba, "Uriah's wife," a woman who, like Mary, is erotically tarnished, but, unlike Mary, is actually punished (by God), nonetheless remains with David and produces another son, King Solomon (2 Samuel 11–12). As Stephanie Buckhanon Crowder points out, we often forget "Bathsheba's role in securing the kingdom for her son, Solomon [see 1 Kings 1:11–31]."[39] Mary is defined relative to this tradition of maternal rebellion and survival.

From Matthew's Gospel we know that however it was that Mary became pregnant, it was not according to the protocols of traditional marriage and family values. Joseph clearly believes Mary has been *un*faithful to him, and so he decides to send her away. It is his resolve to do so discreetly, rather than publicly, that earns him the title, "just man" (1:19). Satisfied with his plan, he falls asleep and dreams. I read his dream in a way that conveys Mary's voice, her defiance of Joseph's will.

In his *Interpretation of Dreams*, a richly complicated text at its theoretical core (VI–VII), Freud observes that "the dream-work cannot actually *create* speeches."[40] The speeches (and conversations) we hear in our dreams, according to Freud, "have really been made or heard."[41] Having said that, the dream-work does a lot with the speeches and conversations we have really heard. For example, what appears as a single speech in a dream is often an effect of the dream-work. The dream-work "drags [fragments of speeches] out of their context . . . incorporating some portions and rejecting others . . . often [abandoning] the meaning the words originally had in the dream-thoughts and give[s] them a fresh one."[42]

Joseph is a literary character, and we cannot ask him about his dream and so better understand the dream-work the speech underwent. And I am not attempting to *apply* Freudian psychoanalysis to this text. I am more interested in what we can make of the basic idea: While speeches may undergo some editing in dreams, in dreams speeches are *not our own*. What is important, in other words, is the Freudian idea that "whatever stands out markedly in dreams as a speech can be traced back to real speeches which have been spoken or heard by the dreamer."[43]

You will note that the angel in Joseph's dream very clearly gives a speech to Joseph, where "speech" in a dream is defined by Freud as having both an acoustic aspect ("angel . . . *said*") and motor aspect (angel . . . *appeared*).[44] The speech in Joseph's dream is, we may therefore suppose, Mary's speech: her resistance to the will of Joseph, a supposedly just man. In her speech, Mary seems to be encouraging Joseph to resist a phobic response to her, for the child conceived in her is of the Spirit that is Holy. Mary seems convinced that her boy will be a Joshua; he will save his people from injustice (1:21). We may, of course, allow some room for the dream-work, perhaps transforming Mary into an angel and a virgin,[45] recombining various conversations the couple may have had, and so forth.

The important point is that Mary's resistance was successful (1:24–25). Rather than allowing herself and her child to be dismissed, either publicly or privately, as a result of *erotized* transgression, Mary defies Joseph's will to drive her out. Her acceptance *and* defiance of social norms and expectations also makes it possible for Jesus to be "the Messiah, son of David, the son of Abraham," as it is Joseph who is a "son of David" (1:20). It is not insignificant that the first act of redemption associated with Jesus' birth is the redemption of Joseph. We owe a lot to Mary. Hillary is of that tradition, and we owe a lot to her too. And that is another reason why I identify with Hillary. It is what Jesus would do.

We have more to learn from Hillary. It is easy (and accurate) to blame Donald Trump for all our current social ills. Yet, let us not forget that it was progressive candidates like Jill Stein and Senator Bernie Sanders who helped lift Trump into the highest office of the land. Trump lives in the White House as a result of the logic of either/or—the logic of total victory or the politics of seriousness. Perhaps "Hillary" can teach us that we need not reject conventionality in order to be defiant, as conventionality and defiance are not mutually exclusive. In certain circumstances conventionality may also be defiance. *Viva la diva!*

NOTES

1. Amy Chozick, "Hillary Clinton's Gay Rights Evolution," *The New York Times*, August 29, 2014, accessed March 21, 2017. https://www.nytimes.com/2014/08/31/fashion/hillary-clinton-gay-rights-evolution.html. The article appeared in the Fashion and Style section. Chozick has since written a book, *Chasing Hillary: Ten Years, Two Presidential Campaigns, and One Intact Glass Ceiling* (New York: HarperCollins, 2018).

2. Amy Chozick, "Hillary Clinton, Loudly and Proudly, Taps into a Vein of Support among Gay Voters," *The New York Times*, July 1, 2015, accessed March 21, 2017. https://www.nytimes.com/2015/07/02/us/politics/hillary-clinton-courts-gay-lgbtq-voters.html.

3. Alex Seitz-Wald, "Hillary Clinton's complex relationship with her LGBT base," MSNBC, July 2, 2015, accessed March 24, 2017. http://www.msnbc.com/msnbc/hillary-clintons-complex-relationship-her-lgbt-base.

4. I am going to return to this video in a moment, but you can take a look at it on *YouTube*, initially accessed March 23, 2017. https://youtu.be/SrEmQk3u88U.

5. See Michelangelo Signorile, "Hillary: Viva la diva!," *Advocate*, September 14, 1999.

6. The citations are from David M. Halperin's *How to Be Gay* (Cambridge: Belknap, 2012), 13. I enthusiastically refer you to his text, a magnificent description of gay counter-acculturation.

7. David M. Halperin, *How to Be Gay*, 362.

8. See, for example, Rose Walano's article for *US Magazine*, "Hillary Clinton Debuted a New Bob with Bangs for International Women's Day 2017," March 9, 2017, accessed June 20, 2017. http://www.usmagazine.com/stylish/news/hillary-clinton-debuts-new-bob-haircut-with-bangs-photo-w471325.

9. John Barrett, *Hair* (New York: Assouline Publishing, 2016). An excerpt of the book, "What makes a hair icon? Hillary Clinton's stylist speaks out," was published for CNN, October 7, 2016, available online: http://www.cnn.com/2016/06/28/fashion/hillary-clinton-hairstylist-historys-most-iconic-hair-styles/index.html, accessed June 13, 2017. The quotes, images and photographs included in the collection are striking and beautiful.

10. John Barrett, *Hair*, 6.

11. Ibid.

12. Ibid.

13. Ibid.

14. This idea is, in fact, conveyed by several quotes in *Hair*. Jane Fonda remarks, "Hair had ruled me for many years. Perhaps I used it to hide behind. I simply said to Paul McGregor, 'Do something.' It was the haircut that became famous in *Klute*, the shag. I knew right away that I could do life differently with this hair." Christiaan Houtenbos contends: "A lot of people hide behind their hair. If you take that veil away, something else happens. A haircut may change your view of the world. It may change your view of your boyfriend. It may change your view of yourself." Rod Stewart thinks his hair made him a rock singer: "I couldn't be anything other than a rock singer with this hair."

15. *Hair*, 7.

16. Ibid.

17. Ibid.

18. Ibid.

19. Ibid., 8.

20. Ibid.

21. Ibid., 10.

22. Ibid., 12.

23. See John Barrett's *Hair*.

24. See Shawn J. Parry-Giles, *Hillary Clinton in the News: Gender and Authenticity* (Urbana, IL: University of Illinois Press, 2014).

25. Ibid., 40. For the moment Parry-Giles is referring to, see the coverage of Hillary's 1992 Democratic Convention appearance at NBC News, accessed June 13, 2017, http://www.nbcnews.com/video/watch-hillary-clinton-s-grand-entrance-at-1992-dnc-733998147787. For more about Hillary's image in the press, see also Amber Jamieson and Adam Gabbatt's piece, "'You Don't Fit the Image': Hillary Clinton's Decades-Long Push against a Sexist Press," *The Guardian*, September 15, 2016, accessed June 13, 2017. https://www.theguardian.com/us-news/2016/sep/15/hillary-clinton-press-sexism-media-interviews.

26. For the details, see Michael Kruse, "The TV Interview That Haunts Hillary Clinton," *Politico*, September 23, 2016, accessed March 27, 2017. http://www.politico.com/magazine/story/2016/09/hillary-clinton-2016-60-minutes-1992-214275.

27. Hillary's lines from 1992 correspond to several other well-known lines she delivered later in her career. The first she delivered on September 5, 1995, in China while she was First Lady, "Women's rights are human rights and human rights are women's rights." The second line was delivered on December 6, 2001, in Geneva while she was Secretary of State, "Gay rights are human rights and human rights are gay rights."

28. Ruby Cramer, "Hillary Clinton Wants to Talk with You about Love and Kindness" *BuzzFeedNews*, January 25, 2016, accessed April 9, 2017. https://www.buzzfeed.com/rubycramer/hllary-clinton-wants-to-talk-to-you-about-love-and-kindness?utm_term=.nivv3MbOQ#.tb1N1BjXY

29. The full text of her speech is available at Wellesley College's website, accessed June 21, 2017. http://www.wellesley.edu/events/commencement/archives/1969commencement/student-speech#lSTBGubuAZOVH4lR.97.

30. The title of the present essay, "Saint Hillary," is a reference to this way of imaging Hillary and not, of course, to ecclesial notions of "sainthood" or "saintliness."

31. The text of Kelly's article for the *New York Times*, "Saint Hillary," May 23, 1993, accessed June 24, 2017. http://www.nytimes.com/1993/05/23/magazine/saint-hillary.html?pagewanted=all.

32. See the photo that is the subject of Oliver Laurent's "The Story Behind Hillary Clinton's Epic Group Selfie," *Time*, September 26, 2016, accessed on July 16, 2018. http://time.com/4508252/hillary-clinton-epic-selfie/. Long hair does not seem appropriate for a woman in politics. Nonetheless, Hillary fans may be telling her to let her hair down? I thank an unnamed source of David M. Halperin's for this lead.

33. See Amber Jamieson and Adam Gabbatt, "'You Don't Fit the Image': Hillary Clinton's Decades-Long Push against the Sexist Press" *The Guardian*, September 15, 2016, accessed July 16, 2018. https://www.theguardian.com/us-news/2016/sep/15/hillary-clinton-press-sexism-media-interviews.

34. Michael Kelly, "Saint Hillary."

35. The names of the nine people who lost their lives are the Reverend Clementa Pinckney, the Reverend Daniel Simmons, Sharonda Coleman-Singleton, Depayne Middleton-Doctor, Cynthia Hurd, Myra Thompson, Ethel Lance, Susie Jackson, and Tywanza Sander.

36. David M. Halperin, citing Foucault's comments in an interview with Jean Le Bitoux, et al., "De l'amitié come mode de vie," *Gai Pied*, no. 25 (April 1981): 38–39, in *Saint Foucault*, 98. The citation is from page 38 of *Gai Pied*. See Michael Foucault, "Friendship as a Way of Life," in *Ethics, Subjectivity, Truth: The Essential Works of Foucault, 1954–1984*, ed. Paul Rainbow, trans. John Johnston (New York: The New Press, 1997). See, further, now Halperin, "Queer Love," *Critical Inquiry*, 45.2 (Winter 2019), forthcoming.

37. I do not know how to do theology without the Bible, hence I adopt Theodore Jennings Jr.'s broad definition of theology as reflection on the Christian mythos. See Jennings, *Introduction to Theology: An Invitation to Reflect Upon the Christian Mythos* (Philadelphia: Fortress Press, 1976), 2: "[B]y theology I mean reflection on the Christian mythos. . . . Mythos is used here to designate that set of symbols, rituals, narratives, and assertions which, taken together . . . represent, orient, communicate, and transform existence in the world for a community of persons."

38. Theodore Jennings, Jr., *An Ethics of Queer Sex: Principles and Improvisations* (Chicago: Exploration Press, 2013), esp. 98–102. I should note that situating Mary in this way is not Jennings's purpose in this context; it is, rather, an implication of his reading of the significance of Rahab. See also Halperin's "The Democratic Body: Prostitution and Citizenship in Classical Athens" in *One Hundred Years of Homosexuality and Other Essays on Greek Love: The New Ancient World* (New York: Routledge, 1990), 88–112, for a very helpful analysis of the politics of prostitution in classical Athens. I think Halperin's work is also helpful for reading several moments in Paul's letters, from issues relating to hairstyle and (the interpolation regarding) women speaking in church. See 1 Cor. 6–14.

39. Stephanie Buckhanon Crowder, *When Momma Speaks: The Bible and Motherhood from a Womanist Perspective,* Kindle edition (Louisville: Westminster John Knox Press, 2016), 63. Buckhanon Crowder also reads Mary's significance, but from within the Gospel of Luke (73–83).

40. See Freud's *Interpretation of Dreams*, vols. 4–5 in the *Standard Edition of the Complete Psychological Works of Sigmund Freud*, ed. James Strachey, esp. 418–420. Citation is from 418, emphasis is Freud's.

41. Ibid., 418.

42. Ibid.

43. Ibid., 420.

44. Ibid.

45. Joseph's strategy, in fact, has become the preferred method of Christendom. See, for example, Marcella Althaus-Reid's *Indecent Theology: Theological Perversions in Sex, Gender, and Politics* (New York: Routledge: 2001).

REFERENCES

Barrett, John. *Hair*. New York: Assouline Publishing, 2016.

Buckhanon Crowder, Stephanie. *When Momma Speaks: The Bible and Motherhood from a Womanist Perspective*. Louisville: Westminster John Knox Press, 2016. Kindle edition.

Chozick, Amy. "Hillary Clinton's Gay Rights Evolution." *The New York Times*, August 29, 2014, accessed March 21, 2017. https://www.nytimes.com/2014/08/31/fashion/hillary-clinton-gay-rights-evolution.html.

———. "Hillary Clinton, Loudly and Proudly, Taps into a Vein of Support among Gay Voters." *The New York Times*, July 1, 2015, accessed March 21, 2017. https://www.nytimes.com/2015/07/02/us/politics/hillary-clinton-courts-gay-lgbtq-voters.html.

Cramer, Ruby. "Hillary Clinton Wants to Talk with You about Love and Kindness." *BuzzFeedNews*, January 25, 2016, accessed April 9, 2017. https://www.buzzfeed.com/rubycramer/hillary-clinton-wants-to-talk-to-you-about-love-and-kindness?utm_term=.nivv3MbOQ#.tb1N1BjXY.

Eastman. Susan. *Recovering Paul's Mother Tongue: Language and Theology in Galatians*. Grand Rapids: Eerdmans, 2007.

Freud, Sigmund. *The Standard Edition of the Complete Psychological Works of Sigmund Freud*, edited and translated by James Strachey. Vols. 4–5. *The Interpretation of Dreams*. London: Hogarth Press and the Institute of Psycho-Analysis, 1953.

Halperin, David M. *Saint Foucault*. New York: Oxford University Press, 1995.

———. *How to Be Gay*. Cambridge, Belknap: 2012.

———. "Queer Love," *Critical Inquiry*, 45.2 (Winter 2019). Forthcoming.

Jamieson, Amber, and Adam Gabbatt. "'You Don't Fit the Image': Hillary Clinton's Decades-Long Push against the Sexist Press." *The Guardian*, September 15, 2016, accessed July 16, 2018. https://www.theguardian.com/us-news/2016/sep/15/hillary-clinton-press-sexism-media-interviews.

Jennings, Jr., Theodore. *Outlaw Justice: The Messianic Politics of Paul*. Stanford: Stanford University Press, 2013.

———. *An Ethics of Queer Sex: Principles and Improvisations*. Chicago: Exploration Press, 2013.

Kelly, Michael. "Saint Hillary." *New York Times*, May 23, 1993, accessed June 24, 2017. http://www.nytimes.com/1993/05/23/magazine/saint-hillary.html?pagewanted=all.

Laurent, Oliver. "The Story Behind Hillary Clinton's Epic Group Selfie." *Time*, September 26, 2016, accessed on July 16, 2018. http://time.com/4508252/hillary-clinton-epic-selfie/.

Parry-Giles, Shawn J. *Hillary Clinton in the News: Gender and Authenticity*. Urbana, IL: University of Illinois Press, 2014.

Seitz-Wald, Alex. "Hillary Clinton's complex relationship with her LGBT base." *MSNBC*, July 2, 2015, accessed March 24, 2017. http://www.msnbc.com/msnbc/hillary-clintons-complex-relationship-her-lgbt-base.

Signorile, Michelangelo. "Hillary: Viva la diva!" *Advocate*, September 14, 1999.

Chapter Nine

Love Trumps Hate

Images of Political Love from Pussyhat Makers

Donna Bowman

Between 2013 and 2015, I interviewed dozens of women involved in prayer shawl ministries. They knit and crochet prayer shawls as gifts of comfort, support, and celebration. As a theologian and researcher, I asked them to express the motivations, responses, and meanings involved in their experience. Knitting with and learning from these women was my life for three years, and resulted in the book *Prayer Shawl Ministries and Women's Theological Imagination* (Lexington Press 2015). However, it wasn't until six days before the Women's March on January 21, 2017, that I realized the same approach was needed for the makers of the pussyhats, the pink square hats that were produced in the tens or perhaps hundreds of thousands by individual knitters, crocheters, sewists, and milliners. Here was a handmade textile object, functional but more importantly symbolic, that burst out onto the streets of American cities and around the world on that day, and became the iconic focus of a mass movement.

This chapter invites us to listen to the people who made those pussyhats on a topic that dominated the political campaign: the dichotomy of love and hate. In this research, as in the prayer shawl project, I adopt the framework of *ordinary theology* pioneered by Jeff Astley and colleagues at the North of England Institute for Christian Education:

> Unfortunately, it is often difficult to *infer* people's beliefs from their practice. Unless one defines beliefs in terms of behaviour, there is rarely a one-to-one relationship between beliefs and their expression in actions, and sometimes only a weak empirical correlation. . . . This is why ordinary theology research normally concentrates on people's beliefs as they are expressed in their words:

> portraying the theology in what people say (or write) rather than the theology implicit in what they do. I want *literally to hear* the theological voice of those who call themselves "just ordinary."[1]

Using qualitative interviews, I sought to elicit through conversation the theological meanings that lay people form out of their resources of religious education and personal experience, and use as lenses for their thinking and doing. These meanings inform us about the theologies that are operative in ordinary people and everyday experience, the ones that emerge from the interaction of historical deposits, cultural settings, and practical wisdom. In talking with pussyhat makers, as with the prayer shawl ministry participants, I sought to create a space in which respondents can bring theological concepts to bear on meaning-making projects that are significant, useful, and/or resonant in their own lives. The pussyhat has no obvious or intentional theological significance. Yet works of love (including caring for others by clothing them, and standing up for and standing in solidarity with the oppressed), and responses to hate and violence, involve attitudes and behaviors that call upon—or perhaps impel the construction of—theological meanings. While only half of my respondents identified themselves with a religious community, American interviewees in particular found it difficult to avoid situating themselves in some relationship to religious meanings, given the cultural importance of religion here. For those in southern, rural, and relatively homogenous areas of the country, politics and religion are already fused, if not for themselves, then in the assumptions of most of their neighbors. For those in coastal, urban, and diverse communities, the 2016 election campaigns focused their attention on the religious beliefs and actions of their fellow citizens, and prompted reflection on their own relationship to claims made and values professed by religious voters.

THE PUSSYHAT PROJECT

The Pussyhat Project began after the November 2016 elections, in response to the call for a Women's March that went viral and began to be organized that same month. As Krista Suh and Jayna Zweiman tell the story, they were brainstorming some sort of unifying wearable for the march at their Los Angeles local yarn shop (LYS, in knitter lingo), and the idea of a hat that would pay ironic homage to Trump's "grab 'em by the pussy" remark emerged.[2] The original online call for hats envisioned "a sea of pink" on the National Mall in Washington, D.C., an image that was repeated to me scores of times by the hatmakers. As designed by Kat Coyle, the pussyhat is a simple rectangle of knitted or crocheted fabric, folded over and sewn up the sides to form a short, squat tube with corners at the top—corners that, when worn, stick out like cat ears. Easy enough for absolute beginners, yet conducive to endless variation and customization, the pussyhat caught on in the knitting and crochet community in December and early January. Instructions in the pattern PDF included an address in Alexandria, Virginia, an LYS that had agreed to collect hats by mail and distribute them to marchers on January 21. Despite the tens of thousands of hats logged and shared online by makers, no one knew whether the "sea of pink" would come off. Makers who also marched told me of their growing realization that the project had succeeded as they traveled to marches in major cities and saw airplanes, vans, buses, subway stations, trains, and finally streets full of people wearing handmade pink pussyhats. The hat became the preeminent icon of the march, appearing on the covers of *Time* and *The New Yorker*.

In February and March 2017, I surveyed 801 people who made pussyhats. Most of their making took place before the January 21 marches; for some it continued afterward, even deep into the year. Participants in this research were invited to the survey on Ravelry, the eight-million-member social network for knitters, crocheters, and weavers, where the Pussyhat Project group as of this writing has about 4,500 members and the various pussyhat patterns have about 20,000 individual projects logged; and on Facebook, where the Pussyhat Project page currently has 33,000 followers. Additional participants arrived at the survey via snowball sampling, as makers were encouraged to share the link with others they knew who made hats. Survey respondents were also invited to volunteer for a follow-up interview; over 400 did so, and between March 20 and August 21, 2017, I conducted phone interviews with 206 of them. The conversations loosely followed a set of qualitative questions designed to elicit the interviewee's background, follow up on the answers given to open-ended questions in the survey, and inquire into perspectives on the pussyhat, the march, political engagement, and the direction of the country at the time of speaking. Interviews lasted an average of 40 minutes, and more than 139 hours of interviews were collected in total.

While not a representative sample of pussyhat makers due to the sampling methodology, the demographics of the surveyed population do hold interest, matching in some respects observations about the women's movement and preliminary findings about participants in the January 21 marches.[3] Respondents were overwhelmingly white, college-educated, upper middle-class, straight, and cisgender female, with an average age in the upper 40s. Sixty-two percent of the pussyhat makers surveyed marched on January 21, in 117 marches across the United States and Canada, and in five other nations abroad. That places members of the surveyed group at about 17% of the 673 official sister marches. Fifty-eight percent of respondents made between one and five hats prior to January 21; 8% made more than 20 hats, the highest response range provided to them on the survey; the single greatest number reported on the survey was 165, by a rare male pussyhat maker in Chicago. Half of respondents reported no religious affiliation; 34.5% identified themselves as Christian, most of whom belonged to mainline denominations; 6.5% identified as Jewish, and 9.5% gave a range of other answers.

POLITICAL RHETORIC OF LOVE AND HATE

To my 206 interviewees I posed the question: Can you endorse the rhetoric of love that was part of the Clinton campaign, the idea that love trumps hate?

Hate became an issue in the presidential campaign in both general and specific ways. The rise of hate groups during the eight years of the Obama administration has been documented by the Southern Poverty Law Center. Xenophobic hate, for example anti-Muslim activities and rhetoric, became a major concern in the United States after the 9/11 terrorist attacks, but resurfaced as the context for political attacks in the Obama years as part of the "birther" conspiracy movement. President Obama's supposed Kenyan origins fueled speculation that he was a secret Muslim, and Islam was once again conflated with anti-American views. The rise of Daesh (the so-called Islamic State, ISIS, or ISIL), with its brutal beheadings of prisoners and journalists widely shared on video, gave cultural and political legitimacy to broad claims about the incompatability of Islam with civilized, democratic, or American values. But the biggest spikes in hate group membership and activity had to do with race. The backlash to the election of the first black president increased the appeal of groups organized around white separatism, white Christian nationalism, and white supremacy. That trend exploded into the open with the candidacy of Donald Trump, whose campaign was staffed by open allies of these groups from far-right media like Breitbart News (whose website had long featured a vertical called "Black Crime"). David Duke, long marginalized for his Ku Klux Klan ties, enthusiastically supported Trump, and neo-Nazi and Klan groups endorsed him.

The association of Trump with hate, even outside of his own words and actions (such as his leadership in the birther movement, calls to execute the Central Park Five, and anti-immigrant/xenophobic "America First" sloganeering), brought questions about the countervailing value of love to the forefront of the campaign. The Clinton campaign, and the National Democratic Convention, began using the phrase "Love Trumps Hate" in the summer of 2016. As anti-Trump and women's rights activism rose in the months following the election, anger, disgust, desperation, and nausea dominated the emotional palette of the movement.

I wondered what participants in the Women's March and its supporting activities, particularly those engaged in the caretaking and supportive activity of hatmaking, thought about the idea of love's power to conquer hate. Were they in agreement with the sentiment during the campaign? Had their views changed since? Is love a political virtue? Why or why not? In discussing and answering these questions, pussyhat makers sketched their own operationalized definitions of love (and of hate, anger, and other associated or countervailing affective states). These images sometimes referred to the pussyhat maker's religious beliefs and practices, including her view of the divine. The images of love also frequently responded to definitions of love, and loving behavior, arising from religious groups with highly active political agendas, either in support of Trumpism or in opposition to it.

LOVE AS CARING ACTION

One of the first women I interviewed was Georgina, a teacher at a Pentecostal school in Rhode Island. She belongs to a theologically orthodox but socially progressive Evangelical Covenant congregation, is a registered Republican, and voted for Jill Stein. She felt caught between two worlds in terms of the political dimension of Christian identity, she told me. The school where she teaches "has a bunch of pro-Trump, keep out the refugees, Trumpisms crap that I don't agree with. So I keep my head low." But her own congregation "feel(s) strongly that all human beings are image bearers, made in the image of God. And as such, they have infinite value. They believe that our motive for everything needs to be love and not hate, and that we are responsible to care for each other." Her church mobilized en masse to show a welcoming face to 200 Syrian refugee families settled in their community when anti-refugee executive orders began emanating from the White House shortly after the election: "[T]he response was so awesome from the community, but it was just we've got to put our money where our mouth is. What can we do to help? We can't fix Trump, but we could give them toilet paper."[4]

Elizabeth, a Presbyterian speech-language pathologist in California in her 50s, sees love as the "theology of Christ Jesus." Exemplifying Christ to others means caring for them:

> [T]hat's what I try to model for my daughter, for that matter for the students that I work with, for my colleagues, that um, you know, that love indeed is more powerful, is—more to the point—than abusing others. We don't have time for acrimony or lies, life's too short for that and the theology of Christ Jesus is that philosophy—that approach to life, that theology, is all about showing love and kindness to others and thinking of others and being Christ to others, and that means that you can't judge others and you have to try to see people through a lens of compassion.[5]

Elizabeth sees her relationship to others as a demonstration of Christ, whom she explains as revealing God precisely in the relationship to others. Jessica, a Lutheran chaplain in Massachusetts in her 30s, expands on this insight. For her, rhetoric about love tends toward the idealistic precisely because it is without an object:

> Christian love is something more difficult than what people would want it to be because we are called to love our enemies and to also be able to love others like we love ourselves, which also implies that we are to be loving ourselves before we can actually love others. I've been kind of cautious in my use of love when I talk about these sorts of issues. I think there is a little bit of wide-eyed idealism in terms of oh, we just need to band together and love is going to fix this. When I think of love in terms of activism as a Christian person, it means speaking truth [to] power, it means standing up for those who don't have a voice, it means some self-sacrifice, not to the point of damaging yourself, and not to the point of being subservient to someone, but being willing to stand up for somebody and put yourself in place of somebody else.[6]

To put love into action means sacrificing one's privilege to stand up for others, putting one's self in their place. Relationship provides the resonating material without which love is merely a sounding gong or a clanging cymbal.

LOVE AS CONNECTION

Love as connection was another theme frequently raised in my conversations with pussyhat makers. Ludmilla, an Eastern Orthodox retiree who was born in Ukraine and now lives in Ohio, told me a story to illustrate the kind of love she saw in the Pussyhat Project:

> One of the priests a few years ago had heart surgery, and I think he might have died, and he said what he saw he could only describe as what the ancients called the music of the spheres of being connected with infinity, with God, the universe, things like that. And that's the kind of love I think is being put out there by women who do these hats. That kind of connectedness. And that's like a building block for what has to be done.[7]

Cornelia, an educator in Michigan in her 40s of Polish extraction who describes herself as an "Easter and Christmas Catholic," emphasized the way knitting materializes love by forming fabric to clothe the body of another:

> [W]hen you look at knitting, to me the thing that's so fascinating about it, I mean it's very meditative. Every stitch a person turns for you. Every stitch a person pushed through for you. So there's this love aspect. And even something that's sewed by hand isn't the same because it's not sewed by hand all over. You have fabric, right? But with knitting, your stitches become the fabric. And so to me, if you make something for somebody then it really becomes more love enveloping them and your strength.[8]

The pussyhats become the way in which the faraway maker was present at the march not only in a symbol, but also in the care for the person who was there, which forges the connection.

FAILED THEOLOGIES OF LOVE

I also heard how inadequate conceptions of love fail in action. In a recent email, Georgina (the Rhode Island teacher quoted above) expressed frustration about the way her movement comrades follow through on their claims about love. She perceives a disconnect in both of the two worlds she stands astride, on the part of both conservative and progressive Christians, between the rhetoric and action of love. She is "tired" and "exhausted" by conservative Christians' "growing levels of authoritarianism and patriarchy," and of the pressure she feels from them "to make myself small and weak when God has made me strong and powerful." But when it comes to *showing* love, "those conservatives are the first ones to bring a meal when you're sick. When they say they'll pray for you, they really do, often on the spot. . . . They do what they say they will do, and if you need them, they are there." A mirror-image disconnect exists on the progressive side, she writes:

> I'm every bit as frustrated with the orthodox but more socially aware group. They see the evil in Trump, they will even march in protests and actively help the poor. They endorse women well. Yet at the same time, they don't care for their people. No one is going to check in to see how you're doing. Although I do believe they genuinely care or at least intend to care, things tend to be done for the furthering of their brand and reputation.[9]

Georgina feels that progressives have a lot to learn from conservatives about moving beyond the rhetoric of love, which provides one with the movement-approved costume of caring, and "showing up" for the work of helping those in need.

Pam, a member of the Uniting Church of Australia in her 50s pursuing a graduate degree, told me about going to a Patti Smith concert on Palm Sunday:

> [S]he actually read out the gospel passage that we had that morning in church, which was about the donkey and Christ going in and sending his disciples to get it and bring the colt back. . . . And then in the end she talked about how she felt that she had great respect for the values and the philosophy and that message about respect and care and love and vulnerability and so she was saying, you know what we need to do is love. Everybody needs to just, we need to have more love. And everybody was saying, "Yeah yeah yeah yeah yeah! We need love!" And so then the person in front of me, I was right up near the back, the person in front of me had been sort of waving and shouting,

"Love! Love! Love! We need love! We need love!" And then stood up and so I didn't see anything more of the concert because all I saw was her back, and I thought it was kind of an example of how we can say, "love, love, love," but then be completely oblivious to the needs of the people around us.[10]

Laura, a Mississipian and artist in her 40s who was raised Southern Baptist but later confirmed in the Episcopal Church, mentioned rhetoric associated with the prosperity gospel, where poverty or want is the fault of the needy. Such a view cannot be reconciled in her mind with the gospel of love:

> I had an interesting conversation with my brother who is conservative and a very, very fundamentalist Christian. I was talking to him about Africa and I was like, they live, you know, people in Africa for the most part live in an environment that's not sustainable. And I said, "It doesn't rain, they can't grow crops. So think about that. So why do you think, you know why do you think God created this way of being?" And he said, "I think they're not praying hard enough." And so that falls right in line with the idea of the American dream and if you are living right and living faithfully then you should be thriving. So where is the true love in that? Where is the love in that statement?[11]

A view of others that sees their outcomes as a demonstration of their worth, their relationship to the divine, is incompatible with true love, Laura claims.

LOVE AS POWER

Power and violence were on the minds of many pussyhat makers when I asked them about love. Georgina emailed me after our interview to expand on one of her answers:

> I was thinking more about your question about how I felt when I saw all the news coverage and pictures of the pussyhats at various marches. I said I felt proud. I do, but there's more to it, and I think I've finally put my finger on it. I felt powerful. Our culture says that power comes from weapons and domination. But as a Christian, I would counter that power does not come from hate and killing, it comes from love and caring for people. Hats are more powerful than guns, because they are life sustaining not life ending. We have the power to sustain life in our needles![12]

But Megan, a Long Island stay-at-home mom in her late 30s, the daughter of a former nun and also a Lutheran, pushed back against this dichotomy. Righteous anger, and even forceful or violent action, is intimately connected with love:

> I think that anyone who has been a daughter to a living mother and anybody who has been a mother to a child at all has a really, really, really innate sense that righteous anger is love. It is a form of love. It's one of the 20-sided die of the emotion of love. The ways that we express love. And what daughter, what teenage daughter hasn't said, "I hate you so much!" and really meant, "Why don't you love me more?" And what parent hasn't recognized, like hasn't said, "I am doing this because I love you. I love you too much to let you get away with this shit." So I don't see the two as necessarily being different, at least not in women's hands.[13]

Megan connected this forceful kind of love to the mystery of Christ's passion. To her, this parental affect, this refusal to yield in the face of wrong or evil, ties together the wrath and the love of God:

> You know, my God is a loving God. And my God is a vengeful God. And look at it in the Christian tradition, in the tradition that I ascribe to here, how did God show us, demonstrate his love for us? You know, he sent us his child to be killed and to live again. And it is the most violent form of love. But if we believe that the resurrection of Christ is God's love for us, then we have to also believe that the murder of Christ is His love for us. And so I think that for people who think about this stuff, it's not, the two go together. Love and hate, terror, fear, and acceptance, it all happens.[14]

LOVE AND GENDER

Some women connected their gender to the theology of love they espoused. Ashley, an Episcopal divinity student in her 20s in Illinois, told me she prayed while making her last pussyhats the night before the march—for right intention, safety for the participants, clarity of message, and determination to be a resource for women in crisis. Her meditations that night centered on the way Jesus treated women:

> Mostly that, and even just being reminded of verses in which God is described, or Jesus was described as really being present and seeing women in where they were and empowering them, even so much as Christ could at the time, or as the socioeconomic status of the people he was engaging with. Remembering those stories helps to push me and motivate me more as well.[15]

Marya, a disabled Catholic former teacher in her 50s in New Jersey, told me she was in a phase of doubt about her faith, sparked by recent images of the Syrian refugee crisis. "I guess I'm just in a place where I'm not sure—you know I question how a loving God can allow such things to happen. And you know, seeing these babies lying on beaches or, you know." But the very movements that such events spark are rooted in the compassion that unites us with people of different experiences, recognizing that bonds of family and community are conditions of common humanity:

> It's important that there has to be an underlying and connecting attribute to each movement so that we can all be—now I'll use the metaphor—stitched together and maybe wrapped in that rainbow flag, because it all comes down to love. Love is the basic ingredient that is the motivator of all of these movements. Women naturally love and nurture. LGBTQ loves quote-unquote differently, and in the black community, black families love each other as much as white families do, even though certain white families don't believe that. . . . And so if they divide, you know if ultimately all these movements divide, it would be a tragedy. But the way to unite them is to unite them through love and through just by the very acceptance of the LGBTQ community, we are saying we have to accept them all in a big, big room, in a big table, in a big nation.[16]

For Marya, an experiential lesson that women and other historically marginalized groups have learned is the power of acceptance and love as a political tool. The need to forge common bonds across diverse life experiences teaches women the craft of solidarity, a tool that can be used to build communities larger than narrow identity categories.

LOVE AS RELATIONALITY

Perhaps what brings together these strands of theologies of love, and weaves them into a nascent political theology, is the recognition that relationality must be fundamental in our theological and political conceptions. Christina, a nursing administrator in her 60s in Washington State, told me about her mother, a German nurse who worked as a nursing assistant after immigrating to the United States because she wasn't fully licensed here. Her father was disabled, and the Catholic hospital where her mother worked begged her to bring little Christina along on her shifts rather than quit; every hand was needed during the postwar baby boom.

> So I grew up in the delivery room, on the nurses' lounge couch. This figures into my knitting and who I am as a woman. My mother taught me how to knit there when I was four years old. I learned how to hold a crayon. And the nurses knit when they were waiting for babies or on a slow night. And my mother taught me how to knit continental. I also learned at that time that I was never around women who were not strong.[17]

She had been to see the movie *Wonder Woman* the night before our interview, and the way that character was raised and taught resonated with her.

Wonder Woman was raised on an island of women who taught her how to be a strong woman, and that is how I was raised. I watched the nursing supervisor, who was a religious sister, tell one of these surgeons that it was her job to protect these women and you cannot do that in my operating room. So that is where I learned I became a real defender of women. I fell in love with women. I love women. I have worked all of my life on the behalf of women. I have a Ph.D. in nursing. In my clinical practice, I have always taken care of women and young children.[18]

At the Women's March in Seattle, Christina took a bag of pussyhats and handed them out to whomever needed one:

Women were very emotional. Now I don't know if it is because I am a nurse and I have this thing where I listen to and comfort people, but a lot of women were crying. Women told me their stories of being raped. Of living in small rural towns, which I have lived in a lot of my life, you know what it's like to feel objectified, like a thing, um you know, and as I am thinking about it, I am very emotional.[19]

So when I asked Christina if the movement's rhetoric of love's power was something she embraced, she was unhesitating: "Absolutely. As you heard me earlier, I love women. My love of women does not diminish my love for anyone else. I love women, I love my country, I love who we are."[20] Caring for women, she said, connected her with every other woman who is a daughter, or the mother of a daughter or son.

I have been behind that message since I was a baby myself. The daughter of a German woman, who by the way was a [Nazi] sympathizer. When I was picked up every night and rocked and went to the delivery room to watch powerful women push their babies out. And when I was treated with tenderness all of the time by those women. Yes this is who we are. This is who we are.[21]

Christina challenged the idea that the relational underpinning of love and belonging is a weakness to be decried: "Me and my daughter are not hardened. We are snowflakes. Yeah, we are. We are not hardened. I proudly claim those labels because I believe in them. And I challenge those people who try to label that thinking and behavior as being weak and not good. I proudly claim that belief."[22]

CONCLUSION

Opposition to hate was a key motivator for activists involved in the Women's Marches in January 2017. Love, however, is not automatically a political value or strategy in such opposition. Whether love as an affective state, an attitude toward others, a practice of caring, or a source of power, can be effective as a motivator or source of political agency was a question with which activists found themselves grappling in the wake of the 2016 elections. Pussyhat makers involved themselves in an activity closely associated with caretaking and nurturing domesticity, and sought to turn this activity into public defiance and resistance. In doing so, they confronted with particular urgency the question of political love. For many, the hats (especially when given away freely) expressed love for fellow women and allies in the movement. Yet the association with Trump's pussy-grabbing comment subverted the "soft" or "fuzzy" associations of handknitting with a sharp edge of anger.

Pussyhat makers who identified with religious communities, or who found themselves inevitably responding to the Christian rhetoric that forms a major strand of conservative politics in the United States, formulated understandings of love that had the potential to support political action in several ways—as caring action, connection, power, and relationality. They asserted a special capacity to understand and engage in the politics of love out of their gendered experiences. And they criticized the empty rhetoric of love, when the concept failed to sensitize its users to the needs of those around them.

In listening to the theology of those engaged in this political movement of resistance, especially as they react out of understandings taught to them in faith communities or that are pervasive in their environments, we can appreciate the hard and unseen labor of meaning-making in which ordinary people are always engaged. Christina, who majored in religious philosophy along with nursing in college, talked to me at great length about her spiritual inspiration, the theology of Mary Daly, who is also a lifelong knitter and cataloger of stitch patterns. She paraphrased a conversation she had with a mentor about knitting, theology, and feminism:

> For generations women have done every day the work that we have never been able to name and claim. Because we have been silenced. It's the mundane work that creates joy and safety and comfort and shelter. The most important foundational work that is important to a community and family. We do it without talking about it. We don't claim our voices. A lot of what we do we take to the graves with us.[23]

The promise of qualitative work like this study is to claim these voices as *theological sources and products*, worthy of being utilized for a variety of reflective and constructive projects. In listening to pussyhat makers, I have tried to "unsilence" and create a discursive space where the foundational labor of meaning-making can be brought to consciousness and expressed in context. We can then put it to work as a robust framework for thinking and practice, in politics and far beyond—legacies and heirlooms that are picked up and used every day, like needles and wool handed down to us, rather than taken to our graves and buried unseen.

NOTES

1. Jeff Astley, "The Analysis, Investigation and Application of Ordinary Theology," in Jeff Astley and Leslie J. Francis, eds., *Exploring Ordinary Theology: Everyday Christian Believing and the Church* (Burlington, VT: Ashgate Publishing Company, 2013), 5.
2. See for example (among many published retellings) Seema Mehta, "How these Los Angeles-born pink hats became a worldwide symbol of the anti-Trump women's march," *Los Angeles Times*, January 15, 2017.
3. See for example Bettina Spencer and Ernesto Verdeja, "Nevertheless, She Persisted: Mobilization after the Women's March," *Interdisciplinary Perspectives on Equality and Diversity* 3(2) (2017): np; Dana R. Fisher, Dawn M. Dow, and Rashawn Ray, "Intersectionality Takes It to the Streets: Mobilizing across Diverse Interests for the Women's March," *Science Advances* 3 (2017): eaao1390.
4. Interview, March 30, 2017.
5. Interview, March 23, 2017.
6. Interview, March 22, 2017
7. Interview, March 28, 2017.
8. Interview, May 8, 2017.
9. Email communication to author, May 26, 2018.
10. Interview, May 9, 2017.
11. Interview, April 20, 2017.
12. Email communication to author, April 2, 2017.
13. Interview, April 5, 2017.
14. Ibid.
15. Interview, April 26, 2017.
16. Interview, April 6, 2017.
17. Interview, June 4, 2017.
18. Ibid.
19. Ibid.
20. Ibid.
21. Ibid.
22. Ibid.
23. Ibid.

REFERENCES

Astley, Jeff. "The Analysis, Investigation and Application of Ordinary Theology." in Jeff Astley and Leslie J. Francis, eds. *Exploring Ordinary Theology: Everyday Christian Believing and the Church.* Burlington, VT: Ashgate Publishing Company, 2013.
Fisher, Dana R., Dawn M. Dow, and Rashawn Ray. "Intersectionality takes it to the streets: Mobilizing across Diverse Interests for the Women's March." *Science Advances* 3 (2017).
Mehta, Seema. "How these Los Angeles-born pink hats became a worldwide symbol of the anti-Trump women's march." *Los Angeles Times*, January 15, 2017.
Spencer, Bettina, and Ernesto Verdeja. "Nevertheless, She Persisted: Mobilization after the Women's March." *Interdisciplinary Perspectives on Equality and Diversity* 3(2) (2017).

Chapter Ten

Achieving Reproductive Justice

Theology and Activism

Thia Cooper

One in every three women in the USA[1] will have an abortion during her life. The recent appointment of Justice Kavanaugh to the US Supreme Court could mean these women may not have access to legal abortion. Black[2] women would be disproportionately affected; they have abortions at three times the rate of white women and twice the rate of all women.[3] Yet, black women are less likely than white women to be pro-choice. A woman's control over her reproduction is determined by many factors: experiences of women differ due to economics, politics, race, gender, religion, and other cultural issues. Abortion dominates the conversation about reproduction in the USA, particularly among white middle-class women. If we expand the horizon of the conversation to include women of color, abortion is not the only reproductive issue and is not framed in terms of life versus choice. This chapter argues: (1) The conversation around abortion cannot remain limited to life versus choice; (2) Reproductive justice includes far more than access to abortion. Both pieces of this argument should be taken forward by activists for reproductive justice.

Reproduction is about far more than abortion. Reproductive justice is "the human right to maintain personal bodily autonomy, have children, not have children, and parent the children we have in safe and sustainable communities." (Sistersong) If a woman has unprotected penetrative sex beginning at age 18, she could conceive children for up to 30 years. Without some reproductive control, in theory, one could have a child at least each year. Reproduction includes being able to have and raise children and being able not to have and raise children. Being able to have children includes issues of surrogacy, infertility treatments, and fetal selection. Being able to raise children includes childcare, safety, and health care. Being able to not have children includes abortion, contraception, and sterilization. Thus, this chapter broadens out the discussion of reproduction from abortion to a broad swath of activism.[4]

I approach the issue of reproductive justice from the perspective of poor women and women of color, rarely seen in the debate. This perspective comes from global feminisms and feminist liberation theology. Liberation theology emerged in Latin America in the 1960s as a response to political and economic poverty. Poor, mainly Catholic, Christians began to read the Bible for themselves. In this reading, they understood God to be on the side of the marginalized, struggling with them toward justice. This theology expanded around the globe to also address race,[5] gender,[6] and the environment.

From the perspective of global feminisms, one learns that being a woman intersects with race, class, gender, religion, environment, and so forth.[7] In this chapter, I interrogate race, gender, and economics, in particular. Most of the data focuses on black women, however, I will bring in statistics of Native American and Latina women where possible.[8] Integrating the perspective of women of color enables us to understand the complexity to find a way forward that relates to all women.

Liberation theology's method is called the hermeneutical circle, a circle of interpretation leading to action in community. The circle begins with a thorough discussion of the problem or situation, analyzing the situation through academics, through sacred text, tradition, and theology. Finally, it acts. This chapter follows that pattern. To achieve reproductive justice, we must integrate and prioritize the perspective of marginalized women, understanding that all human beings are part of the family of God and as such each person should be able to choose whether or not to have and raise children.

A BRIEF HISTORY OF REPRODUCTION IN THE USA

To understand the perspectives of poor women and women of color on reproductive issues, we need to see how the history differs from that of white wealthier women in the USA. During slavery, white men controlled black women's bodies, including reproduction. Black women were supposed to reproduce to give the masters new slaves. The women also had to submit to white male sexual desires. Finally, the women also had to labor in the fields and houses just like black men. Black women (and men) were considered bodies to be used by whites.

In the 19th century, a focus on health and disease emerged with sexist, racist, and classist overtones, which included ending the reproduction of people considered less desirable. Healthy wealthy white people were to procreate. Others considered less desirable due to race, sexuality, religion, ability, and class were not. Certain people were considered "defective," including black men and men with disabilities, considered beasts unable to control their sexuality. White women needed to be protected from such men. Hence, men of color and men with disabilities were sterilized without consent. Women with disabilities, considered too vulnerable to resist any predators, were sterilized too. Finally, homosexuals were added to the "defective" category.

After slavery, black women were not supposed to have children, so the black population would not increase. While black men were lynched supposedly for their "uncontrollable" sexuality, black women continued to be raped by white men. Black women were considered lazy if they stayed home to raise children, continuing the white notion that black people were to labor for whites.

Throughout the 20th century, black women continued to be bodies only used for labor and sex but not for reproduction.[9] For example, in the 1930s, several states aimed to reduce the black population by providing birth control to black women.[10] In the 1960s and 70s, California, Connecticut, Delaware, Georgia, Illinois, Iowa, Louisiana, Maryland, Mississippi, Ohio, South Carolina, Tennessee, and Virginia proposed sterilization laws for women to reduce the population of "illegitimate and poor children."[11] Black women were also subject to the "Mississippi Appendectomy," where women were sterilized without their knowledge when in for unrelated surgery or sometimes directly after birth.[12] This sterilization extended to Native American and Puerto Rican women too. Twenty-five percent of Native women were sterilized without their knowledge by the Indian Health Services (IHS) during the 1970s.[13] By the 1970s, Puerto Rican women in New York City had been sterilized at seven times the rate of white women.

In contrast, white middle- and upper-class women have been consistently encouraged to reproduce. Sterilization and abortion were difficult for these women to access. "Many physicians would not sterilize a white woman until the number of children she had given birth to multiplied by her age added up to 120."[14] Contraception was also difficult to access. Only in 1965 did the Supreme Court overturn a law prohibiting married couples from using contraception. Hence, in the 1970s, during *Roe v. Wade*, white middle-class women wanted legal access to abortion.

However, also in 1973, two black children Minnie and Mary Alice Relf (ages 12 and 14) were sterilized without consent.[15] In 1977, the judge in the *Relf v. Weinberger* case decided there should be no federal funding for "involuntary" sterilization and families access to welfare should not be dependent on being sterilized. While white women wanted access to abortion, women of color wanted the ability to actually have children. Black and white women were both suffering from reproductive injustice but in different ways.

We will consider reproductive justice in the context of this history.

Chapter 10
PREVENTING CHILDREN

Abortion

In the USA, abortion is legal during the first two trimesters. However, accessing an abortion can be difficult. With no federal funding for abortion,[16] poor women, the military, and Native Americans using the Indian Health Services are all affected. In addition, abortion services are available only in 13% of US counties.[17] Thus, women would have to be able to afford an abortion and travel to a location that provides the service.

Why do women abort? For many middle- and upper-class white women, the choice has been between work and motherhood. For example, "*Premarital sex, traditional marriage,* and *traditional family* are significantly related to White women's support for legalized abortion but not Black women's."[18] In particular, "for Whites religious affiliation was by far the most important predictor."[19] White women's perspectives reflect the main argument within the abortion debate of life versus choice.

In a study of 721 women who had abortions, 27% of the women stated they were black, 86% claimed a religious affiliation, 40% were married, and 65% had between one and five children. Further, statistics compiled in the early 1990s show that black women's rate of abortions was increasing relative to white women.[20] Black women often face different circumstances. The incarceration and underemployment of black men due to structural racism means these men cannot be the main provider.[21] This lack of black male contribution to the household means many black women have had to work and single-parent their families. Black women could not choose to either be a wife and mother or to work. Both had to be done.

Most women face some constraints when deciding whether to have a child. These can be legal, social, personal, and economic.[22] For example, if a woman is already a mother, economics can play a particular role. Many poor women, both black and white, have to choose between the lives they are providing for and the fetus. One study showed that 86% of black women with multiple abortions already had at least one child, compared to 57% of white women.[23]

Most commonly, the argument over abortion is framed in terms of life versus choice. However, pro-choice rhetoric assumes women have more than one choice. "The framework of choice assumes that all women can . . . decide for themselves whether and when to have children; . . . that a women's body is *her own*—that she owns it, controls it, and makes her own decisions about her body, her health, and her relationships."[24] Many women do not have multiple options; choices are determined by our systems and societies.

Second, the pro-life argument does not resonate with many women. Jeanette Bushnell, a Seattle-based Native health activist stated, "The fetus is a life—but sometimes that life must be ended."[25] Sometimes one has to choose which life to protect. "The 'right to life' is an empty rhetorical phrase if it is not also focused on addressing social issues such as poverty and drugs that contribute to poor living conditions and crime-related activity—which can have a significant impact on reproductive freedom."[26] Protecting the life of the fetus does not seem to extend to protecting the lives of those born.

Each person should have reproductive rights and responsibilities in community. Neither the pro-life nor pro-choice arguments address how to do this. "The major flaw in the pro-life position is NOT the claim that the fetus is a life, but the conclusion it draws from this assertion: that because the fetus is a life, abortion should be criminalized."[27] People suffer daily in the USA from lack of choice, lack of empowerment. A focus on punishment for women who abort a fetus does not prioritize life after birth, only life before birth. The focus instead needs to be on supporting life throughout life.

Abortion is an important piece of the conversation over reproduction. Legalization makes abortion a safer procedure. "Before *Roe v. Wade* in 1973, women of color died from abortion-related complications nearly four times as often as white women."[28] Poorer women and women of color could only afford the less experienced abortionists. However, the conversation over abortion needs to expand beyond life versus choice, redressing the racism and classism around reproduction.

So to address the issue of abortion in its broader context what other aspects need to be included? Here we consider rape, contraception, sterilization, fetal selection, infertility treatments, surrogacy, miscarriage and infant death, and childcare.[29]

Rape

The simplest way to not conceive is to not have sex. However, it is not always possible to resist sex. Rape is one clear example. Here too the issue affects women of color disproportionately. For example, at least one-third of Native women are raped; 57% of those rapists are white men.[30] Women of color have been seen as bodies to be used for sex throughout US history. Native women face two additional difficulties here. First, women who seek treatment for injuries do not always have access to a facility that provides a forensic examination. Some of the IHS facilities do not. Women may have to travel more than 100 miles in order to access a rape kit,[31] and they may have to pay for it. Second, white men who rape Native women on reservations are sometimes not subject to tribal law or brought to court under federal law. In terms of punishment under US law, more than 50% of violent crimes on reservations were not brought to US court by prosecutors; 67% of these were sexual violence.[32]

Further, in general, stranger rape is less common than acquaintance and partner rape. Women risk being raped by those they are most intimate with. So intimate relationships are dangerous and need close attention, as I argued in Cooper (2017). While women of color have disproportionately been treated as property, so too have white women. For a long part of US history, it was thought rape could not occur within marriage.

Religious groups may pressure the woman to keep the fetus conceived by rape. For example, after the war in Croatia, Pope John Paul II encouraged Croatian women who became pregnant after being raped during the war to "'accept the enemy' into them."[33] This extreme example is the logical outcome of considering the fetus a full human being.

Apart from forced sex, women may also want to have sex but not get pregnant.

Contraception

Women have primary responsibility for preventing pregnancy. Women face both the cost of contraception and the responsibility for ensuring contraception is used. Further, forced contraception has been a way to control the growth of particular populations. Planned Parenthood's history, for example, is tied to eugenics.[34]

Women of color also have been subject to birth control testing, as each new form emerged. In the 1970s, the company producing Depo Provera, a birth control injection, conducted some of its clinical trials on women of color, injecting the birth control for free. However, women were charged for removal, even if there were side effects. In addition, some judges offered Depo Provera as an alternative to prison for women convicted of drug charges.

Further, not all contraception is created equal or is equally available. Male condoms have to be paid for and actually used by a man. The birth control pill must be taken every day. Access to refills can depend on your pharmacy. For example, in the Indian Health Service, only one month at a time is available in some locations. Sometimes the closest pharmacy is over 100 miles away. Injected contraception can cause serious side effects as well as infertility months after being removed. It is also costly. One side effect is irregular bleeding, which can cause difficulties for many women. For example, some Native ceremonies and practices exclude women during menstruation. So irregular bleeding can lead to difficulty with participating in traditional practices.

Contraception is also costly. Even having insurance is no guarantee of inexpensive birth control. Some insurers still charge or "cost share" for IUDs, patches, and vaginal rings though the 2010 Affordable Care Act requires coverage without cost sharing. Hobby Lobby, for example, won its

Supreme Court case, stating its religious beliefs did not allow it to provide coverage for contraception that it considered similar to abortion.[35]

Sterilization

A permanent form of contraception is sterilization, which has had racist, ablest, and classist connotations throughout our history. "The . . . NCEB (North Carolina Eugenics Board) . . . [approved] the sterilization of 'feeble-minded' and epileptic patients. In the 1930s, . . . only 23 percent of those sterilized were black; . . . [by] 1966 there was a dramatic shift in the racial makeup of those the board targeted, as the percentage of blacks sterilized rose to 64 in this period."[36] This board sterilized more than 7,600 people in its 55 years of existence. For many people the choice of reproduction was taken away.

While less common today in the USA than in our previous history, there are still cases of enforcement of long-term contraception and sterilization. Most recently, in February 2018, a judge suggested a woman with seven children would receive consideration at sentencing if she were sterilized. She underwent sterilization and the judge stated in his findings that the woman "will receive a shorter sentence because she made that decision."[37]

Still today, people of color are sterilized at greater rates than white women, in part through "choice." I put "choice" in quotes as, for example, a Native woman who relies on the IHS can have difficulty accessing monthly or longer-term contraception and is only allowed abortion in cases of rape, incest, or when a pregnancy endangers her life. Hence, the only option to prevent pregnancy may be sterilization.

Reproductive justice also includes the ability to have children. Recent technological shifts make it possible for biology to be separate from parenting in ways that were limited previously to adoption.

GETTING PREGNANT

Fetal Selection

One possibility is to select or deselect a fetus. One could deselect a female fetus or a fetus with a disability. Smith argues, "if our response to disability is to simply facilitate the process by which women can abort fetuses that may have disabilities, we never actually focus on changing economic policies that make raising children with disabilities difficult."[38] We also do not reconsider the notion of dis/ability itself. Preferred characteristics can be prioritized. Economic privilege exists here too, where people with access to money can more easily afford the tests on a fetus.

Infertility Treatments

There are ways for infertile women to try to conceive. All are costly, though some excellent insurance plans will cover part of the cost. However, women of color and poor women have higher rates of infertility than middle and upper-class white women.[39] Women at most risk of infertility have the least access to treatments. Further, sperm and egg donation has a history of eugenics as well. One can select donors with particular characteristics just as one can select a fetus.

Middle-class women often get into debt in order to try IVF. IVF has a less than 50% chance of success so there is no guarantee that treatment will lead to having a child. This fact harms even wealthy women, particularly those who may delay having children because of a career. The most recent advance has been for women to freeze eggs when younger, with the plan of using them later, an expensive and not always successful option.

Surrogacy

Another possibility is surrogacy. Surrogacy also has racist and classist undertones. Often, women of color bear children for white women and poor women for rich women. Increasingly, surrogates are used internationally.[40] Wealthy women, whether due to infertility, other health issues, or career choices, can pay others to have children for them, mirroring our history of using other bodies for the benefit of whites. On the other hand, surrogacy enables gay men to have children.[41]

Achieving conception is not the end of the reproductive justice struggle. One still has to bring the pregnancy to term and raise a child.

HAVING CHILDREN

Miscarriage and Infant Death

Miscarriage is common and often hidden in our society. Traditionally, one only announces a pregnancy after the twelfth week. So if a woman miscarries earlier, few know. Estimates range from 15% to 30% that a pregnancy will end in miscarriage. Miscarriages occur more often among poor women and women of color. For example, black women miscarry at a rate 57% higher than white women and 93% higher after the tenth week.[42]

Further, infants of women of color die at much greater rates than white babies. In 2013, the CDC reported 5.1 infant deaths per 100 births for white women and 11.1 for black women.[43] No medical reason has been found. The stress of racism may be the cause, medical researchers argue. Black women more often have lower paying jobs without insurance.⁴⁴ Here too women of color have more difficulty bringing children into the world.

Caring for Children

Finally, one needs to be able to raise children safely and healthily, which means having economic and social resources. Where until recently, white mothers who stayed at home to raise their children were celebrated (as long as they had a male provider), mothers who stayed at home to raise their children but did not have a male provider were shamed for being lazy.

Excellent childcare and education are also crucial for children. Without affordable daycare, poorer children are disadvantaged. Their parent/s have to work due to lack of welfare. Those same parent/s cannot afford the excellent care their children need nor provide it themselves when working. Currently, "care for an infant in a day care center was more expensive than tuition and fees at a public university in half the states in the United States."⁴⁵ Single-parent households are disproportionately affected.

Child care in the USA also contains racist undertones. Poorer women and women from the global South,⁴⁶ provide care for wealthy US women's children.⁴⁷ The US woman turns over the responsibility for child care and often cooking and cleaning, increasing a global gender and economic gap. Many of these women from the global South have to leave their children behind in the home countries, sending money back to the extended families who care for them. In addition, many domestic workers are undocumented. These women are underpaid, without their families, and they lack any access to state support for problems they encounter. White women gained a measure of independence on the backs of women of color.

Finally, related to this is the taking of children from parents and into foster care. Ostensibly, foster care exists to protect children from abusive situations. However, many children are taken into foster care due to lack of parental housing or "neglect," often due to lack of money. Rather than providing housing and money, the children are removed. It can be difficult to get a child back after they have been taken into care.

Hence there are a multitude of arenas in which we need to advocate for reproductive justice.

THEOLOGY

Christianity has supported reproductive injustice in the USA throughout its history. However, Christianity could shift to support reproductive justice. We need to create a new reproductive ethic, a holistic ethic that enables people to have and raise children. Every single person on the planet should be able to choose to have and raise a child in a safe and healthy environment. When any person cannot, that is a sin committed by us as a whole. Usually Christians turn first to sacred text (the Bible) and tradition, so I will too.

First of all, the biblical text does not discuss abortion or when a fetus becomes a full human being. The closest we come is in the Hebrew text (Old Testament), which distinguishes punishment for the death of a pregnant mother and the death of her fetus. "If, in an altercation, a woman suffers a miscarriage, the aggressor is to be fined; if the woman is killed, 'you shall give life for life.'"[48] Not only does the text distinguish between the life of the woman and the fetus, but humans are also not required to procreate. Even the text of Genesis 1:28 is not a mandate for procreation. "God blessed them, and God said to them, 'Be fruitful and multiply, and fill the earth and subdue it." Rather than a direct order, this statement is part of God's blessing. David Daube, scholar of Hebrew scripture and ancient law, notes that when we say "have a nice day" this is not an order to do so. "Ordinarily, one will feel inclined . . . but such an inclination is quite different from being under a requirement to do so."[49] We also need to remember the entire canon of rules regarding reproduction and marriage was to ensure the orderly transition of the male lineage through procreation.

While the Hebrew Bible emphasized family and procreation, the New Testament promoted celibacy. The New Testament Gospels in particular reject the focus on the biological family.[50] Jesus did not prioritize his biological family. "Whoever does the will of God, that one is my brother and sister and mother" (Mark 3:34–35, Matthew 12:46–50, Luke 8:19–21) One was to leave one's biological family and become part of the church family. The earliest Christians, as portrayed in the Book of Acts also prioritized the community of God over their biological families. And they shared all in common: Acts 2:44.[51]

The Christian tradition has also changed its understanding on procreation and when life begins over time. Augustine argued sex should only be within marriage for the purpose of procreation, though he preferred celibacy. The Catholic Church argued throughout its history that sex should take place within marriage for the purpose of procreating.

Prior to the 17th century, abortion was only considered wrong after the fourth month, when the fetus could be felt moving (quickening). In the 17th century, scientists argued the sperm was the complete human, using the egg only for nutrition. With this notion came the idea that any attempt to abort after conception would be wrong. The science has advanced, however, the Catholic Church, in particular, has not shifted its stance. The Pope confirmed in *Humane Vitae:* "directly willed and procured abortion, even if for therapeutic reasons, is to be absolutely excluded as licit means of regulating birth. Equally to be excluded . . . is direct sterilization . . . similarly excluded is every action which . . . proposes . . . to render procreation impossible (14)."[52] Here the Pope condemned abortion, sterilization, and contraception. The

Vatican has also rejected the use of technologies to become pregnant, though this is not an area of activism. For the majority of Catholics, sterilization and contraception are not problematic. Ninety-eight percent of US Catholic women use contraception.[53]

This narrow focus on abortion to the exclusion of other arenas of fetal life and life after birth makes the Catholic Church's theology appear hypocritical. Unfortunately, the Church did not expand its focus on the humanity of the fetus to its dealings with miscarriage or IVF. For a miscarriage, there is no requirement of baptism, blessing, or burial. Neither is there blessing for a fertilized embryo. Only the condemnation of abortion was taken forward.

Text and tradition are interpreted differently over time. Theology can be defined as faith seeking understanding. This understanding shifts in varied time periods and contexts. Protestant traditions, for example, have been more open to regulating procreation, as they tend to see the primary purpose of marriage as the union of a husband and wife. Protestant traditions also focused more on the family and marriage and not celibacy as prioritized by the Catholic tradition.

Our shifts in theology should continue today. From the perspective of liberation theology, God is on the side of marginalized. Ecofeminist theology argues that "The first thing to be affirmed in an ecofeminist perspective is the collective dimension of 'person.' . . . And in this collective dimension the most important thing is . . . relatedness."[54] The Christian tradition can help to elaborate an understanding of community, rejecting the focus on the individual and rejecting a focus on a "nuclear" or biological family. As Christians, we have a covenant with God and each other. As Beverly Wildung Harrison, feminist ethicist, has argued, "the true measure of community building is love infused with justice."[55] From within the Christian tradition, we do not love or do justice to others because they are biologically related to us, we love and do justice because we are all part of the family of God.

The strongest response theology can make to reproductive injustice is to reject the focus on the individual and to help reimagine the "ownership" of children and what it means to be a family. Thinking about reproduction requires considering a fetus, the born child, the mother, and the rest of the family. Theologically speaking, even if the fetus is fully human from conception, it is no more human than any other human being. One individual cannot reproduce alone. None of us chooses to come into this world. None of us can survive without help, particularly early on. Each child who enters the world is either adopted or abandoned by that world. This theology needs to extend beyond the process of reproducing and attend to issues of work and care, and the support needed to raise children. To prioritize life, people must first be able to raise any children they do have.

As Protestantism moved away from the prioritizing of celibacy, to prioritizing marriage and the family, so too can the Christian tradition once again move away from this narrowly defined family and extend to the family of God. Only God owns children; we are all responsible for them. This requires a commitment from us all, not just the biological parents. This covenant is not limited to the "nuclear" family. Our definition of family is a subset of the common good. Our civil and state institutions should support an expanded definition of family, enabling any type of family, enabling any type of family to receive the support it needs.

Further, marriage should not be the framework we use as the basis for the family. Overturning marriage will be difficult as it is seen as the cornerstone both of the church and of the state at the moment. However, it does not have to be and from a Christian perspective, should not be at the base of the definition of "family." In part, this is why same-sex marriage became such an important issue because without the ability to marry, same-sex partners and their children were not considered family. From hospital visitors to insurance to taxes, family is defined in specific ways, privileging some and excluding others. Marriage should not be privileged above other forms of family life. Throughout our history, many people have not had access to marriage, many people are unmarried today, and yet families exist and people continue to raise children.

With this expansion of family, also comes a need to care for each other throughout life. Within the Christian tradition, one can distinguish between charity and justice. Charity is needed when justice does not exist. Charity is the one with more giving to the one without. A move toward justice would require our communities (in part through welfare) to support the poorest among us. Our networks in civil society have tried to address this need to prioritize the marginalized with shelters, food banks, and so forth. Instead of this piecemeal filling in of the gaps, we need to remember that we are in community together and each of us should have access to support.

This support spans the public and private realms. With regard to business, the charity that we provide in the civil realm can, unfortunately, help businesses increase their profit as we help their workers to survive with our charity rather than with appropriate pay. Businesses themselves need to remember that enabling each person to live in the fullness of life is the priority, not profit. In our capitalist system, we put profit before the needs of the workers. Christians working toward justice have not been vocal in their requirement of just business. For example, theologian Elizabeth Hinson-Hasty argues that "if we believe that all human beings are valued by God and created as equals in God's image, then wages should reflect the value of workers by covering workers' basic needs."[56] The minimum wage does not cover workers' basic needs and the majority of people on minimum wage are white women. Further, percentage-wise more Black and Hispanic people earn poverty-level wages than whites.[57] Human beings are more than just workers. Work is a means to survive and thrive in life.

In addition, theologies that work to undo racism are crucial. Women of color have been directly harmed by (white) Christian theology. We know that slaveholders found scripture to back up their assertion that slavery was Christian. However, less obvious is the harm done by white theology that argued sex was for procreation within marriage and then kept people of color from marrying and procreating. Christians working toward reproductive justice have to remember the different contexts in order to elaborate a theology and act in a way that includes white women and women of color.

The Christian tradition, reflected in the life of Jesus and the Gospels in particular, removes the focus on the individual and family and on to the community of Christians: the people of God on earth. Advocating for justice for each human is crucial.

ACTION

"Poor conditions in housing, diet, employment, and health care, as well as the absence of conditions of sustainable life, are the signs of continuous social abortion in daily life. This abortion is a local, national, and international problem, and it must be recognized as such."[58] What actions could help us achieve reproductive justice? Each of our actions in the private and public realm need to aim toward empowerment. Empowerment is "the ability or capacity to do things, that is, to achieve goals, make choices, and be self-determining."[59] First, we need to recognize that our actions affect people's ability to reproduce and raise children. Second, particular attention needs to be paid to redressing the wrongs of racism in US society. Third, attention also needs to be paid to redressing the wrongs of classism in US society. Fourth, we need to recognize that having and raising children is a communal responsibility.

We need to ensure that people have a network of financial and other support to raise the children they do have. For example, the negative understanding of the welfare system in the USA must be challenged. Instead of the negative association with "dependency," as in: she is dependent on welfare, we need to recognize that welfare enables children and other dependents to rely on that adult. Welfare is a support system that enables our society to reproduce and to raise children.[60] The formal welfare system and our communal networks of support need to focus on ensuring the poorest and most marginalized among us can survive and even thrive.

We also need to be more attentive to justice in business, regarding the wages of workers and the products crafted. Classism and racism work together in harmful ways, including using whiteness as a way to separate poor white workers from poor workers of color, both of whom are in the same harmful economic situation. The lowest paid workers in our society are caregivers, who are predominantly women of color.

As the corollary to welfare and proper wages, we also need to provide safe and affordable housing. As womanist theologian Rosetta Ross notes, "One of the fastest-growing homeless groups is families with children, accounting for 33 percent of the homeless population. A significant number of these are women and children fleeing domestic violence."[61] Further, African Americans make up almost half of the homeless, though they are less than 15 percent of the population.[62]

Reproductive justice would include attention to work, social support, and education. Work: A 40-hour workweek with flexible working hours; paid parental leave; a minimum wage that enables a person to pay rent, food, and so forth; excellent and inexpensive family health insurance. Social support: Welfare that is easily accessible and that enables a family to survive; an expanded definition of family, not based on marriage; high-quality affordable daycare; safe affordable housing.[63] Education: High-quality schools; free preschool; school schedules that mimic the 40-hour workweek.

In our society, family is bounded in particular ways, usually biology and marriage. However, as a child of a single mother, my church family was far more important than biological family. Without this network of support, we would not have survived. Rather than rely on charity, our societal structures need to support and empower each person to act.

In whatever field you work, in however you are involved in community, ask: who am I including? Who am I excluding? Work to support the gaps in our society in the civil realm. Advocate for justice in the political realm: call your senators and representatives at state and national level. Participate in your local government. Educate others on issues of racism, classism, and sexism. If you are part of a church, ensure your churches also educate others and treat their workers and members fairly. Reproductive justice requires us to act broadly to ensure each person has the ability to decide whether or not to have a child.

CONCLUSION

Each person should be able to decide whether or not to have (and raise) children. Any policy that prevents a person from having and raising children is an abortive policy. Any policy that enables a person to have and raise children is a policy that supports life. Legalizing abortion has made life safer for some women; however, it has done nothing to enable people to choose to have and raise children safely and healthily. Making abortion illegal again would do nothing to enable people to have and raise children safely and healthily. Activism needs to be focused on providing each human being with the ability and support to choose to have or not to have children through a broad spectrum of issues.

To achieve reproductive justice, we need to:

1. Nest the issue of abortion within the broader issue of reproductive justice.
2. Understand the intersections of race and class with reproduction.
3. To prioritize life, recognize that life continues after birth. Ensure supportive structures are in place enabling each person to raise a child safely and healthily.
4. To prioritize choice, recognize that many people within US society cannot actually make a choice. Ensure supportive structures are in place enabling each person to raise a child safely and healthily.

NOTES

1. The 2010 US Census listed 72% of United Statesians as white, 13% as black, 5% as Asian, 0.9% as Native American; 6% classified themselves as some other race; 3% listed more than one race. In terms of ethnicity, 17% listed themselves as Hispanic. The Pew Forum states that 78.4% of United Statesians are Christian (51% Protestant and 24% Catholic). Sixteen percent are unaffiliated. Next is Judaism at 1.7%.
2. I use the term "black" rather than African American, since the data collected on women through the CDC is separated into white, black, other, and Hispanic.
3. In fact, 2010 data from the CDC estimates the abortion rate to be 8.6 for white women, 31.8 for black women, 18.6 for Hispanic women, and 16 for "other." The overall abortion rate is 14.4. The abortion rate refers to: "number of abortions obtained by women in a given race/ethnicity group per 1,000 women in that same group" (Pazol et al., 31).
4. Laura Briggs's book *How All Politics Became Reproductive Politics* (2017) gives a thorough and detailed examination of the breadth of reproductive politics.
5. Black, womanist, Latino/a, Chicana, Asian American, Native American, and so forth.
6. Feminist liberation theology works against the marginalization of women within and outwith religion.
7. Chandra Mohanty argues that "being a woman has political consequences in the world we live in; that there can be unjust and unfair effects on women depending on our economic and social marginality and/or privilege . . . that sexism, racism, misogyny, and heterosexist underlie and fuel social and political institutions of rule and thus often lead to hatred of women."
8. Asian American women are the most marginalized in the debate, with no data on their abortion-related beliefs or practices.
9. See Threadcraft's excellent book for details, particularly the Introduction.
10. Nelson, *Women of Color and the Reproductive Rights Movement* (New York: New York University Press, 2003). See also Dorothy Roberts, *Killing the Black Body: Race, Reproduction, and the Meaning of Liberty* (New York: Pantheon, 1997).
11. Nelson, 69.
12. Kline, *Bodies of Knowledge: Sexuality, Reproduction, and Women's Health in the Second Wave* (Chicago: University of Chicago Press, 2010), 33.
13. Andrea Smith, "Beyond Pro-Choice Versus Pro-Life: Women of Color and Reproductive Justice," *NWSA Journal*, vol. 17, no. 1 (1995): 42.
14. Nelson, 75.
15. Dorothy Roberts, *Killing the Black Body: Race, Reproduction, and the Meaning of Liberty* (New York: Vintage Press, 93).

16. The Hyde Amendment (1976) restricted federal funding of abortion (Medicaid, for example) to when the "life of the mother would be endangered if the fetus were carried to term" or when pregnancy is "the result of an act of rape or incest." Funding for sterilization, however, continued. 1993 incest and rape added. See: http://www.npr.org/templates/story/story.php?storyId=121402281 for more details.

17. R. Jones and K. Kooistra, "Abortion Incidence and Access to Services in the United States, 2008," *Perspectives in Sexual and Reproductive Health* 43.1 (2011): 46.

18. K. Dugger, "Race Differences in the Determinants of Support for Legalized Abortion," *Social Science Quarterly* 72.3 (1991): 577.

19. Ibid., 579.

20. N. Russo and A. Dabul, "The Relationship of Abortion to Well-Being: Do Race and Religion Make a Difference?" *Professional Psychology: Research and Practice* 28.1 (1997): 30.

21. Dugger, 572.

22. Norsworthy et al. note the legal: "laws vary across and within countries and communities," the social: norms "differ from group to group within countries," and the personal: "who one is; e.g., personal history, beliefs, ethnic/racial/cultural/sexual identity, sense of personal empowerment."

23. Russo and Dabul, 25.

24. J. Chrisler, "Introduction: What Is Reproductive Justice?" in *Reproductive Justice: A Global Concern*, ed. J. Chrisler (Denver: Praeger 2012), 1–2.

25. Smith, 121.

26. Kimala Price, "What Is Reproductive Justice? How Women of Color Activists Are Redefining the Pro-Choice Paradigm,' *Meridians: Feminism, Race, Transnationalism*, 10. 2 (2010): 55.

27. Smith, 121.

28. Nelson, 10.

29. This list is not exclusive. I do not address pregnancy itself, childbirth, or adoption for example.

30. Barbara Gurr, *Reproductive Justice: The Politics of Health Care for Native American Women* (New Brunswick: Rutgers University Press, 2015), 105, 109.

31. Ibid., 110–112 for details of sexual assault care available through the IHS.

32. Ibid., 114)

33. D. Stein, *People Who Count: Population and Politics, Women and Children* (London: Earthscan, 1995), 39–40.

34. Smith, 131–132.

35. So it would provide access to the birth control pill or a condom but not Plan B or some types of IUDs. While churches have been able to do this, now a business can claim "religious beliefs." This business must be "closely held." Closely held means that five or fewer people own more than 50% of the company. That term applies to 90% of US businesses. The insurer can still provide coverage to the employees but cannot charge the business for it.

36. Threadcraft, viii.

37. https://www.washingtonpost.com/news/true-crime/wp/2018/02/08/judge-suggests-drug-addicted-woman-get-sterilized-before-sentencing-and-she-does/?noredirect=on&utm_term=.f4f9159b816a

38. Smith, 130.

39. Ibid. and Rubin and Phillips, 179.

40. https://surrogate.com/about-surrogacy/types-of-surrogacy/what-is-international-surrogacy/ provides a brief overview with links to information about various countries' surrogacy laws.

41. See for example the excellent Radiolab podcast: https://israelstory.org/en/episode/10-birthstory-2/

42. This study controlled for factors such as smoking or drinking, and so forth. Laura Briggs. *How All Politics Became Reproductive Politics: From Welfare Reform to Foreclosure to Trump* (Oakland: University of California Press, 2017), 129.

43. Ibid., 133.

44. Ibid., 131.
45. Ibid.
46. The global South refers to poorer countries within Latin America, Africa, and Asia.
47. Barbara Ehrenreich and Arlie Russell Hoschschild, eds. *Global Woman: Nannies, Maids, and Sex Workers in the New Economy* (New York: Holt Paperbacks, 2004).
48. G. O'Brien, *The Church and Abortion: A Catholic Dissent* (New York: Rowman & Littlefield, 2010), 71–72, citing Exodus 21:22–25.
49. C. Carmichael, *Sex & Religion in the Bible* (New Haven: Yale University Press, 2010).
50. Paul's letters are more complicated. While the letters written by Paul himself focus more on celibacy. Later letters written by others but in Pauls' name return to ideas of marriage and the family. The early church fathers followed more in the tradition of Jesus and Paul by emphasizing celibacy.
51. See Dale Martin's excellent chapter: "Familiar Idolatry and the Christian Case Against Marriage."
52. L. Sjørup, "The Vatican and Women's Reproductive Health and Rights: A Clash of Civilizations?" *Feminist Theology* 21 (1999): 84.
53. Rosemary Ruether, "Women, Reproductive Rights and the Catholic Church," *Feminist Theology*, vol. 16:2, 2008: 187.
54. Gebara, Ivone. *Longing for Running Water: Ecofeminism and Liberation.* (Minneapolis: Fortress Press, 1999), 83.
55. Ibid., 46.
56. Ibid., 2.
57. "A poverty-level wage is defined as an hourly wage which if worked full-time and year-round does not total enough to meet the federal poverty standard for a family of four" (Hinson-Hasty, 3).
58. Ivone Gebara, "The Abortion Debate in Brazil: A Report from an Ecofeminist Philosopher under Siege," *Journal of Feminist Studies in Religion* 11.2 (1995): 131.
59. Norsworthy et al., 62.
60. See Briggs's chapter 2: "Welfare Reform" for details of this negative association and its history (2017).
61. Ross, 88.
62. Ibid.
63. Even mortgages can have an effect on reproductive justice. Some women receive a "baby letter" when applying for a mortgage. "Banks ignore a woman's earnings unless she promises not to have a baby or signs a letter saying that she will continue to work after the birth of a child" (Briggs 207). A male of course does not need to sign such a letter.

REFERENCES

Briggs, Laura. *How All Politics Became Reproductive Politics: From Welfare Reform to Foreclosure to Trump.* Oakland: University of California Press, 2017.
Carmichael, C. *Sex & Religion in the Bible.* New Haven: Yale University Press, 2010.
Chrisler, J. "Introduction: What Is Reproductive Justice?," in *Reproductive Justice: A Global Concern.* ed. J. Chrisler. Denver: Praeger, 2012, 1–10.
Cooper, Thia. *A Christian Guide to Liberating Desire, Sex, Partnership, Work and Reproduction.* New York: Palgrave Pivot, 2017.
Dugger, K. "Race Differences in the Determinants of Support for Legalized Abortion." *Social Science Quarterly* 72.3 1991, 570–587.
Ehrenreich, Barbara, and Arlie Russell Hoschschild, eds.. *Global Woman: Nannies, Maids, and Sex Workers in the New Economy.* New York: Holt Paperbacks, 2004.
Gebara, Ivone. *Longing for Running Water: Ecofeminism and Liberation.* Minneapolis: Fortress Press, 1999.
———. "The Abortion Debate in Brazil: A Report from an Ecofeminist Philosopher under Siege," *Journal of Feminist Studies in Religion*, 11, no 2, 1995, 129–135.

Gurr, Barbara. *Reproductive Justice: The Politics of Health Care for Native American Women.* New Brunswick: Rutgers University Press, 2015.

Harrison, Beverly Wildung. *Justice in the Making: Feminist Social Ethics.* Louisville: Westminster John Knox Press, 2004.

Hinson-Hasty, Elizabeth. "For Workers." In *To Do Justice: A Guide for Progressive Christians,* eds. Rebecca Todd Peters and Elizabeth Hinson-Hasty. Louisville: Westminster John Knox Press, 2008, 2–11.

Jones, R., and K. Kooistra. "Abortion Incidence and Access to Services in the United States, 2008," *Perspectives on Sexual and Reproductive Health,* Volume 43, Issue 1, 2011, 41–50. https://www.guttmacher.org/pubs/journals/4304111.pdf, accessed September 1, 2014.

Kline, W. *Bodies of Knowledge: Sexuality, Reproduction, and Women's Health in the Second Wave.* Chicago: University of Chicago Press, 2010.

Martin, Dale. "Familiar Idolatry and the Christian Case Against Marriage." In *Sexuality and the Sacred: Sources for Theological Reflection,* second edition, eds. Marvin M. Ellison and Kelly Brown Douglas. Louisville: Westminster John Knox Press, 2010, 412–436.

Mohanty, C. *Feminism without Borders: Decolonizing Theory, Practicing Solidarity.* Durham: Duke University Press, 2003.

Nelson, J. *Women of Color and the Reproductive Rights Movement.* New York: New York University Press, 2003.

Norsworthy, K., M. McLaren, and L. Waterfield. "Women's Power in Relationships: A Matter of Social Justice." In *Reproductive Justice: A Global Concern,* ed., J. Chrisler. Denver: Praeger, 2012, 57–75.

O'Brien, G. *The Church and Abortion: A Catholic Dissent.* Lanham, MD: Rowman & Littlefield, 2010.

Pazol, K. et al. "Abortion Surveillance—United States, 2010," in *Surveillance Summaries,* 2010.

Price, Kimala. "What Is Reproductive Justice? How Women of Color Activists Are Redefining the Pro-Choice Paradigm," *Meridians: Feminism, Race, Transnationalism.* 10. 2, 2010: 42–65.

Pope Paul VI. *Gaudium et Spes,* 1965. http://www.vatican.va/archive/hist_councils/ii_vatican_council/documents/vat-ii_cons_19651207_gaudium-et-spes_en.html, accessed September 3, 2014.

Roberts, Dorothy. *Killing the Black Body: Race, Reproduction and the Meaning of Liberty.* New York: Vintage Press, 1997.

Ross, Rosetta. "For People Lacking Affordable Housing." In *To Do Justice: A Guide for Progressive Christians,* eds. Rebecca Todd Peters and Elizabeth Hinson-Hasty. Louisville: Westminster John Knox Press, 2008, 85–96.

Rubin, L. and A. Phillips. "Infertility and Assisted Reproductive Technologies: Matters of Reproductive Justice," in *Reproductive Justice: A Global Concern,* ed., J. Chrisler. Denver: Praeger, 2012, 173–199.

Ruether, Rosemary. "Women, Reproductive Rights and the Catholic Church," *Feminist Theology,* vol. 16:2, 2008: 184–93.

Russo, N., and A. Dabul. "The Relationship of Abortion to Well-Being: Do Race and Religion Make a Difference?" *Professional Psychology: Research and Practice,* vol. 28, no. 1, 1997: 23–31.

Sistersong. *Reproductive Justice.* https://www.sistersong.net/reproductive-justice/ Accessed August 1, 2018.

Sjørup, L. "The Vatican and Women's Reproductive Health and Rights: A Clash of Civilizations?" *Feminist Theology,* vol. 21, 1999: 79–97.

Smith, Andrea. "Beyond Pro-Choice Versus Pro-Life: Women of Color and Reproductive Justice," *NWSA Journal,* vol. 17, no. 1, 2005.

_____. "Women of Color and Reproductive Choice: Combating the Population Paradigm," *Journal of Feminist Studies in Religion,* vol. 11, no. 2, 1995: 39–66.

Stein, D. *People Who Count: Population and Politics, Women and Children.* London: Earthscan, 1995.

Threadcraft, Shatema. *Intimate Justice: The Black Female Body and the Body Politic.* Oxford: Oxford University Press, 2016.

III

Militarism and Resistance to State Violence

Chapter Eleven

Why Resistance Fails?

Olli-Pekka Vainio

While the last century witnessed the rise of various revolutions and resistance movements, many of those had a poor track record. Some of them failed to instantiate reasonable alternatives; sometimes the alternatives were unstable, and the result was even worse than the state that was originally rebelled against. Yet sometimes, the revolutions were successful. As an Eastern European scholar, I have witnessed these movements through my own family history and the history of my home country, Finland.

In this chapter, I offer insights from political history and cognitive sciences on why resistance often fails to achieve its goals and why, as the saying goes, revolutions devour their own children. I will use especially the Polish philosopher Leszek Kolakowski's accounts of the problems of Marxism to offer eyewitness reports on what went wrong in the socialist revolution. Then, I will link Kolakowski's insights to theorization within contemporary cognitive science on cognitive biases that inhibit morally virtuous behavior. This opens up a way to see how a certain type of behavior is natural for humans, but ultimately detrimental to human flourishing. Negatively, this enables us to see which forms of behavior are necessary (but not sufficient) to the flourishing of human societies.

REVOLUTIONS IN THE EAST

This year marks the 100-year anniversary of bloody and traumatic Civil War in Finland that lasted from January to May in 1918.[1] The so-called Reds, backed by Russian Bolsheviks, tried to overthrow the government but the rebellion was ultimately crushed by the "Whites." Behind the uprising was a legitimate concern about the rights of the workers. The protest soon escalated to senseless violence, and in the end-stage prison camps were established to detain the captured Reds, many of which were executed without a proper trial. The total death count of both sides was approximately 37,000. By all accounts, the Finnish Civil War was a failed revolution. Even if essential sociopolitical changes were introduced after the war, we have good reason to believe that the same goals could have been achieved without the bloodshed. In fact, many progressive laws were already processed by the congress when the rebellion started to spiral out of control.[2]

Some decades before the civil war, when Finland was still part of the Russian Empire, there emerged a different kind of revolutionary movement, which was more successful. Finland was occupied by Russia in 1809 (before this Finland had been part of Sweden) but it was given autonomous status as Grand Duchy of Finland, with its own language, religion (Lutheranism), currency, and local government. Russia tried to take away this special status during the Time of Oppression in 1899–1917. During these years of Russification, my great-great-grandfather with his whole family were imprisoned because he was active in the resistance movement, which mostly involved printing journals and giving speeches. Like many others who had stood up to oppression, they were exported to Siberia. Luckily, the sentence was removed when the political climate changed and the whole family made it back alive to Finland. This revolution, which eventually (even if slowly) led to Finnish independence in 1917, was a success.

It is obvious that all historical situations are unique and establishing universal rules for failure or success is not easy or even recommendable. However, what seems to have helped the Finnish independence movement was the fact that basically everyone within the borders of Finland (minus the collaborators, who benefited from the Russian presence) supported the independence or, in the earliest stages, the continuation of autonomous state and ending of the acts of oppression. There was no need for internal quarrel since it was clear where the enemy was. Moreover, Russia had perpetrated horrendous acts of violence during the Great Hatred (1714–1721), and the atrocities were still remembered by the population.[3] This is where the situation in the Civil War differed from the independence movement as it mobilized significant numbers of people to act in opposition with each other.

This historical anecdote is supposed to set a stage for more contemporary revolutions. The downfall of European fascism in Germany and Italy in the aftermath of the Second World War enabled a new kind of socialist presence in Europe, especially in the countries occupied by Russia. Ironically, this victory over Nazism, as important as it was, enabled an even more appalling ideology to rise to power. Today we know that the ethical differences between Nazism and Socialism were to a large extent merely semantic. While Nazism never succeeded to reach similar levels of oppression as Socialism, it was, according to Hannah Arendt, developing in the same direction but this was luckily interrupted by the Allies.[4]

In the end, also Socialism failed, but only after tens of millions of human lives were sacrificed for this inhuman experiment. But why did it fail? Many of the goals of the Karl Marx's philosophy were good and the motivation behind the movement was respectable. Few people would deny that things like the freedom from oppression and fairness should not be among the goods that any human society should strive for. But apparently mere good intentions and will to change the world for the better is not enough, and often the results seem to be exactly the opposite.

One interesting story provided by Alexander Solzhenitsyn in *The Gulag Archipelago* reports unbelievable events in the socialist utopia where the will to promote a good cause had turned on its head. I will quote him in length.

> At the conclusion of the conference, a tribute to Comrade Stalin was called for. Of course, everyone stood up (just as everyone had leaped to his feet during the conference at every mention of his name). . . . For three minutes, four minutes, five minutes, the stormy applause, rising to an ovation, continued. But palms were getting sore and raised arms were already aching. And the older people were panting from exhaustion. It was becoming insufferably silly even to those who really adored Stalin.
>
> However, who would dare to be the first to stop? . . . After all, NKVD men were standing in the hall applauding and watching to see who would quit first! And in the obscure, small hall, unknown to the leader, the applause went on— six, seven, eight minutes! They were done for! Their goose was cooked! They couldn't stop now till they collapsed with heart attacks! At the rear of the hall, which was crowded, they could of course cheat a bit, clap less frequently, less vigorously, not so eagerly—but up there with the presidium where everyone could see them?
>
> The director of the local paper factory, an independent and strong-minded man, stood with the presidium. Aware of all the falsity and all the impossibility of the situation, he still kept on applauding! Nine minutes! Ten! In anguish he watched the secretary of the District Party Committee, but the latter dared not stop. Insanity! To the last man! With make-believe enthusiasm on their faces, looking at each other with faint hope, the district leaders were just going to go on and on applauding till they fell where they stood, till they were carried out of the hall on stretchers! And even then those who were left would not falter. . . .
>
> Then, after eleven minutes, the director of the paper factory assumed a businesslike expression and sat down in his seat. And, oh, a miracle took place! Where had the universal, uninhibited, indescribable enthusiasm gone? To a man, everyone else stopped dead and sat down. They had been saved!

> The squirrel had been smart enough to jump off his revolving wheel. That, however, was how they discovered who the independent people were. And that was how they went about eliminating them. That same night the factory director was arrested. They easily pasted ten years on him on the pretext of something quite different. But after he had signed Form 206, the final document of the interrogation, his interrogator reminded him: "Don't ever be the first to stop applauding."[5]

Here Solzhenitsyn depicts a common scene (several similar occasions are known to historians) where people had become so afraid of the system, which originally was supposed to be a force for the good, that they were willing to put up with blatantly irrational behavior. What is perhaps most intriguing about this is that while the original Marxist thought underlined critical thinking, it soon succumbed to the worst kind of groupthink that made any successful criticism (even being the first to stop applauding was taken as criticism!) virtually impossible.

MEANWHILE IN POLAND

Today, the crimes of Communism are well-reported and analyzed.[6] While Solzhenitsyn has provided detailed accounts of the horrors of Stalinist Russia, Hannah Arendt has offered insightful philosophical critiques of imperialist and totalitarian movements of the 20th century. I wish to concentrate on another similar thinker, who is less well-known in the West despite his remarkable career as a philosopher and historian of thought.

Lezsek Kolakowski (1927–2009) was a staunch socialist in his youth and he served for years as the chair in philosophy at the University Warsaw. In the 1950s he made trips to the Soviet Union that opened his eyes to the reality of socialist dream. After his visits, he started to criticize Marxism from the inside. At first, he did not abandon Marxism but tried to develop a humanist form of Marxism. These essays and talks were published in English in the collection *Marxism and Beyond*.[7] However, this proved to be too much for the party elite, who expelled him from the Polish United Workers' Party in 1966. Eventually, he escaped Poland in 1968 and ended up in UK, where he became Fellow of All Souls College in Oxford. He became known as a prolific writer and a historian of thought who analyzed the events and ideas of the 20th century with soul and wit.

While he first tried to save Marxism, he relatively soon abandoned this idea.[8] Here I will not examine his constructive political thought as this would be beyond the scope of this article. Instead, I refer my reader to read his own brief but insightful account "How to be a Conservative-Liberal Socialist. A Credo."[9] Here I focus on his accounts of Marxist thought and praxis as it is described in his works. I will not asses to which extent the following patterns of thought are explicitly supported by the Marxist though as this would be too onerous and not exactly relevant considering the aims of this chapter.[10] Instead, I take Kolakowski's accounts of the Marxist state of mind as they appear in his writings. Also, it is perhaps good to mention that the following claims do not represent everything that Marxist philosophy claims. Kolakowski is pretty clear that these forms of thought express what were the behavioral patterns that destroyed the system, and it goes without saying that similar features can be found from opposite movements as well (he offers similar critiques of the Right, too). For the sake of brevity, I have formulated some of them in a concise form as follows:

The Relationships between Us and Them

> We live in a surrounded fortress and outside its wall are only enemies. Compromise is never possible.[11]

> "We" cannot be accused of anything. "Them" should be accused of everything. If we fail, it is because we have not been unable to implement our ideology fully and there are remnants of wrong ideology in our thinking, which calls for more ideological purification. Even failure is not argument for the superiority of our ideology.[12]

> Everything that is wrong in the society is attributed to the enemies.[13]

> The enemies of the ideology do not get anything right. We get everything right.[14]

On Truth and Ideology

> Truth is one and totally in our possession. Within our ranks there exists no disagreement, or different interpretations. Ideological purity is guarded to the extreme. If disagreement is voiced, this is evidence that the person has joined the enemy.[15]

> The end justifies the means. A lie is not a lie and a murder is not a murder if the intention is good. The values are not objective but situational, which allows double standards.[16]

> The question of truth is outdated and even harmful. Truth is what we want to be true. Truth is not what the world and its mechanism are really like, but our ideal picture of the world in its perfect state.[17]

On Simplicity

> Complex problems are treated with a simplistic answer. No matter what problems arise, the answer is always the one and same. The logic and grounds of this answer can never be questioned.[18]

On Not Answering the Critics

> Criticism is met not with arguments and discussion but with shaming the opponents.[19]

> Ideology should never be argued for using rational and public arguments. It is enough to show why the enemies are wrong.[20]

COGNITIVE BIASES STRIKE BACK

What is interesting about Kolakowski's accounts is that several of the aforementioned claims latch on nicely with some typical cognitive biases. Cognitive biases are thought patterns that make our thinking fast and frugal. We need biases to think effectively.[21] However, sometimes they harm us when they are used in a wrong context.[22] On the one hand, they help us to succeed and reach our goals, but if they are not tended carefully they will corrupt our thinking and behavior. It must also be noted that biases do not care whether our goals are ethical or not; they are merely interested in our survival, which taken as the ultimate value quickly becomes a destructive force. As Kolakowski states: "But the very conditions which facilitate the seizing of power make it particularly difficult to hold on to it in the long run."[23]

In this section I will list some typical biases that resonate with what Kolakowski describes as the errors in the Marxist praxis. As we know, it is natural for humans to form groups. Some theorists suggest that this group-forming feature of human societies was introduced through particularly efficient forms of religious rituals. Religious rituals enabled effective forms of social grouping behavior that were conducive for the survival of these communities.[24] But this need for group forming is not tied to explicitly religious behavior alone. We humans are naturally "groupish" and there are several biases that cherish groupish behavior.[25] For starters, a group needs a neatly defined set of beliefs that are easily communicated to the members or rituals that successfully tie the group together. These beliefs and rituals do not need to make absolute sense; it is enough that they offer some plausibility and are recognized to some extent as effective.[26] Almost automatically, this group formation creates a distinction between "us" and "them." It becomes very important to recognize who is with us and who is against us. Obviously, this is a depiction of a group that exists in some sense in a primitive state. But apparently our distance from our ancestors is not as great as we would like to think. When groups and ideas are in competition, we tend to resort to the primitive ways of thinking.

In these kinds of contexts, we tend to prefer beliefs that are simple. This is known as *simplicity bias*: we favor the solutions that appear to us simple even if the problem that they are supposed to solve is highly complicated. We also tend to cherish this sense of simplicity through *confirmation bias*. We invest most of our time in practices that enforce our beliefs. If we are faced with conflicting evidence, we neglect it.[27] We even tend to cling to our beliefs even after it has been conclusively demonstrated to us that they are false, or even fabricated precisely in order to fool us. This is called *belief perseverance bias*.[28]

When belief perseverance bias runs rampant, it creates, together with our groupish tendencies, the phenomenon known as *groupthink*. It does not help the situation if there are only a few dissenters in the group. If the person who finds him- or herself in a minority realizes this, he or she tends to shift toward the majority.[29] If belief uniformity is enforced, the group becomes homogenous, and unable even to think that they might be wrong, or that maybe their critics are on to something. Since facts can't falter our convictions, this inevitably leads to naive and blind ideological commitment.[30]

To sum up: various cognitive biases make it very hard to form a large-scale consensus or compromise and very easy to split people into friends and enemies. These same biases also make it difficult for us to form stable and inclusive communities in times of crises because the more prevalent the sense of danger is or more burning the issue seems, we start almost automatically and without any deeper consideration to weed out the heretics and critics (this human feature is of course taken advantage of by the totalitarian leaders). This explains why it is not uncommon for revolutionaries to turn against each other.

BLAMING THE VICTIM?

But is this what I have said just an elaborate way of blaming the victim? During the recent political upheavals in the USA, there has been discussion about "civility" in relation to protests and demands for societal change. Writing for *The Atlantic*, journalist Vann R. New Kirk II claims that demands of civility "are rooted more in preserving the status quo than in addressing ongoing harms and violence" and that "[c]ivility is the sleep-aid of a majority inclined to ignore the violence done in its name [. . .]."[31]

In another article, Newkirk argues that Barack Obama's conciliatory tone fails to take seriously the challenge of Trump and the rise of "ethnonationalism."[32] Effectively, Obama's carefully considered words that aim to de-escalate the crisis will prove ultimately beneficial not for the subaltern groups but for the alt-right cohorts because they do not play fair. Newkirk claims, rightly to my judgment, that "What Trump understands innately is that power is the most real institution, and that with it, most of the others can be disposed." Are we, then, obliged to bargain our values, if they are not recognized or followed by our adversaries?

Notably, the movement toward liberation in, for example, the USA and South Africa has involved not only "careful debate" but also "shame, dispossession, and outright violence." Here Newkirk walks a fine line, and he recognizes it. While admitting that the walk toward freedom has often been violent, he puts his finger into a real problem: "[t]he real consideration for people in the developing world, for youth in South Africa, and for those in danger of political strongmen and ethnonationalism is how to gain that power in an ethical way without repeating the sins of oppressors." At the very point when incivility and even violence become legitimate political tools, we also risk being formed into the image of our adversaries.

BUILDING BRIDGES IN A BROKEN WORLD

I do not wish to deny that sometimes societal changes require measures that are disruptive. However, there is a difference between transgression of civility in the form of legitimate protests and the acts that effectively corrupt democratic ideals. What are these ideals? For example, Jeffrey Stout lists the following principles:

Ability to listen with an open mind
Temperance to avoid taking and causing offense needlessly
The practical wisdom to discern the subtleties of a discursive situation
The courage to speak candidly
The tact to avoid sanctimonious cant
The poise to respond to unexpected arguments
The humility to ask forgiveness from those who have been wronged [33]

While granting the right for disruptive behavior, it needs to be asked whether the behavior ultimately embodies these ideals or whether it makes achieving them harder for me and my peers—and also for adversaries. [34] But choosing this option requires going against our natural tendencies that enhance our trust in our own judgment and make it hard to think that I might be wrong. It is damn hard. [35]

In a recent *New York Times* column, David Brooks notes how our social imagination can be split into two worlds, to the one of myth and to the one of parable. [36] Myth are more inimical to pre- or non-Christian societies, while parables are linked to Judeo-Christian societies (he does admit that this is a rough sketch). Parables are often concerned about the inner states of the characters, not external combat. In parables, "[c]haracters are presented with a moral dilemma or a moral occasion, and the key question is whether they express charity, faithfulness, forgiveness, commitment and love." Myths instead take place in "perilous realm" and their "competitive" virtues are different: "strength, toughness, prowess, righteous indignation, and the capacity to smite your foes and win eternal fame." Brooks argues, convincingly, I think, that contemporary mainstream movies and videogames are through and through mythical.[37] He then offers a word of warning:

> There are many virtues to the mythic worldview—to stand heroically for justice, to be loyal to friends and fierce against foes. But history does offer some sobering lessons about societies that relied too heavily on the competitive virtues. They tend to give short shrift to relationships, which depend on the fragile, intimate bonds of vulnerability, trust, compassion and selfless love. They tend to see life as an eternal competition between warring tribes. They tend to see the line between good and evil as running between groups, not, as in parable, down the middle of every human heart.[38]

Brooks's remarks about the popular culture, which, without a doubt, effectively forms our social imagination are connected with more theoretical currents in political philosophy. Many recent political theories of resistance are built upon the demand of ideological purity. In one of his essays, Kolakowski calls this "consistency."[39] People generally think that consistency is a good thing but often being consistent leads to deeply problematic results. For example, battles fought by consistent soldiers will only end when the other side has been completely wiped off from the face of the earth. Total consistency becomes easily tantamount to fanaticism and intolerance. But the world of values is not consistent. Kolakowski came to recognize that there are values cherished by "the others" and these were real values, which everyone should be able to recognize as such. Failure to recognize this leads to overemphasizing some values (which are real and important) that eventually corrupts these values. In virtue theory, this is known as the unity of virtues thesis: all individual virtues need to be balanced with other virtues lest they become vices. Kolakowski describes this mindset:

> Inconsistency is simply a secret awareness of the contradictions of this world. By contradictions I mean the various values that are, notoriously throughout history, introduced into society by mutually antagonistic forces. If convictions of the absolute and exclusive superiority of a given value to which all else is subordinate were to spread and be practiced widely, they would of necessity transform the world into an ever-larger battleground—which indeed does occur from time to time. The lack of consistency checks this tendency. Inconsistency as an individual attitude is merely a consciously sustained reserve of

uncertainty, a permanent feeling of possible personal error, or if not that, then of the possibility that one's antagonist is right.[40]

However, Kolakowski does not follow the father of virtue theories, Aristotle, in claiming that we should find a mediating golden mean between the vices. He argues that in the real world this often cannot be done. The antinomies of values are irreducible.[41]

> My praise of inconsistency, however, springs from a completely different source. It posits that contradictions in values do not stem from their abuse and therefore are not merely appearances that can be overcome by intelligent moderation. These contradictions inhere in the world of values and cannot be reconciled in any synthesis. Reasonable inconsistency does not seek to forge a synthesis between extremes, knowing it does not exist, since values as such exclude each other integrally. The real world of values is inconsistent; that is to say, it is made up of antagonistic elements. To grant them full recognition simultaneously is impossible, yet each demands total acceptance. This is not a matter of logical contradictions, because values are not theoretical theses. It is a contradiction which lies at the heart of human behavior. Inconsistency is thus a certain attitude which, having realized that this is the situation, knows the extremes to be irreconcilable yet refuses to reject either because it recognizes each as valid.[42]

Finally, I would like to return to the stories from where I started. Soon after the Civil War, Finland had to defend its borders against Russian invasion during the years of the Second World War in 1939–1944. The sons of the families, who had been on the opposite sides in the Civil War now shared same trenches facing a common enemy.[43] We can only imagine the complexity of the situation and internal struggles these men had to go through. Nonetheless, the extreme situation contributed to the conciliation between the Red and White families. The wounds never fully healed, for sure, but small steps of trust were taken during these dark, long and cold winters. While we still wrestle with the memories of the wars, we were offered a better way of cooperation. The flourishing of our small country today, is a proof that many followed this way, even if in imperfect, human, manner.

Contemporary human being is an evolutionary product of the dialectics of trust and competition. For human communities to flourish it is imperative to build relationships of trust among differing societal groups so that our competitive attitudes are kept in check. The larger the community, the more difficult this becomes—and it also becomes more important since the stakes also become higher as more people are influenced by the public policies. This is why those who resist need to understand clearly the task they are undertaking so that they do not make things even worse, which in this broken world is always a real possibility.

Why resistance fails? In one his essays Martin Luther King Jr. wrote: "There is some good in the worst of us and some evil in the best of us."[44] Resistance fails when it denies the first claim and forgets the latter.

NOTES

1. A concise introduction to the history of Finland is (Meinander 2014).
2. One reason for this was probably the claims made in *The Communist Manifesto* (1848) according to which true change cannot come through slow progress and incremental reforms but only through a revolution.
3. However, it must be noted that the 19th century was not all bad and the connections to Russia were in many ways beneficial to us.
4. Arendt 1973; see also Kolakowski 2012, 27.
5. Solzhenitsyn 1973, 69–70.
6. The words socialism and communist do not mean exactly the same thing. Typically, communism is taken to be a more extreme form of socialism, where the party, instead of the collective, is in charge. However, in the 20th century basically all socialist systems developed into communist-like societies. In this essay, I use "socialism" and "Marxism" interchangeably, and "communism" to refer to those systems that identified themselves as communist. See also Courtois 1999.
7. Kolakowski 1971.
8. See his preface to 1971 edition of *Marxism and Beyond*.
9. Kolakowski 1978.
10. This is something that Kolakowski did in his three-volume *The Main Currents of Marxism*.
11. Kolakowski 2012, 9.
12. Ibid.
13. Ibid.
14. Ibid.
15. Kolakowski 2012, 16–18.
16. Kolakowski 2012, 14; 1971, 229.
17. Kolakowski 2012, 56–59; 1971, 59–87.
18. Kolakowski 2012, 126.
19. Kolakowski 2012, 20–24.
20. Notably, in Marxist thought everything that was deemed to be Marxist was called "science." Everything that was not Marxist was called "ideology." See especially Kolakowski's essay "Permanent vs. Transitory Aspects of Marxism" in Kolakowski 1971. This is what George Orwell was referring to with his concept of "Newspeak" in his novel *1984*.
21. Gigerenzer 2006; Stanovich 2011.
22. Kahneman 2011.
23. Kolakowski 2012, 11.
24. Norenzayan 2013; Sosis and Bressler 2003.
25. Haidt 2012.
26. Whitehouse 2004.
27. Harman 2004.
28. Anderson, Lepper, and Ross 1980.
29. Moscovici and Zavalloni 1969; Kruglanski 2006.
30. Hart 1994.
31. Newkirk 2018b.
32. Newkirk 2018a.
33. Stout 2004, 85; see also Langerak 2014.
34. A concrete example of this is Daryl Davis, a black man, who hangs out with and befriends Ku Klux Klan members. https://www.npr.org/2017/08/20/544861933/how-one-man-convinced-200-ku-klux-klan-members-to-give-up-their-robes?t=1533279457516

35. What makes achieving this even harder, is that the masses do not care about the mediating and conciliatory attitudes. In the recent research about the social media behavioral patterns, it was found that posts that tend to understand the differing viewpoints are less popular than posts supporting one-sided or extreme views (Garimella 2018).

36. Brooks 2018.

37. He mentions especially popular Avengers movies, which fit this description perfectly. However, there are movies like *Three Billboards outside Ebbington, Missouri* (2017), which offer more nuanced characters but movies like these hardly can be described as mainstream. He does not mention perhaps the most obvious trend, which is the popularity of zombies. As enemies, they are inhuman and irrational (by definition, zombie is an entity that has only will but no reason), controlled by outside force or power, and their only goal is to devour you or to turn everyone else into zombies. They cannot be reasoned with and the only way to stop them is to stab or shoot them in the head.

38. Ibid.

39. Kolakowski 1971, 228.

40. Kolakowski 1971, 231.

41. Kolakowski (1971, 236) notes that inconsistency cannot be absolute. "Elementary situations," like "open aggression, genocide, torture [and] mistreatment of defenseless," should always be resisted, no matter what the circumstances are.

42. Kolakowski 1971, 233.

43. At that time, Finland did not have female soldiers. However, female volunteers served actively in all nonarmed branches of the military.

44. King 2015, 63.

REFERENCES

Anderson, Craig A., Mark R. Lepper, and Lee Ross. "Perseverance of Social Theories: The Role of Explanation in the Persistence of Discredited Information." *Journal of Personality and Social Psychology* 39 (6): 1037–49, 1980.

Arendt, Hannah. *The Origins of Totalitarianism*. New York: Harcout, Brace, Jovanovich, 1973.

Brooks, David. "The Fourth Great Awakening." *New York Times*, 2018 (June 21). https://www.nytimes.com/2018/06/21/opinion/marvel-video-games-religion.html

Courtois, Stephane, et al. *The Black Book of Communism: Crimes, Terror, Repression*. Cambridge, MA: Harvard University Press, 1999.

Garimella, Kiran. "Quantifying Controversy on Social Media." *ACM Transactions on Social Computing* 1 (1), 2018.

Gigerenzer, Gerd. "Bounded and Rational." In *Contemporary Debates in Cognitive Science*, edited by Robert T. Stainton. Oxford: Wiley-Blackwell, 2006.

Haidt, Jonathan. *The Righteous Mind. Why Good People Are Divided by Politics and Religion*. London: Allen Lane, 2012.

Harman, Gilbert. "Practical Aspects of Theoretical Reasoning." In *The Oxford Handbook of Rationality*, edited by Alfred E. Mele and Piers Rawling, 45–56. Oxford: Oxford University Press, 2004.

Hart, Paul T. *Groupthink in Government: A Study of Small Groups and Policy Failure*. Baltimore: Johns Hopkins University Press, 1994.

Kahneman, Daniel. *Thinking, Fast and Slow*. London: Allen Lane, 2011.

King, Martin Luther. *The Radical King*, edited by Cornel West. Boston: Beacon, 2015.

Kolakowski, Leszek. *Marxism and Beyond*. London: Paladin, 1971.

———. "How to Be a Conservative-Liberal Socialist: A Credo." *Encounter* (1978), 46–49.

———. *Is God Happy? Selected Essays*. London: Penguin, 2012.

Kruglanski, Arie W. "Groups as Epistemic Providers: Need for Closure and the Unfolding of Group-Centrism." *Psychological Review* (2006) 113: 84–100.

Langerak, Edward. *Civil Disagreement: Personal Integrity in a Pluralistic Society*. Washington, DC: Georgetown University Press, 2014.

Meinander, Henrik. *History of Finland*. Oxford: Oxford University Press, 2014.

Moscovici, Serge, and Marisa Zavalloni. "The Group as a Polarizer of Attitudes." *Journal of Personality and Social Psychology* (1969) 12 (2): 125–35.
Newkirk, Vann R. II. "Barack Obama Still Doesn't Understand Donald Trump." *The Atlantic*, 2018a. https://www.theatlantic.com/politics/archive/2018/07/barack-obama-donald-trump-nationalism/565724/
———"Protest Isn't Civil." *The Atlantic*, 2018b. https://www.theatlantic.com/politics/archive/2018/06/the-civility-instinct/563978/.
Norenzayan, Ara. *Big Gods: How Religion Transformed Cooperation and Conflict*. Princeton: Princeton University Press, 2013.
Solzhenitsyn, Alexander I. *The Gulag Archipelago*. New York: Harper & Row, 1973.
Sosis, Richard, and Eric R. Bressler. "Cooperation and Commune Longevity: A Test of the Costly Signaling Theory of Religion." *Cross-Cultural Research* (2003) 37: 211–39.
Stanovich, Keith. *Rationality and Reflective Mind*. Oxford: Oxford University Press, 2011.
Stout, Jeffrey. *Democracy and Tradition*. Princeton: Princeton University Press, 2004.
Whitehouse, Harvey. *Modes of Religiosity: A Cognitive Theory of Religious Transmission*. Walnut Creek, CA: Altamira, 2004.

Chapter Twelve

Homeland Theology?

*Decolonizing Christianity
and the Task of Public Theology*

Hille Haker

THE TASK OF DECOLONIZING CHRISTIANITY

Every time I cross the border to the United States, I thank God that I am a legal immigrant, white, and citizen of the European Union, Germany. Every time my fingerprints and photo are taken, I wonder where these data go, and whether I have a right to ask. To be sure, I never do, because it could mean that I complicate matters with the immigration officer who might have a bad day and "choose me" to be questioned, to be held indeterminately under the rules of Homeland Security. Others are not so lucky. They are not traveling like I do, but rather fleeing from one place to another. They may flee from violence, war, or poverty, ending up at the border between Mexico and the United States, or between Libya and the European Union. There, they are welcomed with a security system that has but one goal: to prevent them from entering the United States or the European Union in a way that the laws determine to be illegal. With almost 70 million people on the move worldwide, the evermore sophisticated technologies of surveillance and the militarization of borders in the United States and in Europe are laughable efforts to keep the migrants, refugees, and asylum seekers out, but these measures are legitimized politically and legally, and increasingly morally justified in the name of national security on the one hand, and cultural identities on the other. What is often called the "refugee crisis" or "migration crisis," is in fact a crisis of *responsibility*, caused by the amnesia in the United States and Europe about the impact its policies have had on the countries people flee from, and due to the indifference toward the suffering of people who literally risk their lives to find security, freedom, and well-being in the countries who claim to protect and promote exactly these human rights for everyone.[1] When it comes to the cultural and national identities of Northern America and Europe, Christianity plays a central role. Its heritage must be defended, we hear. Its values must be defended, we hear. In Hungary, Poland, and the United States, among other countries, national populism is so intertwined with Christianity that no Christian, and certainly no Christian theologian, can look the other way.

The task of "decolonizing" Christian political theology requires one to critically examine the history and the terms we often uncritically use to describe Christian values or the "Christian culture." Its aim is to counter the narrative of the "threatened" culture of Christianity that is promoted today as part of a political agenda; it critically remembers the often-forgotten chapters of Christian history that question the reemerging glorious imagery of the "Christian heritage" in Europe and the United States. Christianity's "culture of life," protecting especially the unborn life, is held against the "culture of death," as Pope John Paul II and Pope Benedict often labeled the modern secular societies. With such a stark juxtaposition, Christianity's own "culture of death" is vastly ignored: the abuse of children in Catholic orphanages, the sexual abuse of minors by Catholic priests, the financial corruption of the Vatican's bank—these structural sins must all be ignored,[2] just as the denial of access of lay men and women to the ecclesial governance structures. Historically speaking, the blending of Protestantism and Capitalism in the United States, analyzed by Max Weber, must be forgotten; pogroms against Jews in the name of Christianity are also not a part of the "culture of life." The lack of resistance against Germany's "Final Solution" under Hitler's dictatorship, killing six million Jews in Europe, are silently "forgotten" in the narrative that depicts the glorious past of the "Christian heritage" in Europe. And the fact that in the "Western" countries, white Christians and the all-male Catholic cleric still act as the "masters" of Christianity remains unacknowledged. Decolonizing the political theology of Christianity unmasks these narratives that shape the current public imagery Christians promote. I believe that the effort to "decolonize" the underlying political theology (or theologies) of Christianity has two sides: the one is the claim by the colonized people to finally be included in the Christian narrative, often holding the mirror at the white Western Christianity; the other is the acknowledgment of how thoroughly Christianity has been entangled with the history of colonization, ultimately leading to the current trope of the defense of the "homeland," echoed in what I call a "homeland theology" which is retrieving a tradition of violence that no public theology can ignore.

THE AMBIGUITY OF CHRISTIAN PUBLIC THEOLOGIES

Modern democracies promised to give everyone a voice in matters concerning all, and to hold those who represent the citizens of a polity accountable. The cosmopolitan vision, from its beginning in the 19th century the main target of nationalism and often functioning as dog whistle for anti-semitism, takes this thought one step further, striving to limit the power of nation-states.[3] After World War II and in view of the victims of the war, the Shoah, and the atom bombs, the international response to the "eclipse of reason" (Horkheimer) began as a "never again" movement that was transformed into the ethics of human rights, the universal ethics in the name of human dignity, independent of sex, race, class, or religion, and a cosmopolitan vision for international politics.[4] The Catholic Church only hesitantly learned not to fear this ethics (and still fears women's rights as human rights), but Catholic and Christian theologians certainly have contributed to its interpretation over the last decades.

Freedom, equality, and solidarity have long been the core values of modern societies, and they define human rights as equal rights to freedom and well-being of all, which need to be respected, protected, and fulfilled.[5] Furthermore, because of the de facto asymmetries of power, social positions, and access to social goods, however, struggles for recognition as well as struggles for rights are an inherent part of civil and political activism.[6] Invoking the universality of rights, groups over time have forced those who de facto determine the interpretation of human rights to expand the material concept as well as the subjects of rights. Solidarity matters both as solidarity *among* the disenfranchised and *with* them by their allies. Religious groups, too, engage in struggles for recognition, demanding respect of their religious freedom rights when they are not granted by states or other social groups, or fighting for exemptions from (secular or religious) norms in order to being able to practice their faiths. Religious freedom as a human right requires the *respect* of religions; it *protects* the free practice and exercise of religious practices, and it demands of societies and their political institutions to *fulfill* the religious freedom right by granting spaces for religious institutions and/or providing institutional arrangements which may well differ in the different contexts and with respect to the practices of the different religions.

The public sphere is the *civil* sphere in which the different forms of social life, i.e., economic, cultural and religious life, and political engagement take place; they are visible publicly, and unsurprisingly, conflicts may arise.[7] In his famous conversation with Joseph Ratzinger, the philosopher of the Frankfurt School Jürgen Habermas argued that in order to participate fully in public discourses, religions must "translate" their value claims into the argumentative language of public reason, so that "communicative action" rather than coercive, violent action is possible.[8] Only with some procedural norms of discourse, he held, can the normative claims underlying the modern values of freedom, equality, tolerance, and solidarity be actualized.[9] In modern societies, values and traditions, Habermas argued, must be subjected to critique by public reason; his student Rainer Forst insisted: everyone has the right that the claims of others are to be justified, and vice versa, the obligation to justify one own's claims on others.[10] After much criticism, especially from the Christian scholars of public theology, Habermas later corrected his view considerably, acknowledging that "secular societies" actually also learn from those dimensions of the religious tradition that go beyond discursive reasoning. And indeed, though not exclusive sources of the "meaning of life," religions do offer, for example, religious rituals such as the "rites des passage" in childhood, marriage, sickness, or death; these are communal practices that structure the personal and social life and foster social cohesion. Furthermore, religions may provide the motivational basis that guides moral agents to act in accordance with their beliefs, something that reason alone cannot offer. In Western societies—no matter how secular they otherwise are—Catholic and other Christian institutions shape multiple parts of the institutional structures, from childcare, health care, or education, and charity organizations to the spaces of contemplation they create over against the dominance of a consumer culture that accompanies the never-resting Capitalist societies. Likewise, the forum of public reason entails the voices of religious-social advocacy, and the practices of conflict-resolution or even civil reconciliation after atrocities. The Truth and Reconciliation Commission of post-apartheid South Africa, for example, has become a model for numerous countries to strengthen the different sides in their efforts of peace after wars or other violent conflicts, incorporating, among others, testimonials of survivors and families of victims, and practices and rituals of reconciliation. Hence, the so-called return of religion around the turn of the millennium only highlighted in public *discourses* what had never disappeared in *practice*, namely the contribution of religions to the individual value systems, to the cohesion of communities, and to the overall public life of Western societies, which have functioned as secularized societies only *politically* throughout modernity.

CATHOLIC NATURAL LAW, HUMAN RIGHTS, AND THE GLOBAL ETHIC PROJECT

Catholicism has long been ambivalent about the human rights ethics: the natural law doctrine rather than the human rights framework serves as the normative framework of theological and ethical reasoning of the Catholic Church. It has been considerably reinterpreted recently, bringing it much closer to the human rights framework than it was the case in the 20th-century

Magisterium's interpretation of moral theology. The reinterpretation, taken on by the *International Theological Commission* and resulting in the 2009 Document[11] is a much welcome move:

> 92. *The norms of natural justice [ius naturalis] are thus the measures of human relationships prior to the will of the legislator.* They are given from the moment that human beings live in society. They express what is naturally just, prior to any legal formulation. *The norms of natural justice [ius naturalis] are expressed in a particular way in the subjective rights of the human person, such as the right to respect for one's own life, the right to the integrity of one's person, the right to religious liberty, the right to freedom of thought, the right to start a family and to educate one's children according to one's convictions, the right to associate with others, the right to participate in the life of the community, etc.* These rights, to which contemporary thought attributes great importance, do not have their source in the fluctuating desires of individuals, but rather in the very structure of human beings and their humanizing relations. The rights of the human person emerge therefore from the order of justice [ius] that must reign in relations among human beings. *To acknowledge these natural rights of man means to acknowledge the objective order of human relations based on the natural law.*[12]

This quote summarizes the tradition that elevates human reason as the capacity to discover the ontological structures of human existence, "the very structure of human beings and their humanizing relations." Whether one follows this ontological metaphysics or not, it creates the space for a public theology that is informed by the sciences and humanities, and human rights. Laws that do not align to the human rights or justice as the structure that enables individuals to realize their natural rights are not binding. "If the law is not just, it is not even a law."[13]

> [F]acing the threats of the abuse of power, and even of totalitarianism, which juridical positivism conceals and which certain ideologies propagate, the Church recalls that civil laws do not bind in conscience when they contradict natural law, and asks for the acknowledgment of the right to conscientious objection, as well as the duty of disobedience in the name of obedience to a higher law (43). The reference to natural law, far from producing conformism, guarantees personal freedom and defends the marginalized and those oppressed by social structures which do not take the common good into account.[14]

Activists who criticize human rights violations of their governments must indeed transcend positive law or policies that are introduced by governments; after all, it is often these laws and policies that allow for specific political procedures that are contested in the name of morality. For example, the so-called Muslim ban, i.e., the prohibition for citizens of particular countries to enter the United States, is a policy that was introduced by the Trump administration in spring 2018 and upheld at least in general terms by the US Supreme Court in early summer 2018. Yet, it declares foreign citizens a security threat merely because of their nationality. Furthermore, the so-called family separation of migrant infants, toddlers, and minors from their parents at the Mexican/US border in spring 2018 was in fact an orchestrated and intentional *state kidnapping* program, *accepting*[15] that this would result in the *torture* of children.[16]

The clash of positive laws and justice must indeed be criticized—however, not in the name of "divine law" but in the name of those who are treated unjustly. Merely referring to the authority of a "higher law" ignores the problematic legacy of religious authoritarianism that it strives to overcome.

Public theologies are not exclusively shaped by the Pope and Bishops' Conferences or by the leaders of Christian churches. They are, likewise, shaped by the activism and efforts of lay Christians and theologians. In 1993, the Global Ethic Project that had been introduced by Catholic theologian Hans Küng, embraced the United Nations framework of human dignity, human rights, and human responsibility, tying it to the moral visions found in all religions, and it was taken up by the Parliament of World Religions, established in Chicago in 1993.[17] It offered a positive vision of a minimal value consensus that it hoped would help to transform the consciousness of billions of people yearning for a good life, with and for others, in just institutions (Ricœur), and in "our common home" (Pope Francis), planet earth. From the beginning, the World Parliament's vision was interreligious and intercultural, reaching out to all people in good faith. Hence, the 1993 text states:

> We are persons who have committed ourselves to the precepts and practices of the world's religions. We confirm that there is already a consensus among the religions which can be the basis for a global ethic—a minimal fundamental consensus concerning binding values, irrevocable standards, and fundamental moral attitudes.
>
> . . . An ethic already exists within the religious teachings of the world which can counter the global distress. Of course this ethic provides no direct solution for all the immense problems of the world, but it does supply the moral foundation for a better individual and global order: A vision which can lead women and men away from despair, and society away from chaos.[18]

The Global Ethic Project sees itself as an inspiration for individuals and civil society to embrace the minimal consensus of values spelled out as a civic ethos, the Global Ethic. It echoes the Human Rights Declaration but formulates it as responsibility of religions. In contrast to the Catholic Catechism that upholds the notion that salvatory role of Christianity,[19] it acknowledges that no singular religion can claim to be in possession of *the* truth of religion, morality, or politics. Hence, an overlapping consensus among all cultures regarding the dignity and rights of human beings seemed to be a precondition for global peace, and the Global Ethic wanted to contribute to this consensus from a religious perspective. It was a necessary and laudable step to declare that

> every human being without distinction of age, sex, race, skin color, physical or mental ability, language, religion, political view, or national or social origin possesses an inalienable and untouchable dignity and everyone, the individual as well as the state, is therefore obliged to honor this dignity and protect it. Humans must always be the subjects of rights, must be ends, never mere means, never objects of commercialization and industrialization in economics, politics and media, in research institutes, and industrial corporations. No one stands "above good and evil"—no human being, no social class, no influential interest group, no cartel, no police apparatus, no army, and no state. On the contrary: Possessed of reason and conscience, every human is obliged to behave in a genuinely human fashion, to do good and avoid evil![20]

THE "NEW POLITICAL THEOLOGY"

Both Hans Küng and Johann Baptist Metz were among the founding members of the International Journal *Concilium* that understands itself as an international forum of Catholic theology that assembles the voices, practices, and reflections from theologians around the world who believe in the Vatican II call to "read the signs of the times."[21] In response to the Global Ethic, Johann Baptist Metz who coined the term "new political theology," articulated the blind spot of an ethos that is based on a minimal consensus shared by all religions. Metz stated, first in 1999:

> ... But from a strictly theological and not just from a religious and political perspective, ethical universalism is not a product of consensus. It is rooted in the unconditional recognition of an authority—which can certainly be appealed to in all great religions and cultures, too: in *the recognition of the authority of those who suffer.*[22]

Indebted to the Critical Theory of the early Frankfurt School, Metz called, in place of a minimal consensus of values, for a negative universalism that centers on suffering and injustice. It defines as its core task to *remember* what—and who—would otherwise be forgotten; it vows to stand in *solidarity* with and to *advocate* for those who are the victims, the left-behinds of modernity's scientific, technological, and economic progress. It strives to render the undignified, suffering people not the recipients and objects of theology but its subject. The Christian and Catholic ethics entailed in the New Political Theology—like the Latin American liberation theologies—allied itself with those whose stakes in the current order are a question of survival. It *can* only speak from this perspective if it positions itself in the places it speaks about—the *hypotopias*, as I want to call these spaces.

In consequence of this Christian theology, the suffering subject must be the center of the theological memory of God: the remembrance, narration, and reflection of God *is* embodied in the remembrance, narration, and reflection of the experiences of suffering people; it is, as Metz famously stated, a dangerous memory that speaks "truth to power." The principle of negative universalism means that the others, "the strangers," and the *aliens'* suffering ("Fremdes Leid," in Metz's term) must be *remembered*, it must be given a voice in *narratives*, it must be *judged* as evil that should not be, and ultimately, it must be *responded* to in actions and political praxis. Its truth claim, though formulated negatively, is as universal as the universal claim of human dignity and human rights. Metz therefore insisted on an *indirect* ecumenism of religions,

> the praxis of a common response, a common resistance to the sources of unjust suffering in the world: racism, xenophobia, and nationalistic or purely ethnic religiosity with its civil war ambitions. But it is also a resistance to the cold alternative of a global community in which increasingly the "human being" vanishes amid self-serving systems of economics, technology, and their culture and communications industries; of a global community in which world politics increasingly loses its primacy to a world economics whose laws of the market were long ago abstracted from "human beings" themselves.[23]

Metz, who had no illusions about the United Nations or the lacking power of NGO's nevertheless agreed with Küng and the Global Ethic that the memory of all religions are needed, *as the dangerous memory of those who pay the price for our inaction, for the global political, economic, and technological order*. Metz's insights may well be taken up by the Parliament of World Religions, which is, after all, an ongoing project.[24] With Metz, I therefore argue that Public theologies must activate the religious narratives for a social and political ethics of compassion, as resistance to unjust and innocent suffering or the passion-less world of reification and alienation.[25] Evidently, theology's deck in the public political and moral discourse entails no trump card. All it has is the knowledge of its own ideological theologies, which it strives to discern in critical analyses. It counters the glowing myths with the experiential knowledge of people who live in the *hypotopias* and the commitment to speak with and respond to those who are wounded by the decisions, actions, and structures of the current regimes.[26] Public theologies must therefore critique the disrespect of human freedom, dignity, and well-being of millions of people, among them the millions who are forced to leave their homes. They must critique the disregard of life on earth, and fight for a political and economic order that enables a true global justice.

WELCOME TO OUR HOME: A CRITICAL POLITICAL THEOLOGY OF LIBERATION TO JUSTICE

We can certainly learn from our plural and diverse religious traditions and narratives and from our different histories in which our religions and cultures originated, and in which our communities emerged, changed, prevailed, or were destroyed. This is the program of interreligious and intercultural dialogues. Ultimately, however, these dialogues require a direction: attending to those who live in the hypotopias, we will feel the *rahamim*, the Hebrew term for compassion, that begins with the screams of the children torn away from their mothers or fathers and the *pain in the gut* that their suffering evokes.[27] We will then see the yearning for justice in the faces of undocumented dreamers who cannot believe how their (!) country is treating them. We will see the desperation and in the faces of those who join the Migrant Caravan on the way to the US border, because they fear for their lives when fleeing alone. We will cry with the mothers and fathers who are still being deported while their children are declared "unaccompanied alien children," who may well end up in foster families as "orphans" whose parents have been "disappeared."[28]

When Christians believe this is no concern for them because they did not cause the crisis, I fear that religions, and Christianity especially, will make the same mistake as the early moderns made: juxtaposing the secular culture of death with a religious culture of life, to be found exclusively within the murals of a church that hides its complicity. The notion of the peaceful coexistence of the "state" and the "church" has always betrayed either the silent acceptance of state policies or the explicit legitimization of them. Public theologies must therefore maintain a position of *critique* not only as a method but as a performative social action.[29] But I am concerned that we become complacent again in our comforting narrative that we all share a minimal, abstract catalogue of values. I fear that we are too happy dwelling on the upper-side of history, while the suffering, once again, are forgotten. I worry that we do not see the multiple signs of a revision history of modern democracies, which places the Christian narrative, again, in the driver seat of national politics. What world we see depends on how—and where—we look. Whose words we hear depends to whom we listen. Public theologies must strive to organize the solidarity with those who do not want to forget the vision of human dignity and human rights. Christian theology is a *counternarrative* to political power, and this narrative must be held against the myth that is re-created by the nationalist populist groups. Religions, I believe, can indeed help us to look differently at our own world, our own identities and societies, because with the notion of the "divine" that calls us to go beyond our family ties as well as beyond our cultural or national bonds, religions themselves entail an "alienness" (Waldenfels) that is but one dimension of the "otherness of ourselves."[30]

We must resist the narrative of "homeland security" that is echoed in the "homeland theology" of Christian patriotism and nationalism, because it has become just another word for xenophobia and anti-immigrant policies. In our resistance to give in to the political realism that calls us dreamers and idealists who know nothing of politics and the complexities of it,[31] we may want to take Dorothe Sölle's words to heart, spoken when the 1980s German Peace Movement was criticized for its insistence on peace as an alternative to the deterrence politics of the Cold War. After all, in 1983 nobody expected that only a few years later, East German citizens would bring their government down with their protests in the streets *and* churches, ending an authoritarian regime that had violated so many of their rights:

> There are issues for which you must go into the streets, and speak a clear "no" in your workplace or in the union. If they tell you it will not do any good, and has no chance whatever, you must do it anyway, if only for the sake of your own human dignity, if only to be able to look your own children in the eye. If you keep silent today and allow yourself to be used, you are already dead. You have armed yourself to death! In the face of such feelings of impotence and defeatism, you must know exactly why you are doing all this and why it is essential for you, so that you do not cave in if they threaten you and intimidate you with censorship and blacklist you in your profession. We do not want to define our life as do those who are arming us to death.[32]

Quoting what she hears as objection to the Peace Movement: "'You are so naive, you pacifists, such wide-eyed innocents. You do not really know what you are talking about, especially not the women,'" she adds a second response:

> This objection is to the point, in as much as we need to become better informed. This is not so hard; don't be intimidated, even though you do have to overcome government propaganda.[33]

Like Metz, Sölle reminds her audiences to remember the activists and those who came before us and who suffered for their resistance to power. Every society—and every religion— has these witnesses. How they are remembered or listened to defines the public discourses. In my view, religions have a crucial role to pay in this respect: as those who remember the victims of unjust policies and structures, and the witnesses of resistance to these structures. And just as the free press who speaks truth to power is labeled today, once again, the "enemy of the people," Christian witnesses, too, will be the targets of the authoritarian regimes and their Christian supporters: they will not accept the unmasking that they are the "kingmakers."[34]

In sum, the theology that I envision is *critical* in its social and political analyses of power asymmetries, wherever they prevent people from claiming their right to have their rights be respected, protected, and fulfilled; it is *public* in the critique of injustice, arguing for a future that secures the freedom and well-being of human beings, the flourishing of animals and plants, and the environment upon which life on earth depends. It is *political* because it is committed to establish structures and institutions in the social life, in the globalized economy, and national as well as international politics that deserve to be called a political vision of justice. It acknowledges that human rights, de facto, are not the rights of the many but the rights of the few, to which theologians often belong. But from our position of this privilege, we, the "Western" Christian theologians whose rights and well-being are secured, must promote a Christian theology that begins with the acknowledgment that we do indeed refuse to accept the responsibility for past injustices and do little to establish support systems for those mostly in need of them today. Granting hospitality to asylum seekers and refugees should not even be worth a debate; finding solutions for migration may, in contrast, require all elements of practical reason that scholastic theology sought to integrate: prudence is the virtue of practical reason, i.e., the disposition to act in view of insights. They may stem from memory, foresight, circumstantial and contextual knowledge as well as entail docility and shrewdness—in fact, practical and ethical reasoning must be interdisciplinary and multidimensional. To found theological and *ethical* reasoning on the harms *and* vulnerable agency of those whose lives, freedom, and dignity are violated by acts, practices, or structures of coercion, discrimination, or dehumanization will help us not to lose sight of those with whom we are struggling for solutions.[35]

With regard to my own tradition, Catholicism, however, there is yet another task. The critical, public, and political theology and ethics must challenge, in the forum internum, the *image of God* as the ultimate law-giver and emperor of the church; it must challenge *the ecclesial structure* as dichotomy between the clerics and the lay people, and men and women of the church, and *the moral theology* of obedience to the moral authority of the Church. In its place, it will remind the master interpreters of the doctrine that the very tradition of the natural law that they claim guides Catholic moral theology not only permits but *demands* that every moral agent habituates the virtue of practical moral reasoning. Furthermore, public theology will challenge *Christian evangelization* when this prioritizes conversion, doctrine, and religious rituals over the praxis of recognition of and respect for others, including other religions. It will stand in solidarity with those whose trust has been betrayed by the Church, and *demand accountability and reparation* in cases of the Church's moral failures to respect, protect, and fulfill the human rights of its members, children and women in particular. This theology will tell the narratives of the compassionate God who dwells in the undersides as well as in the upper-sides of societies; who cries with the children and their parents at the border and in the prisons, and who suffers with everyone who is yearning to belong somewhere. Together with them, God will demand justice. Christian ethics is neither romantic kitsch nor a private affair—it is an ethics of compassion, justice, and responsibility, understood as practical response and the willingness of moral agents to be held accountable for their actions and inactions. After all, Christian theology does not only entail the blessing for those who turn to their neighbors; it also entails the vision of the divine judgment for those who do not respect, protect, or fulfill the human dignity and rights of others:

> For I was hungry and you gave me nothing to eat, I was thirsty and you gave me nothing to drink, I was a stranger and you did not invite me in, I needed clothes and you did not clothe me, I was sick and in prison and you did not look after me.[36]

Public theologies that commit themselves to critique as a social practice and to the struggle for the liberation to justice must embrace all groups who are willing to repair the old ecclesia of Christianity, and Christians will engage alongside with others to *tear down the walls* of the global order of injustice. They will welcome the stranger to their homes and homelands, and strive to provide the hospitable spaces in which all of us who "aim for a good life with and for others in just institutions"[37] can dwell.

NOTES

1. Hille Haker, and Molly Greening, eds. *Unaccompanied Migrant Children: Social, Legal, and Ethical Perspectives* (Lanham, MD: Lexington, 2018).

2. Cf., for example, Barbie Latza Nadeau, "The Vatican's Dirty Money Problem," *The Daily Beast* (December 12, 2017), https://www.thedailybeast.com/the-vaticans-dirty-money-problem.

3. Seyla Benhabib, *Another Cosmopolitanism*, ed. Jeremy Waldron, et al. (Oxford; New York: Oxford University Press, 2006); *Dignity in Adversity: Human Rights in Troubled Times* (Cambridge, UK; Malden, MA: Polity, 2011).

4. Even though this human rights approach has been criticized, too, by Hannah Arendt or more recently by Christoph Menke, for its shortcomings to secure the "right to have rights" (Arendt) I have defended it, pointing to Paul Ricoeur's concept of capability as responsibility and accountability. Cf. Hille Haker, "No Space. Nowhere. Refugees and the Problem of Human Rights in Arendt and Ricoeur" *Ricoeur Studies* 8, no. 2 (2017). For an analysis and defense of cosmopolitanism cf.

5. I follow Michelle Becka in pointing to the triad of "respect, protection, and fulfilment" that orients the implementation of human rights. Cf. Michelle Becka, "Verantwortung Übernehmen. Christliche Sozialethik Und Migration," *Stimmen der Zeit* 143 (2018); Michelle Becka, and Johannes Ulrich, "Blinde Praxis, Taube Theorie? Sozialethische Reflexion Über Das Menschenrecht Auf Gesundheit," in *Christliche Sozialethik—Orientierung Welcher Praxis?*, ed. Bernhard Emunds (Stuttgart: Nomos, 2018).

6. Hille Haker, *Recognition and Responsibility* (2019 (in preparation)); Axel Honneth, *The Struggle for Recognition: The Moral Grammar of Social Conflicts* (Cambridge, MA: Polity Press, 1995).

7. Jeffrey C. Alexander, *The Civil Sphere* (Oxford ; New York: Oxford University Press, 2006).

8. For a critical discussion cf. Maureen Junker-Kenny, *Religion and Public Reason: A Comparison of the Positions of John Rawls, Jürgen Habermas and Paul Ricoeur*, ed. Maureen Junker-Kenny (Berlin, Germany; Boston: De Gruyter, 2014).

9. Jürgen Habermas, *The Theory of Communicative Action* (London: Heinemann, 1984).

10. Rainer Forst, *The Right to Justification : Elements of a Constructivist Theory of Justice*, ed. Jeffrey Flynn (New York: Columbia University Press, 2012).

11. International Theological Commission, "In Search of a Universal Ethic: A New Look at the Natural Law," http://www.vatican.va/roman_curia/congregations/cfaith/cti_documents/rc_con_cfaith_doc_20090520_legge-naturale_en.html

12. Ibid. (translation changed and emphasis added)

13. Ibid.

14. Ibid., Par. 35. (http://www.vatican.va/roman_curia/congregations/cfaith/cti_documents/rc_con_cfaith_doc_20090520_legge-naturale_en.html)

15. Hearings in the US Congress have shown that the administration was indeed warned by the Department of Human Health Services of the harms this policy would cause the children. It was implemented anyway, and Secretary of Justice did not shy away from quoting the bible to warn the Christian churches to keep its distance from state policies.

16. According to Erika Guevara-Rosas, Amnesty International's Americas Director of Amnesty International, this "is a spectacularly cruel policy, where frightened children are being ripped from their parent's arms and taken to overflowing detention centers, which are essentially cages. This is nothing short of torture. The severe mental suffering that officials have intentionally inflicted on these families for coercive purposes, means that these acts meet the definitions of torture under both US and international law. Amnesty International, "USA: Policy of Separating Children from Parents Is Nothing Short of Torture," https://www.amnesty.org/en/latest/news/2018/06/usa-family-separation-torture/. The UN Convention against Torture defines torture a) as the intentional infliction of pain, b) by a public official or someone acting in an official capacity, and c) for a specific purpose. The courts have since ruled that the children's "pain" and "suffering" was illegal according to US laws. The term "family separation" is, therefore, a euphemism that conceals the reality of a kidnapping policy at the border, in order to deter other asylum seekers to come to the border, and the harming of children (and their parents!) have been either accepted as collateral damage or it was part of the deterrence strategy.

17. Cf. https://parliamentofreligions.org/

18. Parliament of World Religions, "Toward a Global Ethic: An Initial Declaration of the Parliament of the World's Religions," https://parliamentofreligions.org/publications/toward-global-ethic-initial-declaration-parliament-worlds-religions.

19. "Hence they could not be saved who, knowing that the Catholic Church was founded as necessary by God through Christ, would refuse either to enter it or to remain in it." Lumen Gentium, quoted in the Libreria Editrice Vaticana, "Catechism of the Catholic Church" (1993), http://www.vatican.va/archive/ENG0015/_INDEX.HTM.

20. Parliament of World Religions, "Toward a Global Ethic."

21. Belonging to the next generation of scholars, I have been an editorial board member of several issues. One example of the direction is the issue on "women's voices in world religion," co-edited by Susan Ross, Marie-Theres Wacker, and me in 2006. For all issues cf. http://www.concilium.in/

22. Johann Baptist Metz, "In the Pluralism of Religious and Cultural Worlds: Notes toward a Theological and Political Program," *CrossCurrents* 49, no. 2 (1999): 232. Emphasis is mine. Translation corrected. Metz elaborated on the Global Ethic in "'Compassion.' Zu Einem Weltprogramm Des Christentums Im Zeitalter Des Pluralismus Der Religionen Und Kulturen," in *Compassion. Weltprogramm Des Christentums. Soziale Verantwortung Lernen*, ed. Lothar Kuld and Adolf Weisbrod Johann Baptist Metz (Freiburg im Breisgau: Herder, 2000).

23. "In the Pluralism of Religious and Cultural Worlds: Notes toward a Theological and Political Program," 233.

24. In preparation of the 2018 Assembly in Toronto, a conference was held in Chicago in April 2018 under the title "Grappling with the Global Ethic: Multi-Religious Perspectives on Global Issues." The contributions can be watched at https://parliamentofreligions.org/parliament/global-ethic/grappling-global-ethic-multi-religious-perspectives-global-issues-conference#1958.

25. Cf. Axel Honneth et al., *Reification: A New Look at an Old Idea* (Oxford; New York: Oxford University Press, 2007). Rahel Jaeggi, *Alienation* (New York: Columbia University Press, 2016).

26. Even though this human rights approach has been criticized, too, by Hannah Arendt or more recently by Christoph Menke, for its shortcomings to secure the "right to have rights" (Arendt) I have defended it, pointing to Paul Ricœur's concept of capability as responsibility and accountability. Cf. Haker, "No Space. Nowhere. Refugees and the Problem of Human Rights in Arendt and Ricoeur." Benhabib, *Another Cosmopolitanism*; *Dignity in Adversity: Human Rights in Troubled Times*.

27. Cf. Hille Haker, "Compassion and Justice," *Concilium*, no. 4 (2017).

28. "Disappearance" was a well-known crime against humanity of South-American and Central American regimes, often backed by the United States of America. Speaking truth to power entails the responsibility to resist the political rhetoric of the anti-immigrant and xenophobic regimes and identify the policies as what they are. In the case of the "family separation," this means to call the policies state kidnapping, the treatment of the children (and parents) imprisonment and torture, and the "deportation" the intentional disappearance of parents while their children are still in the custody of US authorities, and the "zero tolerance" asylum and immigration policies crimes against humanity.

29. Robin Celikates, *Critique as Social Practice: Critical Theory and Social Self-Understanding* (London: Rowman & Littlefield International, 2018).

30. Paul Ricoeur, *Oneself as Another* (Chicago: University of Chicago Press, 1992). Cf. Bernhard Waldenfels, *Phenomenology of the Alien: Basic Concepts* (Evanston, IL: Northwestern University Press, 2011).

31. Hille Haker, "Political Ethics and the Rights of Unaccompanied Migrant Children," in *Unaccompanied Migrant Children: Social, Legal, and Ethical Perspectives*, ed. Hille Haker, Greening, Molly (Lanham, MD: Lexington, 2018).

32. Dorothee Soelle, "Unilaterally for Peace," *Cross Currents* 33, no. 2 (1983): 143.

33. Ibid.

34. Maegan Vazquez, Brusk, Steve, "Pastor at Trump Rally Asks God to Protect President from 'Jungle Journalism,'" *CNN* (August 4, 2018), https://www.cnn.com/2018/08/04/politics/ohio-pastor-invocation-donald-trump-rally/index.html. In his prayer, Pastor Gary Click compared Donald Trump with David, fighting against Goliath.

35. Cf. a thorough examination in Hille Haker, "Vulnerable Agency: A Conceptual and Contextual Analysis," in *Dignity and Conflict: Contemporary Interfaith Dialogue on the Value and Vulnerability of Human Life*, ed. Jonathan Rothschild and Matthew Petrusek (Notre Dame: Notre Dame University Press, 2018).

36. Matthew 25, 42–43.

37. Cf. from a feminist perspective that I fully embrace: Elisabeth Schüssler Fiorenza, *Discipleship of Equals: A Critical Feminist EkklēSia-Logy of Liberation* (New York: Crossroad, 1993); *Empowering Memory and Movement: Thinking and Working across Borders* (Minneapolis: Fortress Press, 2014); Elisabeth Schüssler Fiorenza, *Transforming Vision: Exploration in Feminist Theolgy* (Augsburg Fortress Press, 2014).

REFERENCES

Alexander, Jeffrey C. *The Civil Sphere*. Oxford; New York: Oxford University Press, 2006.

Amnesty International. "USA: Policy of Separating Children from Parents Is Nothing Short of Torture." https://www.amnesty.org/en/latest/news/2018/06/usa-family-separation-torture/.

Becka, Michelle. "Verantwortung Übernehmen. Christliche Sozialethik Und Migration." *Stimmen der Zeit* 143 (2018): 343–52.
Becka, Michelle, and Johannes Ulrich. "Blinde Praxis, Taube Theorie? Sozialethische Reflexion Über Das Menschenrecht Auf Gesundheit." In *Christliche Sozialethik—Orientierung Welcher Praxis?* Edited by Bernhard Emunds, 299–322. Stuttgart: Nomos, 2018.
Benhabib, Seyla. *Another Cosmopolitanism.* Edited by Jeremy Waldron, Bonnie Honig, Will Kymlicka, and Robert Post. Oxford; New York: Oxford University Press, 2006.
———. *Dignity in Adversity: Human Rights in Troubled Times.* Cambridge, UK; Malden, MA: Polity, 2011.
Celikates, Robin. *Critique as Social Practice: Critical Theory and Social Self-Understanding* [in English]. London: Rowman & Littlefield International, 2018.
Forst, Rainer. *The Right to Justification: Elements of a Constructivist Theory of Justice.* Edited by Jeffrey Flynn. New York: Columbia University Press, 2012.
Habermas, Jürgen. *The Theory of Communicative Action.* London: Heinemann, 1984.
Haker, Hille. "Compassion and Justice." *Concilium*, no. 4 (2017): 44–54.
———. "No Space. Nowhere. Refugees and the Problem of Human Rights in Arendt and Ricoeur." *Ricoeur Studies* 8, no. 2 (2017): 21–45.
———. "Political Ethics and the Rights of Unaccompanied Migrant Children." In *Unaccompanied Migrant Children. Social, Legal, and Ethical Responses to the Plight of Child Migration*, edited by Hille Haker and Molly Greening. Lanham, MD: Lexington Books, 2018.
———. *Recognition and Responsibility.* 2019 (in preparation).
———. "Vulnerable Agency: A Conceptual and Contextual Analysis." In *Dignity and Conflict: Contemporary Interfaith Dialogue on the Value and Vulnerability of Human Life.* Edited by Jonathan Rothschild and Matthew Petrusek. Notre Dame: Notre Dame University Press, 2018 (forthcoming).
Haker, Hille, and Molly Greening, eds. *Unaccompanied Migrant Children. Social, Legal, and Ethical Responses to the Plight of Child Migration.* Lanham, MD: Lexington Books, 2018.
Honneth, Axel. *The Struggle for Recognition: The Moral Grammar of Social Conflicts.* Cambridge, MA: Polity Press, 1995.
Honneth, Axel, Judith Butler, Raymond Geuss, Jonathan Lear, and Martin Jay. *Reification : A New Look at an Old Idea* [in English]. Oxford; New York: Oxford University Press, 2007.
International Theological Commission. "In Search of a Universal Ethic: A New Look at the Natural Law." http://www.vatican.va/roman_curia/congregations/cfaith/cti_documents/rc_con_cfaith_doc_20090520_legge-naturale_en.html
Jaeggi, Rahel. *Alienation* [in English]. New York: Columbia University Press, 2016.
Junker-Kenny, Maureen. *Religion and Public Reason: A Comparison of the Positions of John Rawls, Jürgen Habermas and Paul Ricoeur.* Edited by Maureen Junker-Kenny: Berlin, Germany; Boston, MA: De Gruyter, 2014.
Latza Nadeau, Barbie. "The Vatican's Dirty Money Problem." *The Daily Beast* (December 12, 2017). https://www.thedailybeast.com/the-vaticans-dirty-money-problem.
Metz, Johann Baptist. "'Compassion.' Zu Einem Weltprogramm Des Christentums Im Zeitalter Des Pluralismus Der Religionen Und Kulturen." In *Compassion. Weltprogramm Des Christentums. Soziale Verantwortung Lernen.* Edited by Lothar Kuld and Adolf Weisbrod Johann Baptist Metz, 9–20. Freiburg im Breisgau: Herder, 2000.
———. "In the Pluralism of Religious and Cultural Worlds: Notes toward a Theological and Political Program." *CrossCurrents* 49, no. 2 (1999): 227–36.
Parliament of World Religions. "Toward a Global Ethic: An Initial Declaration of the Parliament of the World's Religions." https://parliamentofreligions.org/publications/toward-global-ethic-initial-declaration-parliament-worlds-religions.
Ricoeur, Paul. *Oneself as Another.* Chicago: University of Chicago Press, 1992.
Schüssler Fiorenza, Elisabeth. *Transforming Vision: Exploration in Feminist Theolgy* [in English]. Augsburg Fortress Press, 2014.
———. *Discipleship of Equals: A Critical Feminist EkklēSia-Logy of Liberation.* New York: Crossroad, 1993.
———. *Empowering Memory and Movement: Thinking and Working across Borders.* Minneapolis: Fortress Press, 2014.

Soelle, Dorothee. "Unilaterally for Peace." *Cross Currents* 33, no. 2 (1983): 140–46.
Vaticana, Libreria Editrice. "Catechism of the Catholic Church." (1993). http://www.vatican.va/archive/ENG0015/_INDEX.HTM.
Vazquez, Maegan, and Steve Brusk. "Pastor at Trump Rally Asks God to Protect President from 'Jungle Journalism.'" *CNN* (August 4, 2018). https://www.cnn.com/2018/08/04/politics/ohio-pastor-invocation-donald-trump-rally/index.html.
Waldenfels, Bernhard. *Phenomenology of the Alien: Basic Concepts* [in English]. Evanston, IL: Northwestern University Press, 2011.

Chapter Thirteen

Political Theology in the Trump Era

*Sacrificial Frameworks in the
US "Neoliberal Disimagination Machine"*

Kelly Denton-Borhaug

This chapter builds on the insight from scholar and social critic Henry Giroux, regarding the US "disimagination machine" at the center of public pedagogy. I begin with warning words that we might be surprised to hear coming from a Marine Reserve Officer at the US Naval Academy:

> Uncritical support of all things martial is quickly becoming the new normal for our youth. Hardly any of my students at the Naval Academy remember a time when their nation wasn't at war. Almost all think it ordinary to hear of drone strikes in Yemen or Taliban attacks in Afghanistan. The recent revelation of counterterrorism bases in Africa elicits no surprise in them, nor do the military ceremonies that are now regular features at sporting events. *That which is left unexamined eventually becomes invisible, and as a result, few Americans today are giving sufficient consideration to the full range of violent activities the government undertakes in their names.*[1] (italics mine)

This officer's alarming description is worth further probing: how are we to understand such lack of awareness or concern regarding the growth of violence and militarism in American culture, even as we find ourselves in the midst of the longest war in US history? This chapter investigates how "post-truth" is related to long-standing religio-cultural dynamics that shape what I call "sacrificial U.S. war-culture." The Oxford Dictionary defines "post-truth" as "an adjective . . . 'relating to or denoting circumstances in which objective facts are less influential in shaping public opinion than appeals to emotion and personal belief.'"[2] But I would argue that our contemporary situation is more complex than this definition suggests. We need to probe beyond and beneath the "post-truth" phenomenon to the long and complicated history undergirding our current reality.

First of all, how is it that emotion and personal belief have become stronger shaping forces than objective facts? If objective facts about urgent realities like climate change have become shrouded with a veil of suspicion and distrust, the situation is even worse regarding American reaction to the state of US militarism and violence. The officer from the Naval Academy is right: this reality mostly is invisible to people in the United States, and Americans are inured to its existence, even as their own lives are profoundly negatively impacted, and as US militarism blindly contributes to a march of death and destruction in ever-increasing near and far-flung places around the globe. Though most Americans behave as though they "have no skin in the game" with respect to the size, shape and extent of US militarization and violence both at home and around the world, such a perspective is a false illusion.

The emergence of what is being described as a "post-truth" culture begs for analysis that can help us better understand all the cultural dynamics that have led us to this place. In addition, this investigation must be inward looking as well as outward, because all of us have been shaped by the cultural forces in which we live and work. As cultural critic Henry Giroux sums it up, American intellectuals have become "indifferent"; we have been "tamed" by "a disimagination machine." Our public pedagogy, in other words, the stories, images, institutions and discourses that shape our learning and life increasingly ". . . short-circuit the ability of individuals to think critically, imagine the unimaginable, and engage ways . . . to become critically engaged citizens of the world."[3]

This theme of relative academic indifference and taming was brought home strongly to me when Rev. James Lawson, the Civil Rights icon and teacher of such leaders as Martin Luther King Jr., John Lewis, and Diane Nash, visited the campus where I teach. During a symposium that was eagerly attended by many of my faculty colleagues who were excited to meet him, at one point he turned to us very pointedly and asked why we are so little involved in our research to address the crises that face us, especially the triplet evils King so well outlined, the intersecting realities of poverty, militarism, and racism. An uncomfortable silence spread around the conference room.

Public intellectual Naomi Klein encourages citizens to mount a deep and widespread analysis of the current moment, as she writes,

> . . . the reduction of the current crisis to just one or two factors at the exclusion of all else won't get us any closer to understanding how to defeat these forces the next time out. If we cannot become just a little bit curious about how all

these elements—race, gender, class, economics, history, culture—have intersected with one another to produce the current crisis, we will, at best, be stuck where we were before Trump won. And that was not a safe place.[4]

Klein is right both regarding the importance of an intersectional analysis of the situation in which we find ourselves, as well as the urgency of an intersectional response to address it.

We face multiple and interlocking crises: climate change; gross material inequality linked with race and gender injustice; lack of access regarding basic rights and needs, and enormous potential for control on the part of the very few; degradation of the environment; the threat of militarized (and nuclear) destruction, even annihilation; the loss of democracy and rise of neoliberal frameworks and systems of domination, and more. I will jump into the fray through one entry point in particular, the intersection between religion and US war-culture, and the curious assessment of the Marine officer regarding his students' "uncritical support for all things martial" as the norm of our time.

US WAR-CULTURE

Shortly after the events of 9/11, I began to investigate what I call the "sacrificial war-culture of the United States." The ethos, practices, and institutions of militarization and war have come to predominate in ever-increasing sites of supposed civilian culture in the United States. At the same time, not only are most citizens unaware of such a characterization, but also, in this "post-truth" society many vigorously will deny that the United States *is* a war-culture. Religion plays a definitive role in our resistance to greater awareness, as we will see below.

Countless pieces of evidence may be marshaled to shine a spotlight on the reality of war-culture in the United States; here I make reference only to three of the most outstanding indicators.[5] First, perhaps the most overwhelming sign of our war-culture is the amount of money we pay to sustain it. According to the National Priorities Project, a non-profit dedicated to tracking the US federal budget, the 2015 discretionary budget for the military topped $598.5 billion, or 54% of the total discretionary budget. But the situation will become even more extreme if the first national budget presented by the Trump administration is passed by Congress: "This budget adds $54 billion to the United States military budget—already larger than the military budgets for the next seven countries combined—by taking away from nearly everything else that keeps our society and economy functioning, including spending on education, jobs, and non-military investments in national security."[6] In the fall of 2017, Republicans and Democrats joined together to pass the $700 billion National Defense Authorization Act of

2018, increasing the outlays for war by $80 billion. Critics noted that this amount easily could cover social costs that have been decried as unaffordable, such as free college public tuition, cleaner drinking water in places like Flint, Michigan, and single-payer health insurance.[7]

Second, the growth of U.S. military bases and "lily pads" around the world and domestically is an unmistakable sign of our war-culture. According to scholars, the United States ". . . has increasingly inserted itself into new corners of the globe with the help of small, often secretive "lily pad" bases; today, there are bases in around 80 countries and US territories—roughly twice as many as in 1989."[8] All in all, international US military bases and lily pads number over 800.[9] The military reach of the United States is deeper and wider than in any empire in history.

Finally, third, in addition to international spread, domestically the tentacles of the institutions, culture, and apparatuses of militarization have a fast and vast grasp on the nation itself. War-culture not only includes obscene amounts of funding, and an international net that is unlike any before in history, but it also is naturalized and legitimated by its interpenetrations with unending sites of civilian culture within the United States. For instance, think about the initial description of "the US military industrial complex," (MIC) the term coined by President Dwight Eisenhower in his last presidential address to the nation at the beginning of the 1960s. Eisenhower expressed his concern about the unparalleled growth and linkage of militarization with government, Pentagon and corporate structures, but this early foreboding pales when compared with the updated definition of the MIC from contemporary sociologist Nick Turse, who studies US ways of war and militarism. As Turse writes, in these first decades of the 21st century, people of the United States now live in "a military-industrial-technological-entertainment-academic-scientific-media-intelligence-homeland security-surveillance-national security-corporate complex."[10] The ethos, institutions, and practices of war and militarism intermix with vast civilian sectors of life in the United States; war in essence has become a central aspect of the way many Americans understand their national identity.[11]

What makes it possible for these widespread and deep realities of war-culture to coexist with attitudes such as those young naval cadets, and their "uncritical support" for unabashed and unceasing militarism and violence? On the one hand, the depth and breadth of war-culture itself provides a normalizing force that makes it invisible and largely legitimated; but in addition to this, we must look at the role of religion, and specifically, forms of Christian thinking and understanding, if we are to understand our own reality in the United States I show how "sacrificial war-culture" endures in the presidential administration of Donald Trump as a form of political theology; but simultaneously I emphasize that this is far from a new reality. Sacrificial war-culture in the United States has roots and branches long predating this particular outgrowth and presidential administration. After dwelling on one telling incident of sacrificial war-culture that characterizes the most recent presidential administration, I draw on the thinking of social critic Henry Giroux and French sociologist Pierre Bourdieu to help us better investigate and understand this reality, and reflect on what we may do to address and change it.

THE CULTURAL ROOTS OF TRUMP'S RHETORIC

The character and behavior of President Trump, the particular construction of his administration, and the makeup of his closest advisors all have contributed to the impression that what we are experiencing in this administration is somehow new, or different from what has gone before. But novelist and human rights activist Ariel Dorfman compares Trump's "war on knowledge" with earlier historical dynamics that occurred during the Franco era in Spain, and the Pinochet era in Chile. Just as in those Orwellian chapters of history, so now in the Trump era, intelligence is despised, and death is hailed. If there is something that is new, it has to do with the blatant, unhidden, and utterly unapologetic nature of the attacks on democratic institutions and swift measures to disenfranchise scientists, diplomats, educators, and regulators. Ariel proclaims, "never has an occupant of the White House exhibited such a toxic mix of ignorance and mendacity, such lack of intellectual curiosity and disregard for rigorous analysis."[12]

> Government websites at the White House, the EPA, and the Departments of State, Agriculture, Interior, Labor, Education, and Energy have been scrubbed of previously posted scientific positions that would contradict the new policy program. Advisory councils have been eviscerated or abolished—the Justice Department's National Commission on Forensic Science, no less!—and government scientists have been muzzled and forbidden from attending national forums or international conferences. The administration is obstructing the collection of data and the publication and discussion of research, as if in expectation that inconvenient truths will magically melt away.[13]

At the same time, a very specific and familiar set of rhetorical practices enables the above. Years ago, Bruce Lincoln deftly analyzed the rhetorical code used so effectively by President George W. Bush to "signal his base." With key words and phrases, Bush was able to communicate to conservative evangelical Christians that he was "one of them," and would sway government resources and decision-making to support their ideals, while doing so in a way that could never be accused of violating the First Amendment. Such "double-coding" was a central method through which Bush "signaled his core constituency."[14]

But not only religious signaling, Journalist Juan Cole further writes that President George W. Bush's public career also was complicit with the Republican Party "dog whistle of racism," and he would not have succeeded without it. During the critical 2000 campaign against John McCain, Bush's campaign advisor, Karl Rove, endorsed robo-calls in South Carolina to suggest to voters that McCain's adopted daughter from Bangladesh was the result of an adulterous tryst between McCain and a Black woman.[15] Tactics and rhetoric such as this, or the "super predator" rhetoric of the Clinton era, are signposts that show how multiple presidential administrations expertly exploited citizens through racialized patterns of victimage rhetoric. This language dovetailed with structural racism, such as tax-cuts or welfare reform that benefited the wealthiest (and whitest) citizens, while shredding the social safety net and adding greater insecurity for those at the bottom, including disproportionate numbers of citizens of color.[16] Cole suggests that these strategies may be traced back to Nixon's "Southern Strategy," and infect both the Democratic and Republican parties. I argue that they go back much further, to the very beginnings of US history. "Victimage rhetoric" is a longstanding and commonly practiced tradition in the United States. In every era of US history, citizens have been not-so-subtly encouraged by political leaders to demonize perceived "enemies" as irrational, evil, unredeemably violent, lazy, religiously intolerant, and/or of an inferior racial heritage.[17] Such rhetoric very effectively has been used against people with different languages, religions, minority cultural backgrounds, and skin colors to characterize them as subhuman and deserving of indifference or violence; while the "we" are reaffirmed as innocent, peace-loving, rational, with a higher form of supposedly "secular" government, in fact, as the aggrieved victims of these others. In the end, such rhetorical patterns perfectly provide the ground for unthinking violence.

This is the enduring cultural rhetorical history of the United States we must keep in mind as we analyze what is taking place in the current era. When Trump signals his white-supremacist base, it is, if anything, only an exaggeration of dynamics that are deeply entrenched in US culture. At the same time, these signals provide cover for the power and wealth consolidation that will harm the very population being rallied to support this administration. There is much in our past and relatively recent history that has paved the way for the moment in which we now find ourselves deeply mired. As Trump reacts to the unleashing of white supremacy in the alt-right such as occurred in Charlottesville by tweeting ". . . can't change history, but you can learn from it. Robert E. Lee, Stonewall Jackson–who's next, Washington, Jefferson? So foolish! Also. . . ."—the dog-whistle is unmistakable.[18]

POLITICAL THEOLOGY IN THE TRUMP ERA

Thus, first, what seems like a new high of mendacity and ignorance in this administration has deep roots in very troubling but long-standing aspects of US culture. Understanding this background makes it possible to better analyze the landscape of political theology of the present United States. For not only with respect to a rhetorical set of practices, the era of Trump provides us an opportunity as well to examine the enduring nature of sacrificial war-culture in the United States, and its disciplining effects on citizens' imaginations. Here I turn to an event from relatively early in the Trump presidency, his first major speech to the houses of Congress in February, 2017, in order to highlight and analyze the tradition of sacrificial political theology in the United States.

In President Trump's first major speech to the houses of Congress, CNN reported that the "emotional high point" involved his reference to Carryn Owens, the widow of Chief Petty Officer William "Ryan" Owens. "Lauding her husband's sacrifice," Trump attempted to derail criticism of a widely questioned military action that many felt he approved too quickly, after only two weeks in office, and not in the official Situation Room, but in a much more casual setting, over dinner with advisers. An elite Navy SEAL was killed, and an expensive Osprey aircraft was destroyed in a ground action in Yemen. Later, military officials also acknowledged that over 20 civilians also were killed, women and children, along with 14 (supposed) al-Qaeda militants. In response to Ryan's death, his father, also a military veteran, refused to meet with Trump and publicly questioned the president's motive for the attack:

> Why at this time did there have to be this stupid mission when it wasn't even barely a week into his administration? Why? For two years prior, there were no boots on the ground in Yemen—everything was missiles and drones—because there was not a target worth one American life. Now, all of a sudden we had to make this grand display?[19]

For a brief moment, controversy swirled, as the dissonance of a military veteran *who was also a* grieving father so publicly criticized the Commander in Chief. Would a window of opportunity emerge in which to think more deeply not only about this particular mission, but also the entire thrust of US militarism around the world, and especially in the wars of the Middle East?

Trump and his advisers quickly set to work to silence any questioners and reassert the dominant narrative. Defense Secretary General James Mattis was brought to the stage to emphasize the approval of the Pentagon for the mission; and the formal setting of a presidential address to joint houses of Congress provided the setting. It was no accident, following his earlier criticism, that the young man's father, Bill Ryan, was not present for the speech before Congress; and the administration kept the invitation it did extend to a member of the Owens family a secret, in order to heighten the drama to come. At a pivotal moment in his speech, Trump acknowledged the widow of the deceased military servicemember sitting in the balcony, Carryn Owens:

> "I just spoke to General Mattis, who reconfirmed that, and I quote, 'Ryan was a part of a highly successful raid that generated large amounts of vital intelligence that will lead to many more victories in the future against our enemies,'" Trump said. "Ryan's legacy is etched into eternity. Thank you. *As the Bible teaches us, there is no greater act of love than to lay down one's life for one's friends. Ryan laid down his life for his friends, for his country, and for our freedom*—we will never forget Ryan."[20] (italics mine)

Almost as if she had been cued, Ms. Owens rose to her feet, and raised tear-filled eyes to the ceiling, as if to reference her husband in heaven. The audience erupted into a standing ovation lasting over two minutes. Trump deviated from his script to make the most of the moment: "Ryan is looking down, right now, and you know that, and he is very happy, because I think he just broke a record." Many media talking heads obediently followed through with the required response to such a moment: with this action, they declared, for the first time it was possible to see Trump as "presidential." CNN drew from the commentary of one of its leading media figures, Van Jones, a former Obama administration official, who described the moment:

> He [President Trump] did something extraordinary, and for people who have been hoping that he would become unifying, hoping that he would find some way to become presidential, they should be happy with that moment, [Trump] "became president of the United States in that moment. Period."[21]

In one fell swoop, important questions regarding the decisions of war were silenced, the voice of the father faded to the background, and the dominant narrative of "the necessity of the sacrifices of war" was reasserted, all of the above resulting in a widely agreed upon media assessment of Trump as "presidential." If there is anything surprising about this, it may be that Americans continue to play their role in these moments with so little thought, and so little resistance. But perhaps that is precisely the point.

For truth be told, spectacles such as the first Trump speech are far from new in the American landscape. When one examines Hillary Clinton's presidential campaign, Obama's presidency or the administration of George W. Bush, we see very similar sacrificial tactics to sway voters and mystify the hard realities of war and militarism. The Democratic National Convention (DNC) of 2016 is a case in point, when Hillary Clinton drew on the martyrdom of Army Captain Humayan Kahn to highlight "the necessity of sacrifice-as-war" in an emotional spectacle very similar to the one described above. First a glossy and sophisticated short film narrated Captain Kahn's exemplary life and martyrdom in Iraq. The DNC then brought his parents, Khzir and Ghazala Khan, to the stage, where Mr. Kahn, an immigrant to the United States, contrasted Hillary Clinton's character with Donald Trump's. As he proclaimed, in sharp contrast to Clinton and his own family, Trump had "sacrificed nothing, and no one." Just as in the case of Trump's speech, this sacrificial spectacle elicited a deeply emotional response from the convention, and provided the opportunity for Clinton to unify and centralize her political base, even as the sacrificial rhetoric also smoothly distracted everyone from considering Clinton's own role in the war that eventually took Captain Kahn's life.[22]

THE DISIMAGINATION MACHINE

I argue that we must include analysis of religio-cultural sacrificial mechanisms within the wider dynamics of what social critic Henry Giroux calls "the disimagination machine" that has come to shape life in the U.S.[23] Not only everyday citizens, but intellectuals as well (such as Van Jones) easily are tamed by a cultural apparatus that "consolidates the power of the rich and supports the interconnected grid of military, surveillance, corporate, and academic structures by presenting the ideologies, institutions and relations of the powerful as both commonsense and natural," writes Giroux.[24] Giroux's understanding of "the disimagination machine" deserves further unpacking.

At its base, neoliberalism as "the latest stage of predatory capitalism" is both cause and condition of the disimagination machine.[25] Neoliberalism encourages a "survival-of-the-fittest" ethic that promotes individual and corporate business rights and interests, deregulation, and the privatization of public resources.[26] At the same time it "spews out stories" emphasizing "disdain for community, public life, public values and democracy itself."[27] Neoliberalism depends upon market-centered private modes of political control and has risen hand in glove with the emerging surveillance state and what I call the "war-culture" of the United States.[28] The consolidating and centralizing of economic power to fewer and fewer hands is aided by increasing social control through coercive means. As Giroux emphasizes, neoliberalism thrives as the spectre of permanent war dominates the horizon, in conjunction with the carceral state and national surveillance infrastructure.[29] Moreover, the growing militarization of society encourages increasing esteem for members of the military, and militarized values, practices, and even logic. Giroux writes, "Waging war is one of the nations's most honored virtues, and its militaristic values now bear down on almost every aspect of American life."[30] The cadets at the beginning of this article are just one example of a much wider cultural dynamic that has taken hold in the United States.

This apparatus encourages forgetfulness and distracts citizens from critical thinking about their own reality. In subtle and more active forms of coercion, and through various spectacles that focus their attention elsewhere, citizens' very imagination is tamped down, much less any thought of action to bring about changes in the social structure. It also is important that we recognize that the dynamics of disimagination are not accidental, but purposeful and coordinated. For instance, Giroux describes the rise of the "ever-growing information-illiteracy bubble" that includes the work of conservative think tanks as the training ground for "anti-public pseudo-intellectuals and religious fundamentalists." These individuals and groups create talking points and discipline the rhetoric of a wide variety of news and social media platforms. This bubble

> ... has become a powerful form of public pedagogy in the wider culture and is responsible not only for normalizing the war on science, reason, and critical thought, but also the war on women's reproductive rights, communities of color, low-income families, immigrants, unions, public schools, and any other group or institution that challenges the anti-intellectual, antidemocratic world views of the new extremists.[31]

We might also add that the bubble normalizes the nation's permanent war economy, and war itself.

Thus, the discourse and culture of war in the disimagination machine increasingly intertwines with the material production for war, and the centralizing of war and militarism in the national economy. At the same time, the disproportionate reality of US material support of war is mystified by highly sophisticated commercial and actual spectacles of violence. Giroux writes, "Very little appears to escape the infantilizing influence and moral vacuity of those who run the market. Films, television, video games, children's toys, cartoons, and even high fashion all are shaped to normalize a society centered on war and violence."[32] A long history of widespread interpenetration between military and supposedly civilian sectors characterizes the United States, especially since the WWII era.

We might focus on just one of countless examples to take this a step further. According to William Hartung, the deep interpenetrations between today's "Nuclear-Industrial Complex" and government go back in US history to the Manhattan Project, as he writes, "The techniques that the arms lobby and its allies in government used more than half a century ago to promote sky-high nuclear weapons spending continue to be wielded to this day."[33] Intentional tactics include ensuring that there are at least two nuclear lobbyists for every member of congress, powerful and well-funded think tanks dedicated to creating the discourse of the necessity of nuclear weapons, and careful distribution of jobs related to nuclear weapons' industries across as many different states as possible. In this way, a web of strategies has been crafted carefully to promote and protect the nuclear complex. Historian Paul Boyer shows that though nuclear freeze activists historically have referenced the horrors of Hiroshima to alert citizens to the dangers of nuclearism, overall American memory remains most deeply shaped by "... an official environment marked by concealment and evasion."[34] In addition, as we contemplate the links between war and the economy, it is important to remember that the rise of capitalist markets and professional (and conscripting) militaries historically developed simultaneously in the early 19th century. As Theo Goldberg writes, "Militarization and marketization are mutually constitutive. They are marked by a common social logic of conception, formation, and (re-)production."[35] This is not a new phenomenon. If there is anything new in the Trump era regarding this long-standing reality of the United States, according to Hartung it is only that "He [Trump] has shoved the president's role as arms-purveyor-in-chief in everybody's faces."[36]

RELIGION AND THE DISIMAGINATION MACHINE

Though Henry Giroux's analysis of the "disimagination machine" powerfully assists us to understand cultural and political dynamics that seem illogical, his work may be further augmented by adding a political theological analysis, for this apparatus also employs religious symbol, text, history, rhetoric, and doctrine.

For instance, scholar Julie Ingersoll explores the influence of "Christian Reconstructionist" thinking in American culture and politics.[37] She argues that though this is a very small and therefore sometimes dismissed Christian group, scholars should not underestimate its impact, as she writes, "their influence is subtle, implicit, and hidden." According to the thinking of Christian Reconstructionists, American culture and politics should be based on biblical law as they interpret it. Ingersoll finds not only their ideas, but indeed, their very language across the landscape of a much broader conservative culture of the religious right.[38] Reconstructionists believe in the right of civil authorities' use of violent punishment to enforce biblical law, support the death penalty, and would punish homosexuality. They uphold Christian supersessionist ideas regarding Jews, would "restore a patriarchal social structure in which whites are the dominant group," "assume that slavery for African Americans was a positive good," "endorse a marriage model that requires the complete submission of women, whose primary calling is to produce as many children as possible," and call for "front-line soldiers who are willing to place their bodies where the battle rages . . . in the child killing industry of abortion."[39] Ingersoll dedicates two chapters of her book to investigation of the way these religious ideas have been inculcated in generations of home-schooled children in the United States.

Traces of this religio-cultural influence abounded during the 2016 presidential election season. In the run-up to the election, one day as I was driving, I listened with fascination to a national talk-radio program, not long after the news had exploded regarding the "Access Hollywood" tape. Every news and social media outlet hammered the nation with looping video of then-candidate Trump publicly bragging about various sexual encounters with women.[40] With callous and careless words that shocked the nation, he described his behavior:

> I did try and fuck her. She was married . . . I moved on her like a bitch. But I couldn't get there. And she was married . . . I just start kissing them. It's like a magnet. Just kiss. I don't even wait. And when you're a star, they let you do it. You can do anything . . . Grab 'em by the pussy. You can do anything.

The words from the tape went viral, and were prominent in my own mind as I listened that day in the car to the different talk-radio voices in urgent discussion about the upcoming election. At one point, a woman called in to speak about her reservations about voting for this candidate, given the revelation of the tape. Yes, she didn't approve of this behavior; but as she kept talking and trying to think it all through, she said that in the end, she would vote for Trump, because he would appoint Supreme Court justices that would continue the important war against abortion in the United States. As I listened to this woman sincerely attempt to think through her own logic, I wondered about the way that Reconstructionist thinking and values were embedded in this conservative religious discourse: just how did the dominant religious message of women's submission and secondary status in her religious world view play into the ultimate accommodating of sexual predation against women, in order to continue the overridingly important march against abortion? What kind of "disimagination" is this? A thorough-going interrogation of the disimagination machine requires us to focus on the role religion plays.

"HYPERBOLIC DOUBT" AND SACRIFICIAL WAR-CULTURE

To take the investigation of religion in Giroux's analysis of the disimagination machine past this current president and era, I suggest a turn to what Pierre Bourdieu calls "the most profound truth of the state: . . . its major power to produce and impose categories of thought."[41] Here we get to the heart of the matter in this exploration of sacrificial war-culture in the post-truth era. The problem is not simply that citizens prefer emotion and belief to objective fact, but that the state plays a much stronger defining role in citizens' very cognition that we tend to recognize. Here, I believe, is the ground on which the disimagination machine is built.

If we come to understand this deepest power of the state, with its capacity to shape the very categories of citizens' thought, according to Bourdieu, scholars and citizens alike will arrive at a shared conviction: the task is to question the state, and expose it to "hyperbolic doubt." He claims, "When it comes to the state, one never doubts enough."[42] What is called for is a rupture with state-thought, but this is very difficult to do, as this chapter has demonstrated, because this same thought is so deeply imprinted upon citizens, and appears to be the only thought possible. Bourdieu asks, given this reality, how may it be possible for people to "retrieve the possibility that things could have been and still could be different"?[43]

However, before responding to this question, it must be said that the situation is more complex still, for the deepest hold of the state on citizens is through its symbolic production; it is in this realm of the symbolic that we find the most unshakable ties between citizens and the state. And what comprises the symbolic realm? Here we encounter the relations of religion, the arts, cosmology and yes, even the realm of science. Moreover, it is here, in the symbolic realm, at this deep place, where all the symbols, narratives, and practices of sacrifice reside. Further, the production of this symbolic reality of the state also is deeply enmeshed with the ideology and practices of state violence, as Bourdieu writes, "The most brutal relations of force are always simultaneously symbolic relations."[44] The constraining and shaping of thought goes hand in hand with embodied structures of force and coercion. Through "doxic submission" (this is submission to the point of view of the dominant) citizens are tied subconsciously to the established order.[45]

Bourdieu's highlighting of the subconscious nature of all this is worth underscoring, for it helps us to better understand why sacrificial dynamics are so integral in the symbolic production of war-culture in the United States, and why they are so effective in unifying people behind this rhetoric and symbol, while simultaneously distracting them from critical thought (the primary thrust of the disimagination machine). When audiences jump to their feet in spontaneous standing ovations at the spectre of a sacrificial narrative of war, they are acting in ways that are prereflexive and subconscious. It is not "a free act of clear conscious." As a result, this precisely is the place where "the grip of the state" takes its strongest hold. Bourdieu explains, "one should rethink along those lines the conditions that make possible the supreme sacrifice: *pro patria mori*"[46] Through prereflexive discourse and symbol of "the necessity of war-as-sacrifice," citizens' thought is shaped; citizenship ultimately is defined as willingness to expend human life for the continuance of the state. There is no deeper performance of state legitimacy, *and* disimagination, than this. Bourdieu summarizes, "It is this prereflexive agreement that explains the ease, rather stunning when we think of it, with which the dominant impose their domination."[47] Think back to the example of Trump's first speech to Congress; Bourdieu helps us to understand *why* citizens fall so easily into line with prescribed compliance with state violence in the face of discourse and spectacle centered on "the necessity of war-as-sacrifice." Moreover, this performance is sacralized through its dependence on civil religious symbols, narratives, and practices based in Christianity. The question is, taking this seriously, what are citizens and scholars to do to disrupt these dynamics?

CONCLUSION: GENEALOGY, DETRANSCENDENTALIZING, AND IMAGINING ALTERNATIVES

The conclusion of this chapter returns to Bourdieu's poignant and urgent question: given this reality, how can people "retrieve the possibility that things could have been and still could be different"? Facing the destructive nature of sacrificial war-culture in the United States, and its deep dependence on Christian theology, symbols and ritual, scholars and citizens first must expose it. Bourdieu would agree: the task of social science is to ". . . uncover all the unconscious ties to the social world."[48] But what about the theological task? Again, I emphasize the importance of including an investigation into religious influences as a part of this excavation. This means exploration of the dominant philosophies and theologies that make it possible for these dynamics to flourish under citizens' noses, while at the same time their critical thought is disabled.

For genealogical analysis reveals the tight links between dominant Christian soteriological understandings and war-culture in the United States. "Making the ultimate sacrifice" is the language applied equally to the death of Jesus on the cross for sin, and the soldier who dies on the field of war. In popular thinking, as well as in countless marketed messages across the United States, the dominant metaphor for understanding the work of salvation in Christianity revolves around notions of substitution and satisfaction. "Remember that only two forces have ever agreed to die for you—Jesus Christ and the American soldier!"—so proclaims the popular social media message at Veterans Day or Memorial Day.[49] And when we turn to the medieval theology at the base of such popular and contemporary ways of thinking, especially works like Anselm's *Cur Deus Homo,* we discover cognitive patterns there that are distressingly similar: In Anselm's world, the ultimate "service" that may be paid to the King (the metaphor for the divine) to address the depth of human sin and bring harmony back to the King's city is the freely offered death of a faithful and loyal subject.[50] *Pro Patria Mori.* Even more, note the ironic cognitive dissonance in such logic: the soldier's injury or death in war that is justified by way of the archetype of "a nonviolent Messiah!"[51] Giroux once again sums up the objection to this state-thought: "State violence is *not* a measure of greatness and honor."[52]

In the end, concerned citizens and scholars not only must expose the apparatus of the disimagination machine to "hyperbolic doubt." We also must find ways to "detranscendentalize" the pseudo-civil-religious practices and cognitive assumptions at its core. This means actively exposing and challenging the sacred canopy that protects sacralized notions, such as spectacles based on "the necessity of war-as-sacrifice" that are decorated and justified with symbols, rhetoric, and cognitive frameworks deeply resonating within Christianity.

But if Giroux focuses in particular on the urgency of higher education to "develop a discourse of critique and possibility," and if Bourdieu emphasizes the need to protect whatever autonomy may be had in educational and scientific institutions, to "use against the state the relative freedom that the state grants for this very task"—we also must ask, what about the role of religious institutions, religion academics and theologians, and people of faith?[53] Not only the imaginaries of the state and citizenship are in dire need of hyperbolic doubt, our theological imaginaries are in need as well.

Five hundred years ago this very year, an Augustinian monk and professor determined that a corrupt and death-and-anxiety-producing theology and religious practice must be exposed to deeper questioning. Though there is much about Martin Luther that is deserving of criticism and hesitation, in these days that feel quite dark, I find myself musing on his example and his courage in the face of the ecclesiastical/state monolith in his own time that must have seemed insurmountable.

In our time, Christianity in the public square seems to have been hijacked by dynamics that work hand in glove: on the one hand, by a conservative religious worldview shaped by groups like the Reconstructionists, and on the other hand, by unthinking civil religious exploitation of Christian sacrificial soteriology to sacralize our war machine. The time is ripe to mount a thorough-going resistance to and criticism of this political theology. Only through this process will we struggle and stumble our way toward greater openness and imagination to envision realistic alternatives.

NOTES

1. Aaron B. O'Connell, "The Permanent Militarization of America," *New York Times*, Nov. 4, 2012. Web. Accessed Oct. 9, 2017.

2. "post-truth," *Oxford Living Dictionaries* (New York: Oxford University Press, 2017). Web. Accessed Nov. 27, 2017.

3. Henry Giroux *The Violence of Organized Forgetting: Thinking Beyond America's Disimagination Machine*. (San Francisco: City Lights Books, 2014), 27.

4. Naomi Klein *No Is Not Enough: Resisting Trump's Shock Politics and Winning the World We Need*, (Chicago, IL: Haymarket Books, 2017), 98.

5. See my full analysis, *U.S. War-Culture, Sacrifice and Salvation*. 1st ed. (New York: Routledge, 2014).

6. "National Priorities Project Statement on Trump FY 2018 Budget Proposal," *National Priorities Project*. March 16, 2017. Web. Accessed Nov. 27, 2017.

7. Jake Johnson, "House Approves $700B 'Cash Cow for Weapons Companies'—But Single Payer 'Too Expensive.'" *Common Dreams*. Nov. 15, 2017. Web. Accessed Nov. 16, 2017.

8. Kelly Martin and David Vine, "Mapping the Growth of Bases World-Wide," *Investigative Reporting Workshop*: American University School of Communication, August 25, 2015. Web. Accessed Nov. 10, 2017.

9. David Vine, "Where in the World Is the U.S. Military?" *Politico Magazine*. July/August 2015. Web. Accessed Nov. 28, 2017.

10. Nick Turse, *The Complex: How the Military Invades our Everyday Lives*. (New York: Metropolitan Books, 2008), 16.

11. See Denton-Borhaug, *U.S. War-culture, Sacrifice and Salvation*, chapter 5, "De-transcendentalizing War."

12. Ariel Dorfman, "Trump's War on Knowledge," *New York Review of Books*, Oct. 21, 2017. Web. Accessed Nov. 10, 2017.

13. Dorfman.

14. Bruce Lincoln, "Bus's God Talk: Analyzing the President's Theology," *Christian Century* 121, no. 20 (2004): 23. See also Denton-Borhaug, *U.S. War-Culture, Sacrifice and Salvation*, 66.

15. Juan Cole, "George W. Bush and GOP Lack Standing to Bash Trump for Racism," *RSN*, Oct. 21, 2017. Web. Accessed Nov. 10, 2017.

16. For more on victimage rhetoric, consult *U.S. War-Culture, Sacrifice and Salvation*, 59–63.

17. See Denton-Borhaug, *U.S. War-Culture, Sacrifice and Salvation*, especially chapter 2: "Building and Maintaining the Drive to War: Victimage Rhetoric, Framing and the Language of Sacrifice."

18. Eve Peyser, "A Timeline of Trump's Post-Charlottesville Fuck-Ups," *Vice*. Aug. 18, 2017. Web. Accessed Nov. 10, 2017.

19. Bill Chappell, "Father of Navy SEAL Killed in Yemen Raid Has Harsh Words for Trump," *National Public Radio*, Feb. 27, 2017. Web. Accessed Nov. 10, 2017.

20. Dan Merica, "Navy SEAL's Widow Provides Emotional Highpoint in Trump Speech," *CNN*, Mar. 1, 2017. Web. Accessed Nov. 12, 2017.

21. Ibid.

22. Denton-Borhaug, "Martyrdom Discourse in Contemporary U.S. War-Culture," *The Wiley Blackwell Companion to Christian Martyrdom*. Ed. Paul Middleton. Hoboken, NJ: John Wiley and Sons, forthcoming.

23. Giroux borrows the language of "the disimagination machine" from Georges Did-Huberman. See 26.

24. Ibid.
25. Ibid., 15.
26. Ibid., 16.
27. Ibid., 17.
28. Ibid., 33, 34.
29. Ibid., 47.
30. Ibid., 47.
31. Ibid., 28–29.
32. Ibid., 51.

33. William Hartung, "Massive Overkill: Brought to You by the Nuclear-Industrial Complex," *TomDispatch.com*. November 16, 2017. Web. Accessed Nov. 17, 2017.

34. Paul Boyer, "Exotic Resonances: Hiroshima in American Memory," *Hiroshima in History and Memory*, Ed. Michael J. Hogan. New York: Cambridge University Press, 1996, 159.

35. Theo Goldberg, "Mission Accomplished: Militarizing Social Logic," *Obstruir, Destruir, Ocultar*. Ed. Enrique Ježik 1st ed. Mexico: Universidad Nacional Autónoma de México Museo Universitario Arte Contemporáneo Cuidad, 2011, 185, 190.
36. Hartung, "Massive Overkill."
37. Julie Ingersoll, *Building God's Kingdom: Inside the World of Christian Reconstruction.* New York: Oxford, 2015.
38. Ibid., 6–7.
39. Ibid., 221, 223, 227, 234.
40. "Transcript: Donald Trump's Taped Comments about Women," *New York Times,* Oct. 8, 2016. Web. Accessed Nov. 25, 2017.
41. Pierre Bourdieu, *Practical Reason* (Stanford, CA: Stanford University Press, 1998), 35.
42. Ibid., 36.
43. Ibid., 40.
44. Ibid., 53.
45. Ibid., 57.
46. Ibid., 55.
47. Ibid., 56.
48. Ibid., 39.
49. In addition to many social media sites, such messages have been imprinted on T-shirts, mass produced, and sold through specialty T-shirt companies, such as "Teespring." See: https://teespring.com/shop/only-two-defining-force-shirt1#pid=2&cid=2397&sid=backfootnotetheteeshirts. Accessed Nov. 28, 2017.
50. See Anselm's parable of the King and his City in *Cur Deus Homo: A Scholastic Miscellany: Anselm to Ockham.* Ed. Eugene R. Fairweather (Philadelphia: Westminster Press, 1946), 167.
51. See Denton-Borhaug, "'Like Acid Seeping into Your Soul': Religio-Cultural Violence in Moral Injury," *Exploring Moral Injury in Sacred Texts,* Ed. Joseph McDonald. London: Jessica Kingsley Publishers, 2017.
52. Giroux, 228.
53. Bourdieu, 40.

REFERENCES

Bourdieu, Pierre. *Practical Reason*. Stanford: Stanford University Press, 1998.
Boyer, Paul. "Exotic Resonances: Hiroshima in American Memory," in *Hiroshima in History and Memory*. Ed. Michael J. Hogan. New York: Cambridge University Press, 1996.
Chappell, Bill. "Father of Navy SEAL Killed in Yemen Raid Has Harsh Words for Trump." *National Public Radio*, Feb. 27, 2017. https://www.npr.org/sections/thetwo-way/2017/02/27/517496770/father-of-navy-seal-killed-in-yemen-raid-has-harsh-words-for-trump.
Cole, Juan. "George W. Bush and GOP Lack Standing to Bash Trump for Racism." *RSN*, Oct. 21, 2017. https://www.juancole.com/2017/10/george-standing-racism.html.
Dorfman, Ariel. "Trump's War on Knowledge." *New York Review of Books*, Oct. 21, 2017. https://www.nybooks.com/daily/2017/10/12/trumps-war-on-knowledge/.
Denton-Borhaug, Kelly. *U.S. War-Culture, Sacrifice and Salvation*. 1st ed. New York: Routledge, 2017.
_____. "'Like Acid Seeping into Your Soul': Religio-Cultural Violence in Moral Injury." In *Exploring Moral Injury in Sacred Texts*, Ed. Joseph McDonald. London: Jessica Kingsley Publishers, 2014.
_____."Martyrdom Discourse in Contemporary U.S. War-Culture," *The Wiley Blackwell Companion to Christian Martyrdom*. Ed. Paul Middleton. Hoboken, NJ: John Wiley and Sons, forthcoming.
Fairweather, Eugene R., Ed. Anselm of Canterbury, *Cur Deus Homo. A Scholastic Miscellany: Anselm to Ockham*. Philadelphia: Westminster Press, 1946.
Giroux, Henry. *The Violence of Organized Forgetting: Thinking Beyond America's Disimagination Machine*. San Francisco: City Lights Books, 2014.

Goldberg, Theo. "Mission Accomplished: Militarizing Social Logic," in *Obstruir, Destruir, Ocultar*. Edited by Enrique Ježik. 1st ed. Mexico: Universidad Nacional Autónoma de México Museo Universitario Arte Contemporáneo Cuidad, 2011.

Ingersoll, Julie. *Building God's Kingdom: Inside the World of Christian Reconstruction*. New York: Oxford, 2015.

Johnson, Jake. "House Approves $700B 'Cash Cow for Weapons Companies'—But Single Payer 'Too Expensive.'" *Common Dreams*. Nov. 15, 2017. https://www.commondreams.org/news/2017/11/15/house-approves-700b-cash-cow-weapons-companies-single-payer-too-expensive.

Hartung, William. "Massive Overkill: Brought to You by the Nuclear-Industrial Complex." *TomDispatch.com*. November 16, 2017. http://www.tomdispatch.com/blog/176351/.

Klein, Naomi. *No Is Not Enough: Resisting Trump's Shock Politics and Winning the World We Need*. Chicago, IL: Haymarket Books, 2017.

Lincoln, Bruce. "Bush's God Talk: Analyzing the President's Theology." *Christian Century* 121, 20 (2004): 23.

Martin, Kelly, and David Vine. "Mapping the Growth of Bases World-Wide." *Investigative Reporting Workshop*: American University School of Communication, August 25, 2015. http://www.investigativereportingworkshop.org/investigations/lily-pads/htmlmulti/lily-pad-multimedia/.

Merica, Dan. "Navy SEAL's Widow Provides Emotional Highpoint in Trump Speech." *CNN*, Mar. 1, 2017. https://www.cnn.com/2017/02/28/politics/navy-seal-widow-trump-address/index.html.

No Author. "Teespring." 2018. https://teespring.com/shop/only-two-defining-force-shirt1#pid=2&cid=2397&sid=backfootnote.

O'Connell, Aaron B. "The Permanent Militarization of America." *New York Times*. Nov. 4, 2012. https://www.nytimes.com/2012/11/05/opinion/the-permanent-militarization-of-america.html.

Oxford Living Dictionaries. "post-truth." New York: Oxford University Press, 2017. https://en.oxforddictionaries.com/definition/post-truth.

Peyser, Eve. "A Timeline of Trump's Post-Charlottesville Fuck-Ups." *Vice*. Aug. 18, 2017. https://www.vice.com/en_us/article/vbbbg8/a-timeline-of-trumps-post-charlottesville-fuck-ups.

Stein, Jeff. "U.S. Military Budget Inches Closer to 1 Trillion $ Mark, as Concerns Over Federal Deficit Grow." *Washington Post*, June 19, 2018. https://www.washingtonpost.com/news/wonk/wp/2018/06/19/u-s-military-budget-inches-closer-to-1-trillion-mark-as-concerns-over-federal-deficit-grow/?utm_term=.00b4d1293eb2.

Theoharis, Liz. *Always with Us? What Jesus Really Said about the Poor*. Grand Rapids, MI: Eerdmans, 2017.

"Transcript: Donald Trump's Taped Comments about Women," *New York Times*, Oct. 8, 2016. https://www.nytimes.com/2016/10/08/us/donald-trump-tape-transcript.html.

Turse, Nick. *The Complex: How the Military Invades our Everyday Lives*. New York: Metropolitan Books, 2008.

Vine, David. "Where in the World Is the U.S. Military?" *Politico Magazine*. July/August 2015. https://www.politico.com/magazine/story/2015/06/us-military-bases-around-the-world-119321.

Chapter Fourteen

A Spirituality of Activism

The Chicago Air and Water Show

Robert Bossie

In 1991, my brother Paul, who took private vows of poverty, chastity, and obedience as a young man, came to me and said if we really opposed war and nuclear weapons, why aren't we protesting the Chicago Air and Water Show which is the largest recruitment tool for young women and men. He said that he was going to go to the show to protest it even if no one else joined him.

The annual Chicago Air and Water Show has been conducted since 1959. It is the largest of its kind in the United States, drawing over two million persons to the shores of Lake Michigan over an August weekend. Persons of every stripe come to this show from all over the Midwest: male and female, parents with their young children, young adults and seniors, all of whom are of various nationalities and ethnicities. Numerous high rise buildings along the lakefront afford a special view of the show. It is produced by Shell Oil Products U.S. and the City of Chicago.

It begins at 10 AM and goes to 3 PM both Saturday and Sunday. It features some water activities but the air component is paramount. Current and former military aircraft are featured but the highlight of the day is the climax performance by the Navy's Blue Angels or the Air Force's Thunderbirds aerial acrobatics teams.

So, for the next two years following his challenge to me, Paul had me drive him to the show and back again to our adjacent, single-room-occupancy apartments. He spent the entire day there distributing thousands of leaflets and interacting with the spectators. On the third year, he persuaded me to join him, reluctantly I must add, given my aversion to the sun and heat of August days, the enormous crowds and the unbearable noise. To be honest, I don't really know why I went. Maybe it was just to support him.

That first year of my attendance, Paul had a large banner made which said, *The AandW Show = A Military Commercial for Recruitment and War*. He also composed an attractive leaflet which, on the face of it seemed, unwittingly, like a program for the show. We went onto the footbridge which spans Lake Shore Drive, a major artery next to the lakefront. Thousands of cars pass under this bridge while about one-half of all spectators going to the show cross this same bridge. Paul suggested that we tie the banner onto the railing of the bridge in sight of the passing cars.

As we stood there with the banner attached to the bridge railing, I looked around to see the location of the police who were monitoring the show. I wondered nervously how these good police officers would respond to our presence. It wasn't too long before I had my answer. Officer not-so-friendly appeared and told us in no uncertain terms to remove the banner from the railings. We did so and continued to stand on the bridge but now holding the banner ourselves. The police officer turned red in the face and growled at me, "What are you doing?!" Sheepishly I questioned him, "Holding the banner?" Again he growled, "Get *off* the bridge." We responded promptly to his order or risked, it seemed to me, greater ire than I wished and possible arrest.

Paul and I proceeded to the sidewalk at the end of the bridge near the beach and began to both hold our banner and distribute the leaflets as best as we were able. It quickly became apparent to me that we were now in the most advantageous position to get out our message because everyone in this enormous crowd crossing the bridge was forced to view our banner which measured about five feet high and ten feet wide. I recall thinking, "Thank you good officer."

We conducted this protest until 2011 under various circumstances. At its height, 30 to 40 persons joined us. This number was disappointing given the magnitude of the show, but I partially attributed these low numbers to its timing during the summer months when schools were out and many activists were engaged in other pursuits—not to mention the long hours and the harsh weather conditions.

Each year was a new experience. After twelve years in this same advantageous spot at the end of the footbridge, the police began to coral us into a fenced-in area which separated us from interaction with the spectators and distribution of our very impact-filled leaflet. They threatened us with arrest if we violated these boundaries. Even if members of our group walked along the beachfront distributing leaflets they were subject to arrest. Meanwhile, the military and various commercial enterprises were distributing their free wares and advertisements totally unimpeded. When we appealed to the police about this disparity, they refused to change their policy. It became clear to us that our message was the problem, not our presence or our, very polite, interaction with the spectators. Such, it seems, is freedom of speech in the USA.

One time, four "skin-heads" approached us aggressively and I said to myself. "Here we go, there's going to be trouble now." But Paul, in his cool-headed, nonviolent manner engaged them in conversation and disarmed their aggression. Finally, a few of them said forcefully to the one more actively engaged in conversation with Paul, "Let's go!" He responded, "Not now. I am talking with this guy." Another time, a large, muscular man angrily approached one of our group, Fred, and spit in his face. I saw Fred clench his fist, but he went no further. Later I thanked him for his nonviolent response and he said to me, "I wouldn't hit him, Bob." I am unsure of Fred's motives for restraining himself but I thought he was being respectful of our nonviolent presence at all these events.

Often we heard passing comments like, "You couldn't be here if it wasn't for our military." The best I could mutter on such occasions when they chose to walk on by was, "I relieve them of that responsibility." At other times, we were able to engage some spectators in more thoughtful conversations.

During the course of these protests, we distributed about 10,000 leaflets each year and exposed several million persons to our message. Essentially, we told all who would listen, including the media, those in the military and others, that this was not family entertainment but a tool for recruiting our young into death-dealing activities, wars of oppression, and huge military budgets. We reminded them that these planes were, in fact, weapons of mass destruction and while they themselves looked on the planes and the pilots with admiration and wonder (the proverbial "God's of Metal" from Leviticus 19:4), persons on the receiving end of these weapons cowered in shock and dread simply at the sound and sight of them. We emphasized that the military does not encourage free thinking, that many suffer from Post Traumatic Stress Disorder and learn very few skills that are transferable to civilian life. And we noted that military spending creates far fewer jobs then equal spending in the civilian sector and that the military helps destroy the environment. Clearly, the show was and is a military commercial. We said, *caveat emptor*, buyer beware!

REFLECTIONS

Three experiences are at the root of my two decades-long efforts to help Paul organize others in nonviolent resistance to this show.

First

The first and primary experience was of God many years ago. I lay on a couch in a friend's basement apartment in Hollywood, California, and decided to stop participating in the world unless I could find a reason to do so. I thought of the many persons who were close to me, including my dear mother, but they were all insufficient. I thought of the God whom I knew at that point but all I could say was "I am sorry. You are not good enough." I thought all the way back to my birth but could not think of any reason to continue. I was about to quit when I thought, what about before you were born?

Immediately I thought of my conception. At that very instant, all I "heard" was "God." The word "God." And at once I was immersed in this God beyond any understanding of words or time. I could not distinguish in any way the difference between myself and God. I was fully and completely lost in this state of being God. God and I were one to the extent that I was God. I no longer existed. Only God. Then I knew that I was holy, good, loveable and worthy of reverence as were all other persons, creatures, and things because they too were in and of the living God. This interconnectivity of all being in God is the foundational and life-changing ground for all of my life and all of my activism. To please God by working to achieve Jesus' words, "That they all may be one." (John 17:21)

In my mind, the Air and Water Show is a direct attack against this interconnectivity of all being wherein we are called to build, through the nonviolent love of Jesus, the beloved community living in harmony with all creation. Father Dehon, the 19th-century priest and founder of the congregation the Priests of the Sacred Heart, of which I am a member, understood this reality by focusing upon this same call of Jesus as one of the principle themes of our religious community: *Sint Unum*.

Second

A second experience which prompts my ministry of resistance to this show occurred in the summer of 1979 when I traveled to the South American countries of Bolivia, Ecuador, and Peru with members of the 8th Day Center for Social Justice. Our goal was to learn from the efforts of the churches in societies struggling to make the Gospel come alive among some of the most desperate conditions, including living under oppression by autocratic rulers aided by their military and police. Some of our church hosts there pointed out to us that often such rulers were supported by the US government and US corporations.

In the outskirts of Lima, the capital of Peru, one of my companions and I stayed with a Maryknoll priest, Peter Rogierre, who lived in a small house in the area called *Ciudad de Dios*, the City of God. This city was inhabited by families driven off their lands—where they were able to live meager lives through subsistence farming—by economic and political changes far beyond their control.

Through the years, these internally displaced migrants arrived in the dead of night in waves of thousands of men, women, and children and set up temporary shelters made of scrap cardboard, wood, sticks, and stones on the harsh, desert-like outskirts of this sprawling city. The sheer number of immigrants made it impossible for local authorities to displace them. Each new invasion expanded these young towns, or *pueblos jovenes* as they were called, to hundreds of thousands of inhabitants.

One morning, Fr. Peter took us to an area where a woman, looking more aged than her years, stood—in a state of shock and thoroughly forlorn—with her two small children amid the rubble of their shelter, their home, which was destroyed during the previous night's storm. (For some reason, I imagined, probably correctly, that her husband was in the city looking for work to buy food for the day.) Fr. Peter gave her a few Peruvian dollars, to which I added a few more, to help her buy one 6 x 10 foot straw mat which would act as one wall of another, better home, similar to the homes some of the other families in the area were able to build after saving enough to purchase "upgraded" materials. To this day, I feel guilty that I only gave her those few dollars, and I wonder where she would have gotten the money to buy the three other mats and roof necessary for the immediate shelter she needed for herself, her husband, and children.

When I returned to the comfort of my community house in Chicago, I realized that if I didn't factor this woman and her family, and many other such families, into my life, my relationship with God would be a sham. Thus, I chose to make this woman and her children an icon for me which asked, "What will my life, my faith, and my choices do to give her and her children greater control over their lives?"

Initially, I forced myself to consider just such questions when preparing my weekly homily. Thereafter, I followed the guidance of three bishops we encountered on our trip who left their comfortable chancery homes to live in more humble settings near the rural poor. Independently, each of them said that they wanted to allow the poor to convert them. Thus, instead of making a weekly journey from comfortable surroundings to minister to the poor, they made such journeys from their home among the poor to minister to those of greater comfort.

I made a similar choice in 1983, when my religious superior allowed me to move from the community house in Chicago, where I was the acting local superior and formation director for those in initial formation for the brotherhood or priesthood, to a poor, multiethnic neighborhood where I hoped to make those who were poor some of my friends. My purpose, again, was to allow the poor to convert me, *Inshallah* (God willing), that is to say, to try to live more in solidarity with those who are poor.

For me, the Air and Water protest is another step in showing solidarity with this Peruvian family. The show is the antithesis of the solidarity to which we are called. The weapons displayed there as family entertainment support oppressive autocratic rulers and economic policies. While such weapons at the show delight spectators, the sight and sound of them drive fear into the hearts of those on the receiving end as they rain down death and destruction on the people and the earth of which we are a part. For me, not to oppose this show and all that it stands for is, intentionally or not, to be complicit in their oppression.

To this day, this woman and her children, and others living in such desperate conditions, continue to challenge the integrity of my relationship with God.

Father Dehon, founder of the Priests of the Sacred Heart, of which I have been a vowed member since 1968, said it well when calling us to the works of justice: "Charity is a palliative which is always welcome and often necessary; but it does not attack the root of the evil." For these many years, I have tried to stay true to this call of God I first recognized in this woman and her children. In a very large manner, their suffering and lack of control over their own lives is the result of policies enforced by the US military. The Air and Water Show is a significant manifestation of that reality.

I must admit that the journey has not always been easy as I have struggled with my own privilege, limitations, and prejudices as well as the criticism of others. In the end, however, I know that this internal and public struggle is the fasting of which Isaiah speaks.

Is this not, rather, the fast that I choose:

releasing those bound unjustly,
untying the thongs of the yoke;
Setting free the oppressed, breaking off every yoke?
Is it not sharing your bread with the hungry,
bringing the afflicted and the homeless into your house;
Clothing the naked when you see them,
and not turning your back on your own flesh? (Isaiah 75:6–7)

Third

A final source for my activism, especially at the Chicago Air and Water Show, comes from an insight I had during the 1980s, at the height of the Cold War, while working against nuclear weapons at the 8th Day Center for Justice in Chicago. At that time, I came to the realization that by the time I was 27 years of age I had already spent nine years of my life working for the military and the military-industrial complex, including working on nuclear weapons systems. During all those years, no one in my social circles—family, work, church and friends—ever asked me if what I was doing was moral or not. I am not sure what my response would have been if they had done so, but it was clear to me that it was not only acceptable but honorable and a sign of success to have worked in these capacities. After all, we call it military "service," do we not?

I am not casting aspersions or promoting guilt here but simply acknowledging the degree to which the military is so entrenched in our national psyche. Even today, we hear people say to present and past members of the military, "thank you for your service." In fact, the military is currently the most trusted institution in our country.

This reflection led me to further question assumptions about the institutions that make up our collective lives and to always try to see the world from the point of view of the minority or the poor rather than from my place of privilege. Clearly, it is essential to acknowledge where and with whom we stand. And to stand there.

But my reflection went deeper. I came to realize that the Air and Water Show is one manifestation of the Sin of the World (John 1:29), original sin, in that it is so ensconced in the public psyche as to be normative. Into this type of reality we are born and it becomes the ground out of which we live and move and have, in a very real sense, our being. Intentionally or not, this is an act of idolatry for it is to God alone we are to give such allegiance. Our protest of this show, then, is an attempt to unmask this state of sin, this idolatry.

To question the show raises many fundamental issues, assumptions, and societal agreements about the military. Is the military there to serve and protect and are its wars really just and defensive? What role does it play in furthering US economic and political interests? Can we truly justify yearly expenditures on the military that reach as much as $1 trillion, an amount larger than the Gross National Product of many countries? What are we to make of the fact that the military is one of the most polluting entities in the world? Do we want to blindly accept the military's recruitment of our young to kill or be killed, especially though such, seemingly, innocuous spectacles as the Air and Water Show? For, you see, if we ask these questions, we are, by default, asking the most threatening of questions: are the death and life changing injuries endured by our loved ones done in vain?

In considering this reality, we must take into account both the objective and subjective dimensions of our moral agency. On the subjective level, the sacrifice of life and limb in such endeavors are of the most honorable and heroic kind. But objectively, we must decide if they comport with the God of Jesus, the Kin_dom of God. Therein lies our struggle with the principalities and powers.

Such questions go to the core of our being in the world but not of it. Again, they raise the question of our allegiance. Is it to God or Mammon? These are heartrending questions which most would rather ignore or reject out of hand as being insensitive to the sacrifices made.

Just as Air and Water Show is a manifestation of the economic and military structures which hold the Peruvian woman and her children in bondage, so does it hold citizens of the United States in bondage and make us complicit in her oppression and that of so many others. That is to say, we participate in the sin of the world, intentionally or not, unless we elect to unmask and confront it. ". . . and the truth will set you free" (John 8:31).

This brings me to yet, another very important consideration. Just as Gandhi said "we must be the change we wish to see in the world," so must our methods for opposing the show foster the beloved community living in harmony with all creation which we all seek. For this reason, we approached organizing the protest from the perspective of Jesus' nonviolent love for all, including our enemies. We do so in as inclusive and collaborative manner as possible wherein each person's voice is honored. Thus we are called to treat those in the military, their leaders, and the spectators as our sisters and brothers. In the spirit of Jesus and Martin Luther King Jr., we hope to make our "enemies" our friends in the struggle for a world of love, justice, and peace. After all, Cornell West reminds us that "Justice is what love looks like in public."

CLOSING THOUGHTS

It seems clear from this reflection that activism for social justice, peace, and care for creation is essentially a spiritual activity. The founder of my religious order, Fr. Leo John Dehon, who lived during the height of the industrial revolution, called for his followers to address the world with the Bible in one hand and the newspaper in the other so as to show the presence of the living God in our daily lives. The Biblical themes motivating his life and ministry, and thus me and all the members of our community, include "Adveniat Regnum Tuum" (Your Kin_dom Come), *Sint Unum* (that they might all be one). But they are rooted in our union with Christ's self-offering to God for the good of all creation as expressed in the Psalmists words, "Ecce Venio" (Behold I come to do your will, Oh God) (Ps 40:7–8). In his spirit, we strive each day to bring about the "Reign of the heart of Jesus in souls and societies."

The purpose of all this is not only to take a strong stance about the oppression and horror infecting our world but, with the vision of Jesus, to do so in such a way that it begins to create that new world for which Christ offered himself. This necessitates that it be conducted in nonviolent love, in a community that fosters inclusion and consensus because in doing so it changes the model that promotes oppression, weapons and war. It plants seeds that emphasize communion rather than competition. Rather than claiming that I am better when you are less, it says we are better when we act as partners in and with God in furthering the creation story. As St. John Paul II has said, we are cocreators with God.

My question even for myself today remains, if I am fully committed to loving my sisters and brothers, does that not also require me to challenge them, and myself, to consider the impact of their actions even if, as some would say, it weakens their resolve in the face of danger. The reality of just such a challenge was brought home to me in 1991 when returning from a peace camp in the desert of Iraq where over 100 of us from 17 different countries interposed ourselves between the Iraqi forces and the Western coalition during the first Gulf War. During one of the many talks I gave upon my return, a young woman spoke to the audience and said that she had written her brother who was in the military in Iraq to say she didn't think he was acting morally by participating in this war. Her family, she said, was deeply troubled by her actions because she risked challenging his resolve and making him more likely to be injured or killed. It seems to me that this brave young woman considered not just her brother but those Iraqis whose lives and well-being were also being seriously threatened by her brother and his fellow soldiers.

In my quest to live the afore-described life, I am driven to stand in the presence of the living God, the God of my life, in the deepest form of prayer.

> Prayer—
> where we stand naked before God
> allowing
> even inviting
> our soul to be tested
> to be refined in fire
>
> to be shown things
> we'd rather not see
> to be presented with a vision
> too wonderful to attain
> yet, which ignites our hearts
> in unexpected ways.
>
> Prayer—
> tests and refines
> our allegiance
>
> now
> flag
> nation
> family
> culture
> are no longer sufficient
> to claim our loyalty
>
> but the living God

>   who sends us out
>   again
>   to subvert
>   redeem
>   all that we touch
>   including our own hearts

Prayer is a subversive activity. Martin Luther King reminded us that, "The arc of the moral universe is long but it bends toward justice." The question is, how will we influence this arc? By our baptism, we are commissioned to ensure that the arc bends more and more radically toward justice so that our oppressed sisters and brothers, and the very earth itself, ". . . may have life and may have it more abundantly" (John 10:10). The Air and Water Show protest has been part of that effort. Or so it seems to me.

Index

abortion, xi, 129–133, 134–135, 138–139, 141–143, 143n3, 143n8, 144n16, 144n17, 144n18, 145–146, 145n48, 145n58, 146, 189, 190
aesthetic, xi, 68, 102, 103
anger, viii–ix, xiii, 21, 28, 65, 66, 92, 96, 118, 122–123, 125
anti-oppression, 17, 55n30
Arendt, Hannah, 77, 79, 83, 86, 150, 152, 160, 177
authority, xi, 76–84, 86, 168, 169, 173

Bourdieu, Pierre, 182, 190–195

Classism, 133, 141, 142
Clinton, Hillary, 23, 101–113, 118, 186
cognitive biases, xii, 149, 154, 155
communism, 152, 159n6, 160
compassion, ix–xiii, 26–40, 40n1, 40n10, 41, 44, 67, 68, 107, 119, 123, 157, 170, 171, 173, 175n22, 176n27, 177

dignity, 26, 32, 34, 36, 39, 93, 165, 168–177, 174n3, 176n26, 176n35
disruption, xii, 45, 48, 50, 51, 53, 60, 64, 72, 72n9

election, x, 6–7, 16, 17, 19, 21, 23, 25, 60, 69, 116, 118, 119, 125, 190
emotion, viii, 11, 27, 28, 29, 50, 65, 85n4, 88, 118, 123, 125, 179, 180, 185, 186, 190, 196
Evans, John, 82, 86

Families Belong Together, 60, 64, 69
feminism, 126, 130, 144n26, 145n54, 146
freedom, x, xi, 8, 21, 27, 84, 87, 93, 94, 95, 97, 132, 151, 156, 163, 165, 167, 170, 173, 186, 193, 198

gay, xi, 27, 30, 37, 101–103, 106, 107, 112, 136
Gerkin, Charles V., 44, 46, 47, 48, 49–50, 56
Giroux, Henry, 179, 180, 182, 187, 188, 189, 190, 192, 193, 195
Global Ethic Project, 166, 168
Graham, Larry Kent, 44, 46, 48, 49, 49–51, 56, 57
groupthink, 152, 155, 160

hate, 4, 5, 12, 12n4, 13, 17, 26, 32, 115, 116, 118, 120, 122, 123, 125
healing, xii, 27, 28, 45, 49, 50, 51, 52, 54n7, 88
hip-hop, xi, 87–97, 98n16, 99
human rights, 101, 111n27, 163–177, 174n3, 174n4, 174n5, 176n26, 183

idolatry, 145n51, 146, 203
immigration, 13, 13n16, 27, 47, 55n20, 70, 163, 176n29

Internal Family Systems, xi, 27–28, 40n1, 41, 52
intersectionality, 18, 127, 127n3
intolerance, 66–68, 157

Jesus, vii–viii, 8, 12, 26, 34, 40n10, 55n20, 64–67, 87, 92, 94–97, 109, 119, 123, 138, 141, 145n50, 192, 196, 199–200, 204
justice, viii–xiii, 22, 27, 30–31, 33, 40n1, 41, 45–47, 49–56, 54n19, 55n26, 55n29, 56n36, 65–71, 90–93, 96, 103, 112, 129–131, 135, 136, 137, 139–146, 145, 145n63, 157, 167–168, 170–177, 175n15, 183, 200, 202, 204, 206

Kolakowski, Leszek, 149, 152, 154, 157–158, 160

liturgy, xi, 61–64, 68–72
love, vii, xi, 9, 18, 26, 29, 32–34, 39–41, 67, 92–93, 106–107, 112, 115, 116–126, 139, 156–157, 186, 200, 204

March for Our Lives, 43, 51, 53n1, 60
March for Science, xi, 60, 75–76, 80–86
Marxism, 149, 152, 159n6, 159n20, 160
migration, 163, 173, 177

narrative therapy, 49–50, 57
natural law, 166–167, 173, 177
neoliberalism, 187
nonviolence, 31

Obama, Barack, 15, 18–19, 22–23, 101, 118, 155, 161, 186
oppression, ix, xi–xiii, 9, 16, 17–18, 44–45, 48–53, 57, 61, 64–66, 87, 91–97, 150–151, 199, 200, 201, 203–204
ordinary theology, 115, 127

pastoral care, xi, 44–57
Poling, James N., 51–52, 57
political objectivity, 84
populism, 69–70, 72, 163
power, viii–xi, 3, 4–5, 7–8, 8, 16, 19, 21, 30–32, 33–34, 37–39, 41, 43, 46, 48–50, 57, 60, 64–70, 82, 90–99, 104, 107, 118, 120, 122, 124–126, 146, 150, 154–156, 165, 165–173, 184, 187, 190–191
practical theology, 44, 51, 57
prayer, 8, 62, 95, 115, 205, 206
pride, viii, 26, 60, 67, 88
procreation, 138–141
protest, x–xiii, 4, 13, 44, 47, 59–71, 86, 121, 149, 155–156, 161, 172, 197–199, 201, 203–204, 206
public theology, x, 44, 57, 164–167, 173
public truth, 76, 83–84

racism, 4, 17, 37, 48, 87–88, 92–93, 96–97, 132–133, 136, 141–142, 170, 180, 184, 195
rap, viii, 88, 94–97, 99
Rauschenbusch, Walter, 65–66, 72
relationality, 62, 124, 126
reproduction, 129–131, 133, 135, 138–139, 143–146

sacrifice, xii, 94, 120, 151, 185–186, 191–193, 203
sibling, 15–18
sin, 9, 61–68, 92, 97, 137, 156, 164, 192, 203
socialism, 150, 151
solidarity, 44, 67, 116, 124, 146, 165, 169–173, 201
Solzhenitsyn, Alexander, 151–152, 161
soteriology, 193
spectacle, 186–193, 203
spirituality, xii, 51, 57, 93
subculture, xi, 102–103, 106
subversive, xi, 70, 88, 206

transformation, 27, 30, 51–52, 59, 62
trauma, vii–xiii, 6, 18, 37, 44–45, 50–53, 57, 62–64, 71–72, 90, 99, 149, 199
travel ban protest, ix, 69

Unite the Right, 60, 63

Walker, Alice, 17

Zerillli, Linda, 76, 83–84, 86

About the Contributors

Jennifer Baldwin is director of Grounding Flight Wellness Center, Woodstock, Georgia. Her primary area of scholarship is the intersection of traumatology and systematic theology. Rev. Dr. Baldwin's publications include edited volumes, *Embracing the Ivory and Stained Glass: A Festschrift in Honor of Archbishop Antje Jackelén* (Springer 2015), *Sensing Sacred: Exploring the Human Senses in Practical Theology and Pastoral Care* (Lexington Books 2016), *Navigating Alternative Facts and Post Truth: Religion and Science as Political Theology* (Lexington Books 2018); monograph, *Trauma Sensitive Theology: Thinking Theologically in the Era of Trauma* (Cascade 2018). She is currently developing a comprehensive outpatient trauma program that incorporates individual therapy, group therapy, aromatherapy specific for trauma and dissociation support, and progressive movement practices designed to address many of the neurosomatic injuries of trauma. Dr. Baldwin offers training for clergy in trauma and congregational care. For more information, www.groundingflight.com.

Robert (Bob) Bossie is a Roman Catholic priest, a fifty-year-long member of the international religious community, the Priests of the Sacred Heart of Jesus which has members on five continents. As a young man, he spent four years as an enlisted man in the US Air Force working on nuclear weapons carrying aircraft and other weapon systems, and five years working for the military-industrial complex. For more than 30 years, thereafter, he worked at the 8th Day Center for Justice, a faith-based organization working for social change. In this role, he focused most of his energies on anti-nuclear and anti-war efforts along with concerns for economic disparity and oppression. In his later years at the Center, he focused his concern around environmental issues.

He is retired now, lives in Chicago and continues to write, speak, and be as active as he is able.

Donna Bowman is professor of Interdisciplinary Studies in the Norbert O. Schedler Honors College, University of Central Arkansas. She holds a doctorate in theology from the University of Virginia, and degrees from the University of Georgia and Wake Forest University. She is the author of *The Divine Decision: A Process Doctrine of Election* (Westminster John Knox, 2002), *Prayer Shawl Ministries and Women's Theological Imagination* (Lexington 2015), and *The Homebrewed Christianity Guide to Being Human* (Fortress 2018). In addition, she is coeditor of *Handbook of Process Theology* (Chalice 2006, with Jay McDaniel) and *Cosmology, Ecology, and the Energy of God* (Fordham University Press 2011, with Clayton Crockett). Since 2013 her research has explored the intersection of theology, women's spirituality, care ministries, activism, and the material work of fiber arts. She hopes to publish the results of her 2017 conversations with pussyhat makers in multiple forms over the next several years. She also writes about television for the A.V. Club. Along with her husband (freelance writer Noel Murray) and two teenage children, she lives, walks, knits, teaches, and persists in Conway, Arkansas. She can be found on Twitter at @donnadb, and on Ravelry under the username paksenarrion.

Thia Cooper is liberation theologian and professor of Religion and Latin American, Latina/o, and Caribbean Studies at Gustavus Adolphus College, Minnesota, where she also teaches in the Gender, Women, and Sexuality Studies program. She is the author of *A Christian Guide to Liberating Desire, Sex, Partnership, Work and Reproduction* (Palgrave 2017) and *Controversies in Political Theology: Development or Liberation* (SCM Press 2007).

Kelly Denton-Borhaug is professor of Global Religions and Peace and Justice Studies at Moravian College in Bethlehem. She has been studying and writing about the nexus of Christian soteriology and US war-culture since not long after 9/11/2001. Her first book was *U.S. War-culture, Sacrifice and Salvation* (Routledge 2014), and currently she is writing *Moral Injury and the Triangle of Violence: Seeing War Through a Different Lens*, in addition to publishing many articles and book chapters. She is the executive director of "InFocus"—a college initiative that focuses each year on one of four challenge areas to involve students, faculty, and staff in research, learning and activism addressing the urgent issues facing human beings: war, peacebuilding and the just society, health, sustainability, and poverty and inequality. She is ordained in the Evangelical Lutheran Church in America.

Hille Haker holds the Richard McCormick S.J. Endowed Chair of Catholic Moral Theology at Loyola University Chicago since 2010, after teaching at Frankfurt University, Germany, and Harvard Divinity School, Cambridge, Massachusetts. She served on several bioethics committees, including the European Group on Ethics in Science and New Technologies to the European Commission, and on the board of editors for the journal *Concilium*. Her research focuses on questions of moral identity and narrative ethics, social ethics, bioethics, and feminist ethics. Books include *Moralische Identität. Literarische Lebensgeschichten als Medium ethischer Reflexion* (1999), *Ethik der genetischen Frühdiagnostik* (2002), and *Hauptsache gesund* (2011). *A Critical Political Ethics—A Revision of Catholic Social Ethics* is forthcoming (2019). She recently coedited a book titled *Unaccompanied Migrant Children: Social, Legal, and Ethical Responses to the Plight of Child Migration* (Lexington 2018 [with Molly Greening]); and coedited several journal issues for *Concilium*, among them "Theology, Anthropology, and Neurosciences" (2015), "The Return of Apocalypticism" (2014), "Postcolonial Theology" (2013), "Human Trafficking" (2011), "Natural Law—A Controversy" (2010), "HIV/AIDS" (2007), and "The Structural Betrayal of Trust: Sexual Abuse in the Catholic Church" (2004). Her present research is a book project on Recognition and Responsibility.

Tony Hoshaw is a PhD candidate in Theology, Ethics, and the Human Sciences at the Chicago Theological Seminary. His theological research takes place at the intersection of gay cultural studies, early Christian thought, and biblical theology. He currently lives in Cary, North Carolina, with his husband, Justin, and son, William.

Willie Hudson is director of Bible Enrichment School of Theology in Inglewood, California. Rev. Dr. Hudson completed his formal ministry training under the direction of Dr. Frederick K.C. Price through the Crenshaw Ministry Training Institute, Bachelor's in Christian Ministry from Facultad De Teologia, and Master of Divinity and Doctor of Ministry degrees from Azusa Pacific Seminary. Dr. Hudson has published *The Holy Ghost Got a New Dance: An Examination of Black Theology and Holy Hip Hop in the Inner-City* and is a pioneer in bridging the gap between Black Theology, Hip-hop Theology and Christian Worship. His ministry focuses on meeting the needs of urban youth and creating ways for "religion" to reach the youth of his community. Dr. Hudson states, "As churches get older, the streets get younger." Dr. Hudson (affectionately known as "Pops" or "The Bridge") has served the community as a pastor for over 10 years.

Frank Rogers is the Muriel Bernice Roberts Professor of Spiritual Formation and Narrative Pedagogy and the codirector of the Center for Engaged

Compassion at the Claremont School of Theology. His research and teaching focus is on spiritual formation that is contemplative, creative, and socially liberative. A trained spiritual director and experienced retreat leader, he has written on the interconnections between spirituality, social engagement, and compassion. He is the author of *Practicing Compassion*; *Compassion in Practice: The Way of Jesus* (and its supplemental curriculum, *The Way of Radical Compassion*); *The God of Shattered Glass, A Novel*, and *Finding God in the Graffiti: Empowering Teenagers through Stories*, which explores the role of the narrative arts (storytelling, drama, creative writing, and autobiography) in the spiritual formation of marginalized and abused youth and children.

Lisa Stenmark teaches Humanities and Comparative Religious Studies at a San Jose State University. She is the author of *Religion, Science and Democracy: A Disputational Friendship* (Lexington Books 2103) on scientific and religious authority in public life, and is active in the American Academy of Religion and the Arendt Circle. She has written numerous articles on the relationship between religion and science particularly in the context of democratic discourse and within the broader culture. She earned an MDiv/MA from Pacific Lutheran Theological Seminary/the Graduate Theological Union, and a PhD in Religious Studies from Vanderbilt University. In her spare time she runs, practices Aikido and reads too much science fiction.

Susan Brooks Thistlethwaite is professor of Theology at Chicago Theological Seminary. From June of 1998 until June of 2008, she served as the 11th president of CTS. Prior to the presidency, she had been a professor of Theology at CTS for 20 years and director of the PhD Center for five years. She has a PhD from Duke University, a Masters of Divinity (Summa Cum Laude) from Duke Divinity School and a BA from Smith College. An ordained minister of the United Church of Christ since 1974, she is the author or editor of thirteen academic books, including two different translations of the Bible. She is also now the author of two mystery novels, and is at work on a third. She is a frequent columnist in several online publications on religion and public life. Dr. Thistlethwaite's most recent academic book (Palgrave-Macmillan, 2015) is called *Women's Bodies as Battlefield: Christian Theologies and the Global War on Women*. The book has been #1 on Amazon's "Hot New Bestsellers" in the Human Rights category.

Linda Thomas has engaged students, scholars, and communities as a scholar for almost 20 years. She studies, researches, writes, speaks, and teaches about the intersection and mutual influence of culture and religion. Her work is rooted intransitively in a womanist perspective. Dr. Thomas has taught in the fields of anthropology, cultural studies, ethics, and theology. She is particularly focused on the experience of African American women, and is passionate about uncovering and exploring historical and contemporary experiences and ideologies that govern actions, policies, and norms surrounding sex, race, and class. She always incorporates multiple teaching and learning methods in the classroom; in addition to traditional sources, she regularly uses literature, music, and film to provide variety and relevance for her students. Dr. Thomas's publications include *Under the Canopy: Ritual Process and Spiritual Resilience in South Africa* (1999), *Living Stones in the Household of God* (2004), and dozens of articles in academic journals and contributed essays to several scholarly books. Dr. Thomas's work has taken her to South Africa, Peru, Cuba, and Russia. She has been recognized as an Association of Theological Schools Faculty Fellow as well as a Pew Charitable Trust Scholar.

Olli-Pekka Vainio is University Lecturer of Systematic Theology at Faculty of Theology, University of Helsinki, and has the title of docent in Ecumenical Theology. Previously, he has taught theology at the University of Oxford and he is a member of the Center of Theological Inquiry, Princeton, New Jersey. His research interests include history of philosophy and theology, political theology, and contemporary philosophy of religion. His articles have appeared, among others, in the *International Journal of Public Theology*, *Kerygma und Dogma*, *Neue Zeitschrift für Systematische Theologie und Religionsphilosophie*, and *Journal of Analytic Theology*. His most recent publications include *Disagreeing Virtuously* (Eerdmans 2017) and *Cosmology in Theological Perspective* (Baker 2018).

Michelle Walsh is a lecturer at the School of Social Work, Boston University, USA. She is a licensed independent clinical social worker, scholar activist, and holds a PhD in practical theology. She is the author of *Violent Trauma, Culture, and Power: An Interdisciplinary Exploration in Lived Religion*, as well as chapters in other edited volumes, including in *Post-Traumatic Public Theology*, edited by Stephanie N. Arel and Shelly Rambo. Her writing draws from her lived experiences in urban ministry and clinical trauma social work for many years and from her scholarly interests in interdisciplinary and transdisciplinary approaches to social justice initiatives and theory. She teaches in the areas of racial justice and cultural oppressions, ethics, and religion and spirituality. Dr. Walsh also is ordained as a Unitarian Universalist community minister and maintains a private therapeutic, consulting, and spiritual coaching/direction practice called Sacred Play Explorations at www.revmichellewalsh.com. Her private practice specifically is focused on assisting human service professionals, clergy, and academic scholars to develop and maintain centered on their unique gifts, passion, and vision for their work in mending our shared wounded world.

www.ingramcontent.com/pod-product-compliance
Lightning Source LLC
Chambersburg PA
CBHW031550300426
44111CB00006BA/246